SHOOTING

OUT THE

LIGHTS

A MEMOIR

SHOOTING

OUT THE

LIGHTS

KIM FAIRLEY

She Writes Press, a BookSparks imprint
A Division of SparkPointStudio, LLC.

Published 2021

Printed in the United States of America

Paperback ISBN: 978-1-64742-134-2
Hardcover ISBN: 978-1-64742-067-3
E-ISBN: 978-1-64742-135-9
Library of Congress Control Number: 2021900773

For information, address:
She Writes Press
1569 Solano Ave #546
Berkeley, CA 94707

She Writes Press is a division of SparkPoint Studio, LLC.

In memory of

Stanislaus Bury Coxe

April 8, 1971 – September 26, 2017

PROLOGUE

Nobody could give me answers.
For years, I tried to put together what had happened on New Year's Eve, 1977. It was only two years before I moved to Hillsboro, the historic town tucked in the middle of Highland County, Ohio. And nobody who had lived there before me, not even members of my own family—who could talk about anything—seemed to know what had happened. Most people weren't even willing to speak about it.

If I'd been smart, I would've followed their lead. But how does one block out a single story without erasing dozens of others?

The Ben story had become a part of *my* life. So I went with it. I was determined to fill in the blank page.

In a chalky brick Greek Revival house at the corner of West South and Oak, two boys sat on a long couch facing a built-in bookcase the color of driftwood. Its shelves were filled with life-size carved and painted birds. Against the wall, and hovering over them, stood a tall blood-red, black, and blue totem pole from the Pacific Northwest. It was sculpted with sharpened stones from a single cedar log. And near their knees, on an abraded antique blanket chest, was a box of shells and a revolver. Ben, fourteen, his face creased in concentration, used something—*a pair of needle nose pliers?*—to pull the projectile and gun powder out of each shell casing, then showed his twelve-year-old friend how to make blanks to create a loud explosion.

"You sure it's safe?" the boy undoubtedly asked. Ben was familiar with guns, but the younger boy was not.

"Look . . ." Ben placed several rounds in the revolver and may have been lifting the gun to demonstrate when the phone rang. "Just a minute." He placed the revolver on the coffee table and hurried to the kitchen, where the clock on the wall showed a few minutes before midnight. As he grabbed the phone, firecrackers sounded in the neighborhood.

"This Ben?" It was Paul Captain, his father's friend, who sometimes helped with deliveries in the family hardware business. Later, he told his wife he'd had a bad feeling.

"Hi, Mr. Captain." In my mind's eye, I can see Ben wrapping the long telephone cord around his wrist.

"How you doin'?"

"Just hanging out." Ben slid back to the family room, his shoulder squeezing the phone to his cheek. Like his father, he may've raised his index finger to the younger boy, signaling the call wouldn't take long.

"Your daddy there?" Paul coughed and waited.

"He's at Harsha's," Ben said. "At a party." He leaned into the hallway to listen to the television report of the New Year's celebrations around the world.

Paul's warm, intoxicated laugh held on to Ben. "You okay?" Paul paused for a moment. When Ben didn't answer, he said, "Look, you tell your daddy I called to wish him Happy New Year's, and you stay out of trouble . . . you hear?"

"Okay, Mr. Captain," Ben said, grinning to his friend. "I'll tell him." And from what I could piece together, Ben hung up the phone, then raised the television volume in the living room. "Happy New Year! You want to try it?" He handed the younger boy the revolver.

"You sure?"

"Of course. Shoot it."

The boy cocked the gun, aimed at Ben, and squeezed the trigger.

A few blocks away, at 216 East Main Street, a party was well underway. The dark gray brick Italianate with its black iron fence and elaborate porch with iron fretwork hadn't changed much since the Temperance Movement swept through the town in the mid-1870s. Its tall front and central double doors, decorated with Christmas wreaths, were surrounded by greenery. The porch's yellow lights flickered; its cold windows sweated. Inside each room, candles cast shadows that danced off twelve-foot walls. The dining table was filled with a display of hors d'oeuvres on tiered silver trays. As more than one hundred guests, dressed to the nines, mingled, they kissed and clinked glasses. Several guests, to gales of laughter, sang "Auld Lang Syne," their arms wrapped around each other as they swayed to the music.

Then, like a sudden change of wind, the kitchen phone rang out through the merriment. A frantic call for Vernon Fairley.

A moment later, Vern's hands shook as he placed the phone on the hook. He bent over to speak to his friend Jerry. "Ben's been shot. Could you go and tell Caroline?"

"History is not the past.

It is the present.

We carry our history with us.

We are our history."

—James Baldwin

CHAPTER 1

Vern was not the kind of husband I'd ever dreamed of as a child. All my boyfriends had been fellow competitive swimmers—tall, blond, and muscular, with pasty skin. Vern was short and tan, with the carriage of a taller man and rugged good looks, but in questionable health due to an addiction to unfiltered Pall Malls from his years in the Navy. I was a leggy athlete, bigger and more muscular, and felt like a moose standing next to him. But the most obvious difference between us was that he was thirty-two years older.

I know. Thirty-two years. It's odd. And I know what you're thinking: she must've been after his money, his social status, a sense of security. And, okay, maybe these things *were* a part of the attraction. Vern didn't have creditors calling or men in dark suits from the IRS poring over restaurant receipts, like my parents did. He owned a car and a truck and a house and a hardware store, and as far as I could tell, he paid his bills. He had time to live without chasing his tail.

But I did feel odd falling in love with him. He was the kind of man who would invite me to lunch at Magee's diner, and we'd enter through the kitchen off the back alley so he could greet the cook and lift the lids of the pots and pans to smell what was cooking. When I was in a rush, he would say things like, "Now therefore, while the youthful hue sits on thy skin like morning dew, and while thy willing soul transpires at every pore with instant fires"—quoting from Marvell's "To His Coy Mistress," I later learned. Our relationship must've reminded him of life's fragility. To me, the poem was yet one more charming aspect of his personality. Nobody in *my* world had ever memorized poems. Or had such an interesting cast of characters around him.

Vern seemed to assume he could make his way in the world unashamed, without asking permission or so much as "if you please." On an early trip to Cincinnati, as we strolled down a sidewalk arm in arm and a strange woman glowered, Vern spoke to her directly. "Hello there, Georgette, how's the world treating you?" Attending a funeral for a friend, when someone asked, "Doesn't she look peaceful?" he answered, "She looks dead."

In winter, he wore baggy wool socks, flannel shirts, and funny hats. His Brooks Brothers shirts must've awakened some deeply buried longing in me, because I could hardly resist the hint of spray laundry starch around his collar. He liked paw-paws and vichyssoise, pine fragrance, and eucalyptus. He loved Chopin, JTS Brown bourbon, and limericks. And he loved auctions. Once, when I asked him if he liked most vegetables, he said he'd lost his taste for Brussels sprouts after being hounded by the Little Old Ladies' Protective Association. He would make things up like that, right on the spot. He was not afraid to admit that he avoided golf courses and country clubs and detested salmon patties, okra, and sushi. Always one to look at things up close, he had an antique brass telescope in his living room and read books with a magnifying glass. His first gift to me was an antique bottle of perfume called "You're the Fire."

I was twenty-four, living at home with my parents after college, and had been hired as a researcher for the Ohio State Historic Preservation Office. I was to gather the local history, jot down the architectural details, and nominate the most significant buildings in the area to the National Register of Historic Places. Joe Rockhold—who was known as Uncle Orrie for his mustached, bespectacled character in a live children's television program of the 1950s and '60s and who served as president of the Highland County Historical

Society—provided me with a small desk and telephone in the Highland House from which to work.

One morning, arriving at the office, I found a note in Joe's handwriting—he was always leaving me notes—taped to my desk. "Call Vern Fairley," the note read. It gave a local phone number.

I called Joe immediately. "Who's Vern Fairley?" I asked. I knew there was a Fairley Hardware Store, but I'd never met any of the Fairleys.

"You don't know him? They call him 'Brother' Fairley. He was there last night."

I had helped my boss, Lois Rock, show a film about historic preservation to the Hillsboro Retail Merchants and the Chamber of Commerce the previous night. But she'd done all the work of introducing the film. I'd hardly spoken to anyone.

I dialed the number as Joe hovered nearby, shuffling through old photographs. After briefly introducing himself, Mr. Fairley said, "I'd like to make you an offer."

"An offer?"

He chuckled, his voice scratchy. "How would you like to join me for lunch?"

Something about his formality amused me. *Is this going to be a job interview? What kind of offer is he talking about?*

"Meet me at the hardware store, and we'll go from there."

I hung up the phone and stared out the back window of the Highland House.

"What did he want?" Joe asked.

"He invited me to lunch." My mouth twisted with uncertainty. "Is he okay? I mean, he's not a weirdo or anything?"

Joe chuckled, paused, then put on his serious face. "Watch out for that guy, you understand? I don't want to say anything more. You be careful."

I went directly to the Administration Building a half hour before our lunch to ask around about Vern. Had he mistaken me for my attractive thirty-something boss? I'd spent most of the preservation meeting the previous night hugging the Colony Theater wall behind her. But Doris Edgington, a woman in the tax map office, told me about Vern's son Ben, about how the town came together after the tragedy. My heart cracked open even before that lunch with Vern, and he and I became fast friends.

"You were a preservationist, and I needed preserving," he quipped when I asked what he remembered from that first day at lunch.

He thought I needed a boyfriend, and would set up meetings on his front stoop as a ruse to introduce me to his friends. He made a game of inviting people he considered "lonely hearts" and swore he was planning a big party to introduce all of us. It wasn't until state funding ran dry and I moved to Los Angeles for a new job that I realized Vern had become my best friend.

From the beginning, I felt lucky to have met him. And my parents treated him like they were grateful to have someone to pass me off to. When my father told Vern I worried a lot and he couldn't handle it as a father, my mother was pleased when Vern answered, "I'm not the father, and therein lies the difference."

I could go on and on about Vern—his quirkiness, his unique style of speech—but what can I say, I was married for the first time at twenty-four. He was fifty-seven and had been divorced for a couple of years. I was starting my life, and he, though I didn't know it, was nearing the end of his.

It was May of 1982, my twenty-fifth birthday. We had been married three months when I pulled into the gravel parking space we called a driveway and entered the back door, giddy with excitement.

"You look radiant, darling." Vern's warm upturned face glowed. "How was the appointment?"

"You ready?" I played with a few tendrils of my shoulder-length brown hair.

Vern nodded.

"We're having a baby."

"Really?" Vern leapt from his seat to hug me. "I'm delighted, honey."

"Around the time of your birthday." Which also happened to be our wedding anniversary—something he had insisted on so he would never forget the date.

"I'm so happy, sweetheart. It's wonderful news." He stared at me, tapping a fresh cigarette on the kitchen counter. "You must be fertile myrtle." He grinned. "How did that happen so fast?"

I could feel my cheeks getting red. I had just learned at the doctor's office that his ex-wife, Caroline, and I shared the same gynecologist, and the awkwardness of that moment with my doctor swept through me now. But I decided to wait to mention the embarrassment. This was *our* moment. I didn't want it spoiled with thoughts of Vern's past life. I was sure he was thinking of his first family—how could he not—but for this one moment, I wanted to bask in the joy of our own relationship.

We spoke briefly about planning a nursery. Vern seemed to be giving me carte blanche to plan it however I wanted.

"We men know so little," he said. "Whatever your dreams were and however they might have changed in maturity, pursue, my darling. Make them come true."

For a split second, I remembered Vern's face on our wedding day. The bright glow that showed me I was loved and appreciated, and the residue of sadness at the corners of his eyes, those deep lines that made me want to wrap my arms around him.

"I can't wait to plan a nursery," I said. "I have so many ideas." I could feel every cell in my body glowing. Maybe it would be a boy, a child who could carry on the Fairley name. A child to look like Vern and remind me of him long after he was gone. *Oh, God*, I thought. *What am I thinking?*

Vern glanced out the window at two mourning doves resting on the window sill. "They mate for life, you know. Mourning doves."

Vern considered himself an ornithologist and pointed out every species of bird that visited our yard. "These two have been visiting for some time."

We watched for a moment as the male approached the female—tentatively, a few steps at a time—as she bowed and cooed. Again, I wondered if Vern was thinking of Caroline. *Have the doves been visiting for years, or is this something new?*

Stop! I told myself. *Don't even go there.*

"Well, I'm on cloud nine, my dear," he said. "I expect we should head over to the Irish Pub." This was one of Vern's names for his group of Friday night drinking buddies. "I'll try not to let it slip." Keeping his eyes on me, he opened the small junk drawer over the liquor cabinet and, from under a zippered black pistol case, pulled out a single cigarette from a pack. He held it in front of me for a moment, then dropped it in his chest pocket. "When does the doctor say it's safe to tell people?"

"One month. Maybe two?"

"I'm thrilled, darling. We should celebrate!" He kissed me again as he escorted me out the door.

CHAPTER 2

With its broad, tree-lined streets and magnificent nineteenth-century architecture, Hillsboro was one of the most picturesque small towns in southern Ohio. An early center of education, it had been home to two of Ohio's governors, Foraker and Trimble, as well as other statesmen, famous abolitionists, artists, inventors, and even television personalities. But above all else, Hillsboro was known as the "Cradle of the Crusade," from 1873 when Governor Trimble's daughter, Eliza Jane—known as "Mother Thompson"—started the National Women's Temperance Movement.

Vern loved the irony of belonging to a drinking club in the exact area where one hundred years earlier, Presbyterian women in their dark coats had marched down Main Street to the drugstores, pubs, and liquor stores singing religious hymns and praying for total abstinence from intoxicating liquors. He loved the early photographs of women burning whiskey barrels in the street.

I think his feeling of connection to Hillsboro's history—a history of defiance, after all—was a part of the allure of the club. He loved that at times the Friday Night Club called itself a "literary society." Several Friday Nighters joked before our wedding that the society page of the *Hillsboro Press-Gazette* would, in their announcement of our impending marriage, describe our china as having been owned by "Queen Marie Antoinette, who used it in the cow's barn of her toy dairy farm." The article would refer to me as "Miss Kimberly" and describe me as "wearing puce and winter white" and would say that Vern was, "as always, immaculately dressed in his Sears best work pants and Pendleton work shirt." Fortunately, the wedding announcement never made it to the paper.

The way I understood it, the Friday Nighters got started after Ben's death, when Vern began dropping by Jerry's construction company's office (which, back then, was located in the basement of the Mother Thompson House). Vern would carry his bottle of JTS Brown and fill a glass with straight bourbon. After an hour of drinking and discussing with Jerry all the town's problems, Vern would nod off in his chair, and Jerry would leave him there and return to his paperwork. Jerry was a big guy, a former West Point quarterback, who was so quiet around me I thought my presence made him uncomfortable.

When I spoke with Jerry a few years ago, he said the Friday Nighters developed organically, growing larger over time. When I asked him what he thought the draw was, he said, "I don't know why they followed me around, but every Friday a bunch of drunks would show up with a bottle, no matter where I was working, and call themselves the Friday Night Club."

By the time I learned of my pregnancy, Jerry's office had moved to a circa 1840 two-story brick on West Walnut. The building sat near the sidewalk with a wide gravel driveway, loaded with rust-spackled trucks and building equipment, to one side.

That night, Jim Gibbs waved us in the side door. "I just got here and they're all drunk," he said, poking fun. Jim was a bona fide Highland County original and owned the Wooden Spoon, a classy restaurant—classy for Hillsboro—with white linen tablecloths and candlelight dining on the north side of town.

The first time I ate at Jim's restaurant was the day I met Vern. Jim greeted me at the table when he caught Vern searching the restaurant for an ashtray.

"Hasn't anyone told you to watch out for this guy?" he needled.

"As a matter of fact, they have," I said, smiling.

Jim had pestered Vern about smoking and insisted that he'd quit the nasty habit himself. Jim was part salesman, part local historian, and also part "fraternity brother," with his shock of brown hair, brilliant white monogrammed shirt, khakis, loafers with no socks, and the Greek letters ΦΓΔ tattooed on his ankle. He had a gift for making everyone feel like his best friend.

Jim handed me a small glass of what looked and smelled like straight bourbon. "I'm the designated driver," I said with a wink, and before I could touch the glass, Vern grabbed the drink away. I'd previously joined Vern for one or two drinks every night before dinner—he made me whiskey sours with little packs of sour mix and bright red maraschino cherries—but now that I'd learned I was pregnant, I was giving up alcohol.

"Today's the day of something or other." Vern beamed.

I thought he might mention my recent birthday, but he didn't.

Jim glanced in my direction. "Let's hear it, Vern. What's the news?"

Vern wore a fiendish smile. He pulled the cigarette from his breast pocket with one hand and tapped it on his left wrist as he held his drink. "Well . . ." He laughed. "I was wool gathering today. Working on my house-boy routine. It was somewhat serendipitous . . ."

"Yes, and? Come on, Vern. Spit it out." Jim pointed to a scorched area of Vern's shirt and elbowed me. "Couldn't you make him presentable?"

"Presentable isn't his style," I teased.

"Where are we, honey?" Vern tried to hold back a smile. "Did we take a wrong turn and end up at the WCTU? I thought this was the Drunk and Disorderly Society."

I loved the Friday Night Club. I had been one of the youngest in my swimming group growing up, and here I was again, one of the youngest—*the* youngest—of the Friday Nighters. There's something validating about being the youngest. You get more attention.

You're reminded of your smooth skin and youthful appearance, your strength, your energy, your enthusiasm, your youthful attitude and ideas. And if you're the only young one—whether you know anything about it or not—you become the authority on popular culture.

Vern placed his hand on my shoulder to lead me toward the group, and Jim nodded at the cigarette smoldering near my blouse. "Careful, Vern. You'll set her hair on fire."

Eight or nine regulars were huddled together inside, and as we entered, the conversation sputtered. I was sure Vern was about to spill the beans. Instead, one of the men, Jon Hapner, our restrained municipal judge, finished a story about John Thompson, one of Hillsboro's citizens who was a descendant of Mother Thompson. He said Mother Thompson may've been the governor's daughter, and the leader of the women's march toward prohibition, but her descendants had veered off in another direction. According to the judge, when the Mother Thompson House had gone up for auction, on the day the furniture was set out so people could inspect it, a drunken John Thompson had lain stark naked with his buddy on one of the beds in an upstairs bedroom.

"Last I heard, Thompson was writing a book," Vern joked. "*From Governor to Gutter in Four Generations.*"

The group howled. Somebody complimented me on Vern's appearance, saying I'd helped him look younger—that for a while he'd been so worn out he'd looked as run-down as the old family hardware store. Another kidded Vern about the saltpeter Jon's brother, Jim Hapner, had given him at Vern's so-called "Bachelor Party."

Vern left for a moment to dilute his drink with tap water. A woman with feathered hair like Farrah Fawcett, a tight knit top, and layers of gold jewelry gave me a limp handshake. "I'm with what's-his-name over there." She pointed toward Bill, whom I'd met a month earlier.

Bill Bear looked like a genuine bear. He was short and roundish, had narrow-set eyes and bushy brows, and wore a pair of overalls with no shirt and lots of curly black hair hanging out. He worked as a plumber who'd started his own portable toilet company—Bear Necessity—and liked to hand out promotional pens with the slogan "Your shit is our bread and butter." He and his wife were raising six kids between them.

Bill patted Vern on the back. "How you been, Vern?"

"I've been getting these morning-afters, Bill, without the night-befores."

Bill let out a hearty laugh. He knew Vern had plenty of night-befores. "You said it," he said. "I got a new wife, new life, new house, new job, bald head, flooded basement, midlife crisis. You know, same old story." Bill was like Norm Petersen in *Cheers*, with one-liners and quips that tasted homemade in Highland County. "I tell my wife she has the most even disposition of anyone I know," he said. "She's a pain in the ass all the time."

"Stop!" Bill's wife gave him a playful slap as he planted a kiss on her cheek.

I stood against a tall filing cabinet, sipping my Sprite, watching them tease each other. I felt lucky too—the exciting news that I was pregnant, Vern's spirited reaction to my news, and now this crowded, laughter-infused room. Yet something told me there were surprises coming.

If I asked Vern what he was up to, he often responded, "Is there a need to know?" Questions about his physical health, his past marriage, or our financial situation made him chafe or shut down. There seemed to be a "no-talk" rule in the family, and I was beginning to think, *Heck yes there's a need to know, or I wouldn't be asking the damn question.*

I'd grown up with open bathroom doors and interrogations from my father that felt like strip searches. I knew how invasive questions could feel. I wanted to give Vern his privacy. At the same time, I sensed there were serious conversations we hadn't yet had.

And the more Vern resisted, the more I found myself modeling my father's intrusive behavior.

Before I met Vern, my life had been, for the most part, a solitary one. I'd grown up in Cincinnati as a competitive distance swimmer, racing up and down the lanes of a swimming pool twice a day, six days a week. I had four younger siblings, but when we were home, our parents were often gone, traveling the Midwest in a motor-home, selling gift items to small boutiques. I'd majored in fine arts and continued my swimming at the University of Southern California. Later, I'd served as an LA County Beach lifeguard, alone in a lonely tower on the beach. I'd eventually returned to live with my parents—by then, they'd moved to Hillsboro—after which I'd found myself working as an independent researcher for the State Historic Preservation Office, spending a full year digging through old tax duplicates in the basement of the Highland County Administration Building.

In my experience, people were here one minute, gone the next. Now for the first time, I had someone who'd promised to be there. Someone who could protect me—someone intelligent, articulate, with a sense of humor. By marrying Vern, I'd gone from vulnerable girl to mature woman, and yet because of our age difference, I was constantly aware of my youth and lack of experience. *Is there a need to know?* Maybe not. All I knew was, I couldn't wait to push a stroller, nurse in a cozy chair, and rock our baby to sleep at night, nurturing our child as Vern was nurturing me.

Mine was a typical pregnancy. Smells were the biggest problem. An open can of greasy wet dog food made me queasy enough that we had to switch solely to the dry stuff. I was tired; had mood swings, sore breasts, and a blinding headache; and, like most women pregnant for the first time, wanted everything to be perfect. I had the idea that adults were supposed to do kind things for each other when a baby was on the way. I wanted a good haircut and a pedicure. A kneaded eraser and a sketch pad. Beethoven's "Moonlight Sonata." A single red rose. Dark chocolate. Italian herbs and fresh olive oil. A clean dog. An open window. And Vern. I wanted him all to myself. I wanted that feeling of absolute buoyancy you get when you're sure you're in the right place with the right man doing the right thing at exactly the right moment.

And that's how I felt the morning I woke to Vern's doleful voice downstairs on the telephone. He spent a long time listening, and lighting one cigarette after another, as I puttered around the kitchen. I thought he was talking to Caroline, who he now jokingly called Brand X, after the television commercials comparing Tide laundry detergent to the old Brand X, which was no longer desirable. But his lack of emotion worried me.

When he hung up, he stared at the framed photographs of his three children—Cassie, Laura, and Ben, reminders of his past life—resting on the antique pie safe we used for kitchen storage.

I set the last dirty breakfast dish in the dishwasher. "Who was that?" It sounded like one more problem to be sorted out.

Vern didn't say anything. He wore cuffed gray wool trousers and a bleached T-shirt under a knee-length green plaid bathrobe and slippers. The bathrobe was pulled tight under his chin, and he looked cold.

"You okay?" I asked.

He slowly twisted the tip of his cigarette on a saucer of ash and then, with a poor attempt at a British accent, said, "I forgot my damned pills." He stood and reached into the cabinet for five plastic medicine bottles. He counted the tablets—Lanoxin, ranitidine, Lasix, and lithium—and tossed the handful down his throat in a single gulp.

"Who was that on the phone?" I asked again.

"The wife of an old friend."

"And?"

Vern held up two fingers. "For two weeks; that's all. He's eleven years old and needs some attention." As he spoke, he made clicking noises with his mouth.

"Wait, what? Who are you talking about?" It seemed he was speaking in riddles, and I was curious if he was being deliberately obtuse.

It took me a few minutes to grasp what Vern was saying. His dear friend Sam had died, and Sam's widow was involved in a lawsuit to save their thirty-four-acre farm and historic Thomas Sill House on the Lieutenant River in Old Lyme, Connecticut. She had called to ask if she could send her son to Ohio to stay with us for two weeks while she wrapped up her husband's estate and, she hoped, put the lawsuit behind her.

"He will be practice for you," Vern said. He opened a cabinet and reached for a glass.

"Practice!" I'd raised three of my siblings. I didn't need *practice*. With our parents on the road, my younger sister Jacquie and I had taken over at home starting when I was twelve.

"If he's anything like his father . . ."

"What?"

Vern didn't answer. He reached down to our Welsh terrier, Chippie, and scratched him around his collar.

"You know, we've only been married—what, three months? And now you want—"

Vern shushed me. "Honey, two weeks isn't long."

I cocked my head and glared. *Could the boy be Vern's son? Does he have a . . . no, that's not possible. Why is my mind going there?* This was a faint possibility with my father, since he'd had an affair, but not Vern. Still, something about what he was saying didn't make sense.

The night before, he had slugged down two strong bourbons while telling me about having to close another one of his hardware stores in Blanchester—I knew he was hung over. I also knew the loss of a store hurt him. On the other hand, he'd been so big on telling me I needed to hire people to help at home, especially now that I was pregnant. It wasn't like him to unilaterally decide on something that would mean more work for both of us.

"Vern, are you serious? What are we supposed to *do* with him?" I was imagining softball games or roller skating, and I was in no condition for either one.

"He can stay up in Laura's old room. Hell, we have the room for him."

"That's not what I mean. I mean, how will we deal with all the other projects in our lives?" My job with the preservation office had ended, but I was involved with the Historical Society now, and those of us on the board had plans to paint the second floor; Vern, meanwhile, had two guys he called his "elves," Herman and Tony, who were refinishing furniture in our basement. Vern had asked me to design the store windows and attend hardware shows with him in Chicago. Then there was the summer place out on Cave Road at the convergence of Rocky Fork and Paint Creek, called The Point, with two houses and a rustic pool that needed attention, not to mention my pregnancy.

"You don't have to fill up your dance card. You delegate," Vern said. "That's all . . . and Ruth will help." Ruth was our cleaning lady. Her husband, Paul, was the one who had called the night of Ben's death, asking for Vern. Ruth had worked three days a week for Vern's first family and was now working once a week for me.

When he introduced me to Ruth and I'd asked her about Vern's first family, she'd immediately mentioned Ben. "I raised him," she'd said, which made me uncomfortable. She was nice enough, but nobody was ever going to say they raised *my* child. I wasn't sure I really wanted her help.

That night, I climbed into bed early and stared at the blue paint, thinking the walls needed freshening. *Is there something I missed when two of Vern's friends warned me—jokingly, right?—to watch out for Vern?*

I glanced at his cherry military dresser covered with cigarette burns in the corner, the clutter of books on a shelf near the bed. Everything in the room belonged to Vern. I asked myself, *Why am I so irritated with him?* I thought of the way he sometimes bossed me around and how it didn't faze me. I guess I wanted someone to tell me what to do. A daddy figure or mentor. I knew that wasn't the ideal kind of relationship, but it felt cozy. Truth was, with most decisions, I didn't mind his issuing marching orders. I'd made a habit of asking for his blessing on everything. *Do I look pregnant in this dress? Should I buy pickles at the grocery? What do you think about these colors? These fabrics? These photos?* If he picked the kind of restaurant, the model of car, or type of movie, I didn't have to.

So why not this time? Why am I resisting? Why not help Vern enjoy this kid, especially after what happened to Ben?

Vern wandered into our room a few minutes later, talking more than usual, apparently wanting forgiveness for saying yes to the two-week visit without asking me first. "Honey, the boy's been having some problems, and his mother may be a strange bird, but I want you to make the best of this."

"Wait. What? The boy has problems?" I grimaced. "Strange bird? What are you saying?" I'd never heard of Sam before. I knew nothing of Vern's friendship with him. Did Vern even know Sam's wife? I felt a chill and pulled our navy coverlet up under my chin. *Not only do we have a boy coming to stay for two weeks, but there's some-thing—what, weird about him?*

"Well . . . we'll have to see. This might've been a mistake, but the decision has been made. The boy is coming, and I want you to support me in this."

"The decision *has not* been made, Vern. All you have to do is pick up the phone and call the woman back. It's not too late." I was thinking *any* woman would understand.

"We've already committed."

"*We* haven't committed at all. Call her back tomorrow. What's her name?"

"Ruthann Coxe."

"Okay, fine. Ruthann Coxe. Tell Ruthann you discussed the idea with your wife, and she didn't think she could handle it. Tell her I'm pregnant. I may not look it, Vern, but I really *am*." I didn't have the energy, or the calm stomach, at one month into this pregnancy to deal with this situation.

This may've been our first serious squabble. The only other time I can think of was when Vern made a weird assumption that he and I would hate each other's music and purchased a car without a radio. I'd later found a letter he'd written to a friend, saying he'd made the decision so there would be no dissension about whose music we listened to. I wondered at the time if the decision to nix the radio was a carryover from a disagreement with Caroline or his daughters.

I gave Vern a long, penetrating look, and for a moment it seemed he might renege. "It wasn't right for me not to mention it to you, darling," he said, "but try to make the best of this. Maybe we can take him out to Rocky Fork and go sailing." Vern was passionate about sailing. We owned a thirteen-foot sailboat, which he enjoyed sailing on Rocky Fork, the scenic lake and state park east of Hillsboro where my parents' house was situated.

In a letter to his sister long before he was married to Caroline, Vern wrote, *I'm in the midst of a violent affair and am going to get married this weekend—to a sailboat.* I wasn't sure if Vern had ever sailed with Ben. It had been four years since his death. Maybe Vern was needing closure. It had to have been traumatic arriving at the hospital that New Year's night. I couldn't imagine the pain and suffering, the lack of warning. We'd chatted briefly about Ben early in our friendship, but Vern could only approach the edge of his grief— that was all he could take of the conversation. I'd learned to tread lightly, to respect his need to deal with Ben's death privately and in his own time.

Most of our friends, knowing Ben's death had led to Vern's divorce, never mentioned the name "Ben" in his presence. I knew I was Vern's chance for a do-over. He was giving me a sense of security in my life, and I was giving him a way to walk away from Ben's dark shadow.

As he leaned on his elbows against his tall military dresser, a thin stream of smoke curling around him, I said, "I'll try to make the best of the boy's visit."

Vern seemed visibly relieved. "Thank you."

But as I said this, I felt tension in my shoulders. I felt like I was being thrust into a game show of *Is Kim a Grown-up Yet?*

When I was younger, my parents had liked to give me grief for not being the natural babysitter that my one-year-younger sister, Jacquie, always was. The neighbors invariably asked for Jacquie first. I knew that Vern wanted to spend more time at the hardware store, which meant caring for the boy would be largely my responsibility.

I wondered if Vern considered this a "teaching moment." He was a natural teacher. It seemed he was testing my parenting skills. He often shared stories from his past, like how his mother had once tied him to a post in the basement with his food, and that he remembered her throwing a coffee cup at him and saying, "Damn you," once. I mostly appreciated his stories. I didn't mind feeling like the conveyor of history to his future children. But his testing my parenting skills one month into my pregnancy struck me as annoying and distrustful.

"So you know, Vern, I'm not agreeing because I *want* to," I said. "I'm only doing this because it's important to you."

By the time we'd finished breakfast the following morning, I had buyer's remorse. I wanted so badly to support Vern, but I felt peevish thinking about how much of a pushover I'd become.

Vern sat at the table, hunched over the *Press-Gazette*, his oversize jean jacket buttoned up to his neck. "Let's go see your parents."

I gulped. "My parents? Why?" I knew where he was going with this.

"They may be helpful in assisting with the boy." Vern chugged his last bit of coffee, then broke into a smile like a man about to show his winning hand in poker.

"Bad idea, Vern." I shook my head and scowled. I'd learned over many years that my parents didn't do "favors." They were the ones to ask for help, not the other way around. "I guarantee they won't have the time."

Vern wanted to believe he could be the bridge that would improve my relationship with my parents. He had gotten over the three thousand dollars my father had borrowed just before our wedding—even reminded Dad periodically, "That was a gift, Dick, don't ever mention it again"—but *I* couldn't get over it. Every time we'd seen them since, Dad had patted Vern on the back. *I haven't forgotten that damn money, Vern . . . I promise to pay you back . . . The business is doing better . . . We're selling the hell out of our wooden Christmas ornaments . . . Blah, blah, blah.* He sure could tell stories.

But I was sick of Dad's florid stories. They sounded like excuses. His delivery, always spot-on, could make you laugh, but I didn't like having to pretend that I believed him.

CHAPTER 3

I **was in no mood to go,** but I tried to focus on the positive. My parents lived fifteen minutes east of town in a lovely home on the north side of Rocky Fork Lake, where they'd moved while Jacquie and I were off at college. Tucked away and screened off by a steep hill and cluster of oak, maple, and tulip trees along the shoreline, the house included a dock, a rowboat, and an occasional deer. My parents viewed their home as a sanctuary from the frenetic pace of their gift business, a quiet corner where they could watch sun glittering on the water's surface and hear owls hooting at night.

Vern and I took off in Vern's light blue S10 pickup, full of old pallets and scrap metal from the appliance store rattling in the bed. I tried to look nice—donned a fitted shirt (I wasn't showing from the pregnancy yet) and loose-fitting pants. Vern looked like an appliance store delivery man with his zip-up-the-front light gray jumpsuit and work boots and his wiry salt-and-pepper hair, which needed a wash. Every time the muffler popped, I would recoil, and Vern would pick up and swig his bourbon, which was jiggling in a glass of ice on the floor in front of the stick shift.

We drove out Route 124, the winding rural highway of rolling hills and large, scenic farms with dark brown split-rail fences and gravel driveways east of Hillsboro, the landscape darkened by looming clouds and the possibility of a storm.

The last visit I'd made to my parents' house haunted me. It had been a spur-of-the-moment decision on a Sunday morning soon after I learned I was pregnant. I think some part of me had hoped my father would weasel the news out of me—you know, say something about my beautiful complexion (Weren't pregnant women supposed to have good skin?), and I'd have to tell him the news.

But as I wound around their gravel drive that day, a dull haze had hung over the house. My eyes had landed on something shiny in one of the forsythias. *A beer can?* Weird. The wide lawn that sloped down to the house looked like it'd been trampled by a herd of elephants.

Turned out Mom and Dad weren't there; their motorhome was missing from the driveway. Empty kegs lay scattered on the back porch with long flexible plastic tubing attached. There was a pile of wet bathmats and several overstuffed lawn bags by the door, and the place reeked of beer.

Rick, pushing the upright vacuum, could hardly hear me over its loud clatter. David, my other brother, a junior in high school, was at work on the couch with his feet propped up on the coffee table, apparently working on a school paper. Carlos, the family's Brazilian exchange student, swiped at a side table with a stained dust rag. "What are you guys doing?" I asked.

"What does it look like?" Rick hissed. "We had a party."

David was hard of hearing and couldn't hear Rick. "Ask Mr. Bigshot," he said with a snort.

Rick was Dad's alter ego—his namesake—with good looks, charisma, and lots of mostly good ideas. David was more like Mom, with his high intelligence and the ability to get things done.

Rick kicked the vacuum's flexible hose against the couch. "Shut up, David."

"You shut up!" David said, gathering his things to leave. "I had to spend the whole night keeping people out of Mom and Dad's room and office. Where were *you*?"

Carlos gave me an embarrassed smile. He had come to live with the family when my sister Pam heard at school that he had been rejected by his host family for giving them a special bottle of tequila with a worm in it as a gift upon his arrival from Brazil. "We can't have a boy like that living in our house," the host family told the school.

"Those sons of bitches," my father said. "Tell the school we'll take him." By the next day, Carlos had become a member of the family.

"You missed it," Carlos said. "There were thirty cars here less than an hour ago. Kids were passed out everywhere."

Rick glowered. "Don't say another word, Carlos." He wiped the surface of Mom's piano and bent over to look closer. "Shoot."

"What?" Carlos rushed over. David and I did too.

On the top of the brown upright piano, Mom's most valued piece of furniture, was a big black cigarette burn. Mom had bought the piano with money she inherited when her own mother died. It was pushed against the wood paneling under a bronze-colored painting of a crashing wave. Nobody ever played the piano. For ten years, it had sat in the living room as a symbol of our missing grandmother. Now it had a black burn the size of a dirty fingerprint on it.

"We're in big trouble," Rick said.

"No, *you're* in big trouble. I had nothing to do with it." David disappeared into his room.

Rick glared toward the hallway. "David, you say one more thing and I'll beat your head in!"

Something was terribly wrong. This wasn't the first time they'd thrown a party. Other impromptu gatherings had resulted in funny stories. This one was different: a three-way game of tug of war that, I sensed, was over something much bigger than a burn on the piano.

I followed Carlos into my parents' bedroom, and over the next half hour, while he Windexed the windows, I tried to coax out whatever it was they were hiding.

Carlos was short and muscular, with a wrestler's build and a full head of loose brown curls. He had skin the color of milk chocolate and soft eyes that were often droopy from lack of sleep. Of the three boys, he was the softest touch. I was sure that if I pushed hard enough, he would tell me.

But Carlos was locked up tighter than a mouse in a trap. He held my gaze, his eyes ringed in red, stubble on his face. "It was terrible, Kim. Terrible."

"*What* was terrible? How did it get damaged?"

He raised his voice above the vacuum's clatter. "It wasn't the piano."

"Then what *was* it?" My mind went blank. "Was there a fight? Did somebody get hurt? Raped?" I waited, but Carlos didn't answer. "Carlos?"

"No, Kim. That's all I can say."

"No, they didn't get raped? If they didn't get raped, then what?" I was almost shouting. "Carlos, you have to tell me. Look, just answer this: Was it bad enough to get Rick kicked out of the University of Dayton?"

Carlos nodded.

"To send you back to Brazil?"

He nodded again.

"If it's criminal, you have to tell someone, Carlos."

"I can't." I trailed him back to the living room, where Rick was gathering the plastic tubing from the porch and wrapping it around his shoulder like a cattle roper.

"We had a pig roast, okay?" Rick said. "It was supposed to be at the Coonhunter's Lodge, but it ended up here. That's all you need to know."

The three boys were afraid to tell me what had happened for fear I would tell Vern and my parents, or both. But there it was again: the need to know.

Rick was eighteen, Carlos twenty. These were grown men. What had they done? Or witnessed? I knew it was something violent. And yet I hadn't mentioned it to Vern. I couldn't. I hadn't grown up enough to say to myself, "Hey, I have my own life now, my own responsibilities. I don't need to protect my brothers." I was still reporting to my parents, playing the responsible older sister. I was so afraid something scary was about to leap out of the shadows and I would be held responsible.

"Darling," Vern said, **"where are you?** You look like you're deep in thought." He cracked his side window to let out the smoke.

"Just thinking, that's all."

While Vern hoped to twist my parents' arms to get them to help me with the boy who was coming, I was imagining all the beer-bingeing kids passed out on the lawn or in various bedrooms of my parents' house. *Those damn boys*, I thought. What had they done?

"Let's think about inviting your parents for cocktails one of these days," Vern said as we turned onto North Shore Drive. "Do you think they'd like the Friday Nighters?"

"Of course they'd like the Friday Nighters. But would the Friday Nighters like *them*?" Knowing Dad, he would try to sell them something. Vern's friends didn't know me that well yet. I didn't want them seeing me through Dad's constantly running but distorted narrative. He was always making me a part of *his* story.

Vern didn't flinch. "I enjoy your parents. I find your father amusing, and your mother sweet."

"Yes, but—"

"Honey!" Vern interrupted. "You're only thinking of the 'yes, but.'" He leaned over, one hand on the wheel; the truck swerved as he lifted his bourbon from the floor.

I didn't say anything more. Listening to my own voice, I did sound judgmental. *Who am I to talk?* It had been less than six months earlier that Vern and I had knocked back one too many whiskey sours and passed out on the maroon couch in the family room only to have the whole bunch of them—Mom, Dad, Rick, Carlos, and several of Rick's friends—show up without warning, at which point Vern had bolted up, au naturel, to answer the door.

Vern thought he needed only a few drinks and jokes with my parents, and they'd offer to help with the boy in some way. But I knew my parents were overloaded with their business struggles. At the same time, Vern could be charming. And every now and then, Mom and Dad could surprise me. I resolved to keep my mouth shut.

We dodged squirrels and groundhogs as they raced across the road near the tiny Highland County Airport. We passed the entrance to Rocky Fork Lake, climbed a hill, turned right, and made our way down my parents' winding gravel driveway.

It amazed me that in a few short weeks, the grass had come back lush and dense, with iris and daffodil clumps near the house and day lilies along the gravel drive on our right, as if the big blowout had never happened.

"Let's not stay too long," I said as Vern pulled our truck up to one of their two garage doors.

"Whiskey, whiskey. It shortens distance and lengthens conversation." Vern thought himself a quipster and had memorized the quote from Doc Hogsett, a large-animal vet in town. For me, it had soured from overuse.

Vern left notes all over the house, in his pockets, tucked into the spines of books, with pithy quotations and jokes for the novel he intended to write someday. As we sat there outside my parents' house, I had the distinct impression he was having another one of his teaching moments. Before we got out of the car, his whole demeanor lit up. "Look up at the sky. Smile!" He was going to show me how it was done.

"Vern. Can we make this brief?"

He put on his straight face like a mask. "Remember that nagging headache I told you I had?" He was referring to a cartoon on his wall where the guy leans over to his buddy and asks if he remembers his having a headache. When his wife walks in the room, he says, "Here she comes."

"Very funny, Vern."

From the truck bed, he grabbed a packing blanket from the hardware store and unwrapped a bottle of Old Granddad, which he swung in his hand by the neck. We sauntered along the railroad tie path and up the steps to the back door. Looking out from the porch, the surface of Rocky Fork Lake glistened.

My parents' section of the lake was only three feet deep, so it was rare to see boats or people down there. But the seclusion, the peacefulness, the natural beauty of the house and its setting were awe-inspiring. It reminded me of the kind of place set up by the Episcopal Church as a religious retreat for wayward boys. A place to clear your mind. But my father . . . Well, let's just say he didn't match the landscape.

As soon as I stepped onto their cedar deck, I felt my stomach tie itself in knots. *Why am I anxious? Are the prenatal vitamins changing my body chemistry? The lack of alcohol and coffee?*

Dad was chipper, wearing a huge grin and puffing out his rock-solid gut. He combed through his cowlick, not a single gray hair on his head, and shook Vern's hand, then patted him on the shoulder. Before we had a chance to greet Mom, he peppered me with questions. "How have you been? How's married life? How was your birthday?"

Vern handed him the bottle. "For Cinco de Mayo, Dick. Wasn't that a week or two ago?"

Dad beamed as he inspected the label, clearly not connecting Old Granddad to a possible pregnancy. I'd never given Dad alcohol, and he looked surprised. "It's a gift from Vern, not me," I said.

"You always have to go and ruin things, don't you, Butch?" He jabbed an elbow in my side, and I winced.

I hugged Dad's bulky midsection—it was like hugging a refrigerator—and up close I noticed his puffy face, how his eyes were swollen behind his oversize glasses. Now that he was more than a hundred pounds overweight, it was hard for me to view him as the young, handsome man he'd once been.

Behind the stove, Mom stirred her savory meat sauce and pretended she didn't hear. She looked pale, her short gray hair falling in frizzy curls around her drawn face, as she greeted us. For all the efforts Mom made to support Dad and their business—and they were countless—there seemed to be something unnatural and inexplicable about the way she was always exhausted. I couldn't help but wonder, *Is she covering for Dad the way I'm covering for my brothers? Or for Vern?*

The cuckoo clock struck seven, punctuating Dad's booming voice, as we set Mom's dinner on the table.

"Oh, me," Dad said, patting his stomach. As soon as he sat, he was piling spaghetti on our plates, smothering each pile with a load of meaty sauce.

"I see the house is back to normal," I said, swirling the spaghetti around my fork.

"Those damn boys," Dad said. "You heard about the pig roast? What did you hear?"

"Not much," I lied.

"Did you see what they did to the piano?" Mom was shaking her head. "They had over two hundred kids here." She looked directly at Vern.

"Next time they try something like that, I swear to God, I'm comin' after them," Dad said. "All three of 'em."

"David had nothing to do with it," I said.

Dad swigged his drink. "I don't give a damn. He was there. David has been just as big a pain in the ass. Tell her, Beejay." He glanced at Mom.

Rick had been his high school class president and was attending the University of Dayton on a full football scholarship. David, a straight-A student, was popular in his own right. Carlos had already completed his stint as a foreign exchange student and graduated from high school, so David resented that before his own senior year, Carlos had returned from Brazil to live again with the family, stealing what was left of Mom and Dad's attention.

"David wasn't a part of it, but he was there," Mom said.

According to her, Rick's musician friends in Cincinnati had been home from college the same weekend as Rick. They had set up on the front stoop and blasted their music out into the front yard. She said the Wards next door, their only neighbors, were upset by the loud music and threatened to notify the police.

"Rick told them the police were here, that they should come over and join the party." Mom seemed full of admiration. "I don't know how he manages," she said, chuckling. "He gets away with things like your father does. In all the times he's been stopped, I don't think your father has ever once gotten a speeding ticket. If it hadn't been for the burn in the piano, they would've gotten away with it."

Mom's admiration of the boys' ingenuity didn't surprise me, since she made so many excuses for Dad. But Dad's bad behavior could boomerang. I knew there was trouble in the offing.

Dad silently chuckled, his shoulders shaking. "They wouldn't have gotten past me."

Mom laughed and slapped at the air.

I smiled tersely. I knew something criminal had occurred, and questioned if my silence and passivity made me an accomplice. I was doing the same thing I'd done as a child: smiling and pretending it was all enormously amusing, when inside I was nervous and panicked.

I finished Mom's spaghetti and dropped my dirty napkin on my plate.

In the kitchen, I pulled Vern aside and whispered, "Tell them about the boy, and then let's go."

He lit a cigarette in his cupped hand and leaned in to tell my parents, "Your daughter has a bee in her bonnet." He glanced from them to me, gauging my reaction. "We have a visitor coming, and he's caused some trepidation."

"What *kind* of visitor?" Dad's eyes glinted. He thought Vern was about to bring up one of my ex-boyfriends.

Vern started on a long tale about his friend Sam from San Francisco, a constitutional lawyer, who had an eleven-year-old son. I interrupted. "What's the boy's name, anyway?"

"I believe she said Stanislaus."

"Santa Claus?" Dad said.

The three of us chuckled.

The name Stanislaus made me think of a cute little nerd with thick glasses, his nose in a comic book, who liked dinosaurs and magic tricks. I found myself smiling from curiosity, even though the conversation rekindled my irritation with Vern.

"Is there anything to entertain an eleven-year-old out here at the lake?" I asked my father.

"Tons of things. I'm sure Beejay would like to have you over. All three of you." Dad gave Mom a hard wink. Ever since the day Vern went out to tell them he wanted to marry me, Dad had taken every opportunity to imply that Mom had the hots for Vern, that he had to keep an eye on her because she enjoyed Vern's visits more than he did. That was my father. *He*, of course, was the one we had to watch.

Dad was fearless when it came to signing up for trouble. When Mom was a student at Cornell and Dad at Colgate, he invited Mom to drive down with him to Sandwich, Massachusetts, for her spring break so he could show off his parents. His father, whom we called Pop-Pop, had been a surgeon in Plainfield, New Jersey. He had retired after serving thirty-seven years on the hospital staff of Muhlenberg Hospital, the last five as chief of staff. His mother—Mom-Mom— was a former nurse who appreciated antiques and fine craftsmanship. During their worldwide travels, she had collected glass paperweights and chiming clocks, as well as Turkish and Asian rugs.

After hearing about them from my father, Mom had hoped for a romantic weekend in the lap of luxury—relaxing at the Cape, going out to dinner, possibly seeing a movie in town. Instead, for two solid weeks, Mom helped my grandmother put blanket insulation in their attic. Then, in the midst of Hurricane Carol, a high-velocity acorn smacked Dad in the middle of the forehead as he brought furniture in from his parents' porch. As the wind whipped around, slamming tree branches against the house, the two of them hunkered down in Dad's parents' dank basement, Mom holding a wet rag to the giant bulge forming on Dad's forehead. Peering at her from under the rag, he asked, "Will you marry me?"

Mom grinned. "I'd love to."

The image of her with the insulation and, later, comforting Dad with a lump on his head in the middle of a devastating hurricane seemed a fitting metaphor for their relationship—Dad stormy, Mom buffering and tending. For her, happiness and duty to my father were inseparably connected. I told her the acorn story explained a lot about Dad, and since then every time she told it, we fell into hysterics.

"Send the boy over for a day or so," Dad said. "What's the problem?" There was hardly a stranger Dad didn't like. "What do we have going over the next two weeks, Beej?"

Mom sipped her drink, rattling the ice as she swallowed. "Don't even think about it. We have to get back on the road, Dick. We need to get ready for the sample sale."

Mom launched into a story Vern hadn't heard from the previous summer:

She and Dad had a booth at the Columbus Gift Mart and were living in their motorhome for the week, expecting a large number of customers for their annual sample sale. She said she and Dad had asked the boys to load the truck with gift samples, and at seven in the morning the kids were to drop by White's Cake Box to pick up a layer cake and then drive the hour to Columbus, deliver the cake, and unload the merchandise for the sale. David and Rick; Rick's girlfriend, Toni; and Carlos, all in the front seat with hot chocolate and the cake, had wrapped the vehicle around a telephone pole out in the middle of the country somewhere.

Dad went into great detail about Rick's girlfriend, who ended up in a nearby field with a patch torn out of her white pants.

"I think Toni grabbed the wheel," Mom said. "You know those kids . . . operating on only a few hours' sleep."

Vern said, "So what *did* happen? With the accident?" He sounded concerned.

"Well." Dad frowned. "The damned truck was totaled. We were conked out in the motorhome and some damn fool banged on the door at seven o'clock in the morning."

"It was a policeman, Dick. It was a serious accident."

"Serious, my ass, Beejay. The serious part was having to sign David out of the damn hospital because he was under eighteen. And right in the middle of the damn gift show."

Mom fixed her eyes on Dad as if to send a message. *That's enough, Dick. Don't say another word.* There was an awkward silence.

"What?"

"Nothing." She shook her head.

"Well, you gave me a look, Beejay. What are you trying to say?"

"Nothing, Dick. Nothing at all." She set some plates in the sink and ran water over them in a gesture of ending the conversation.

I could feel a sour taste in my mouth and swallowed. I knew the drill. I had to let them work out their differences. Vern pulled a cigarette from his breast pocket and bent over to light it from a candle on the kitchen counter. He said something about their being lucky; the accident could've been worse.

Dad kept on yakking. "Oh, hell. We had to pay for the damn telephone pole, and you pay based on the life of the pole."

By then, Vern was staring at the floor, sucking his cigarette. I wanted to reach over and hug him, but he had escaped into his own private space. It was a look I'd seen on him many times before.

Dad stirred his ice, and in the momentary silence, he caught on that the rest of us were thinking of Vern's son, Ben. "Oh, hell, I'm sorry, Vern." Dad pulled up the sides of his trousers and tucked his shirt in with his thumbs. "I never did hear the details of the accident. Can I ask how it happened?"

"No, you can't," Vern said.

I was used to Dad's endless poking and prying, but Vern was not. Vern's reaction was one of the reasons I loved him so much. He had the ability to stop Dad in his tracks. Not me. As a child, I'd let Dad dig into every closed closet of my daily life, believing his mantra—"Secrets are dangerous"—even when I insisted he was getting too personal.

As an adult, I understood his obsession. I found out Dad's grandfather had been a bigamist—that he'd left a wife and two children in England, married a second time in College Point, New York, then had six children, including Dad's mother, all born with congenital syphilis.

Secrets were corrosive; they strained family relationships. And yet here I was, with Vern's help, continuing to embrace the "no-talk" rule. The secret that I was pregnant. And the secret that something violent had occurred at my parents' house.

I rubbed Vern's shoulder and waited. "I think we should head out. I'm tired. Aren't you?"

Dad patted the taut boulder that was his midsection. "Life's a bitch," he said, shaking his head. "I *am* sorry, Vern."

"At any rate, we'd sure love to have you visit when the boy is in town," Vern said again.

Mom looked genuinely apologetic. "I wish we could."

"Why *can't* we, Beej?" Dad asked. "If we get those kids helping us, we should have at least one evening to drop by and say hello." I could tell by Dad's expression that he thought we were leaving too early. He genuinely wanted to help and was very close to suggesting they cancel some of their appointments. But Mom knew her limits. She knew if she helped in any way, it would compound her work. Dad was the kid who needed to be taken care of. And as much as I knew that wasn't the way it was supposed to be, I'd accepted it.

"I'm sure you have chickens to pick," Vern said, "but a visit would be beneficial to your daughter."

That's when I knew he'd blown it. I could see a subtle movement in their shoulders. Dad's lip straightened as Mom busied herself behind the counter. They would do something for Vern—after all, they owed him money—but not for me. To be fair, I couldn't really blame them. I wasn't able to be direct when I sensed their judgment.

On some level, I was sure, it tickled Mom and Dad to think of my taking care of an eleven-year-old boy, since I'd been considered such a lousy babysitter as a child.

"I'm sorry we can't help," Mom insisted. Then she added, "You think you have it rough. Try raising five."

Vern and I left my mother with a sink of dirty dishes. We climbed into the blue truck and drove out into the dark landscape toward Hillsboro. I thought of the moments as a child when I'd prayed for Mom and Dad to be there—to allay fears, to help in difficult situations. Time had healed so much of the hurt. But that night I realized I'd guessed correctly: once again, I couldn't count on them. Not even Vern could change their thinking. I had no doubt I'd be alone with Stanislaus for the duration of his two-week visit.

CHAPTER 4

Stanislaus was tall and gaunt. Maybe scrawny is a better word—think Macaulay Culkin as Kevin in *Home Alone*, with blond gossamer hair, high-water jeans, and a striped shirt. It was mid-May, 1982, and he bopped into the family room in the middle of the afternoon. Vern had picked him up at the airport, his first plane ride since he was an infant, and he was slurping a chocolate milkshake they had picked up somewhere along the way home. Chippie rushed out, yapping and growling, to greet him.

Vern tucked a manila envelope under my arm like a secretary handing me a file before an interview. I raised my eyebrows and shrugged.

"Hold on to it," he said. "It's from his mother."

I stood beside the totem pole in our family room as if it were a symbol of our house and family, its meaning and history bracing me. In front of me, Chippie rolled and rolled, rubbing his back on the red rug we'd purchased in Santorini on our honeymoon. Vern showed Stanislaus the way Chippie enjoyed being scratched behind the ear.

"Why don't you try it," Vern suggested. "Go ahead and give him a scratch."

"Animals smell," Stanislaus said. He turned down his nose, pinching it with his fingers.

A car stopped at the corner, and Stanislaus rushed to the open window. He peered outside, nervously kicking the floor with the tip of his sneaker. He darted from one side of the room to another, running his fingers across every carved bird and book on the shelf, repeatedly punching his toe into the wool nap of the Greek rug. An antique wood ironing board covered with houseplants vibrated by the window. I glanced up at the room's cathedral ceiling; the eagle's beak on the totem pole hovered over us precariously.

"Why are you kicking? Please stop, Stanislaus. You can damage the rug," Vern said.

I rolled my eyes and then caught Vern smiling as if his behavior was adorable. Chippie had already ruined the rug, christening three of the four corners as soon as we brought it home. Since it was made with unstable vegetable dye, its maroon color bled. The rug had become a reminder to me of the brief time in the beginning of a relationship when everything is perfect, and how quickly that perfection is spoiled.

Stanislaus removed the straw from his drink with his teeth, dripping chocolate in a dotted line across the rug.

"This is why you must be careful," Vern said, taking the straw away from him. He took a few deep breaths, pulled a linen handkerchief from his pocket, and leaned over to sop up the mess when he noticed a spot on the boy's shirt. "You'll have to give your shirt to Ruth, and she'll spot-clean it for you." Aware I hadn't yet forgiven him for taking Stan without a discussion, Vern was careful not to suggest that *I* clean the shirt.

"Who's Ruth?" Stan asked.

Vern chuckled. "Ruth is a good friend, and she will help you get acquainted."

"Here, let me help," I said. I held out my hands.

Vern lifted the shirt over Stan's head, revealing a clean but well-worn undershirt. I strode six steps to the laundry room by the back door, scrubbed the stain, and tossed the shirt into the dryer. Vern was still standing over the boy, trying to impart some common sense—or at least, that was what it sounded like to me. Vern lit a cigarette, and we watched Stanislaus fiddle with the loose latch

41

on the sliding glass door, which thrummed as he knocked it with his elbow. For a moment, he held still, scanning the yard full of squirrels.

He looked so out of place—his darting eyes, his twisted expression—that he seemed in a different world altogether, not knowing what to explore first.

"You shouldn't smoke, sir," Stanislaus said, jerking his head toward us.

Vern inhaled and smiled approvingly. "I know."

Stanislaus bent over and rubbed Chippie's ear, then sniffed his fingertips and groaned. I covered my mouth with my collar to hide my amusement.

Chippie was quick. Like a naughty two-year-old, he went for the nearest shoelace. Stanislaus responded with a swift strike.

"Whoa. We don't kick," Vern said. Before I met Vern, Chippie had been Vern's closest companion. I'd been told he was lovable as a pup, a cute little rascal. As an old dog, though, he had his issues. By the time I met him, everything made him scratch. He'd developed a severe anal sac problem and would scoot along the floor, leaving oily anal juice on everything. He had a wet beard and matted hair, and when I went to pet him, well, let's just say he made an odorous impression. No amount of grooming could fix the problem.

Vern's mantra was "Love me, love my dog." He told me Chippie had comforted him when Ben died so I tried to concentrate on Chippie's more redeeming qualities. There were times when he *could* be cute. A soft little Brillo pad with a long square face and grayish, matted hair, at the hardware store he would jump on Vern's desk, curl up, and snooze on his sales reports. Vern liked to tell customers, "Chippie sits on the payroll."

Vern lifted the wooden dowel from the door's track and slid open the sliding glass panel. "What if Stanislaus were to go outside and play with the dog for a while so you can make dinner, honey?"

Stanislaus didn't wait for an answer. He scooted out the door and whipped around the yard, holding a small branch in the air as he chased Chippie or Chippie chased him. Vern winked at me, wonderstruck, like we were staring at our new puppy.

I'll be honest. I didn't like him. He was fidgety, touching things, in constant motion—just watching him exhausted me—and he didn't listen. For the life of me, I couldn't understand why Vern didn't seem to share my reaction to him.

I tried to put myself in Stan's shoes. He'd been through a lot. He'd been through his father's sudden death from diabetes the previous year—he'd gone into a diabetic coma—and his mother's absorption in her legal battle. And his face *was* angelic. Some might even describe him as cute, the way he darted in one direction, then another. Kind of like a mouse in a maze at a pet store. You'd never want to take one home, but he was fun to watch, as long as you knew he couldn't get out to run through the back of your kitchen cabinets or across your floor when you turned out the lights.

Vern eventually called Stanislaus from the back door, then gave him a tour while I browsed the contents of the manila envelope from his mother. Mostly printed material from the La Leche League, it promoted breastfeeding for children up to a certain age—*eight?* Whatever it was, it was too long—and after that, no milk. In the margins were handwritten supporting comments with multiple exclamation points. Ruthann was clear: absolutely no milk.

It wasn't long before Vern and I began firing questions at Stanislaus. What kind of foods are you used to? Do you eat only fresh vegetables? What else? What do you grow on the farm? Call me naïve, but this was what normal families did when kids came home from school, wasn't it? Parents gathered in the kitchen, focused on their children. The wife mashing potatoes, the husband looking up from the local paper, both parents weary from a long day at work. I didn't know what normal was, as I think of it now, but Vern and I were as comfortable as I could imagine for a couple married barely four months. And with Stanislaus there, I could see down the road to a life with our own child, seated at the table, discussing the day's highlights.

I glanced at Stanislaus—rhythmically kicking his shoe against Vern's chair leg one minute, then getting all shifty-eyed watching Chippie scooting around the kitchen the next. This had to be good for him, I reasoned. Living on a farm near the Atlantic Ocean had to be vastly different from living on the western edge of Appalachia. With luck, his visit with us would be a much-needed vacation from the misery of losing a parent.

I asked him if he could describe one of his favorite meals. Did he like chicken or beef? Lamb? Pork? Fish? What was his favorite? Having grown up in Cincinnati and then attended college in Los Angeles, I couldn't remember ever experiencing a real farm. My idea of farm food was heavy in fat, starch, and sugar.

"We only eat organic."

"What do you mean by organic, Stanislaus? Organic what?" In Hillsboro, organic meant expensive and shipped from California.

Stanislaus shook his head, seemingly reluctant to say more.

"What is it?"

There was a click, and then the antique banjo clock struck seven. Stanislaus leapt from his seat, scaring both of us. "What was that?"

Vern held on to the back of the boy's chair and shoved it under the table as soon as he sat back down. "Mother's clock chimes every hour," Vern said. "I've gotten so I hardly notice it anymore."

We went back to our questioning. "Do you like vegetables?" My mind went right to frozen veggies, the kind I ate as a kid.

"As long as they're organic."

Vern folded the *Press-Gazette* and set it on the table with a hard thwack. "You're on vacation now. You can eat whatever you want." The way he said it was as if he were protecting Stan from the harsh treatment he assumed he received at home.

"Well, I don't drink milk."

"*Any* milk?" Despite having read his mother's notes, I assumed he meant whole milk and preferred 2 percent or nonfat, since he'd nearly inhaled a chocolate milkshake a few hours earlier.

Stanislaus locked his eyes on Vern. He looked ready to fight.

And Vern picked up on this. "In *our* house you'll eat what *we* eat," he said. His voice could sound tough when he needed it to be, but I couldn't help but smile, remembering meals as a kid with the five of us wailing at the dinner table, my father's face strained as he waited, determined that we eat every painful bite, while my sister Pam defiantly packed lima beans on a ledge underneath the table. Some part of me was amused—but just as my mother humored my father, I sat back and took a deep breath, smiling and telling myself this was not going to end well.

By the time dinner was ready, Vern had stumbled over Stanislaus's name a couple of times.

"Your name is unusual," he finally said. "Did you know there is a park in California named Stanislaus?" Vern remembered it from the days before he met Caroline in San Francisco.

Stanislaus gazed over Vern's shoulder.

"Is it Stanis-laus or Stanis-law? How do you pronounce it?" Vern asked.

"Stanis-*laus*," the boy said, exaggerating the third syllable.

Vern coughed up some mucus. With his brown fingertips clutching a dirty napkin, he spit out something resembling rubber cement. He took a minute to catch his breath. "Stanislaus is a mouthful, isn't it? How 'bout if we call you Stan for short? Would that be okay?"

The boy shrugged. *Are his feelings hurt?* I wondered.

But it was too late. Vern started saying, "Stan. Stan, the man," and Stan didn't seem to mind.

"What do they call you in school?" I asked.

"They must call you Stan, right? What do they call you?" Vern seemed sure he had a nickname.

"They don't call me anything. I don't go to school."

"You don't go to *school*? You're homeschooled?" *Jesus.* This had not yet become a "thing" in the early '80s. In our area, nobody homeschooled their kids. It was seen as something that weird religious cults did to isolate their members.

"Your mother failed to mention school." Vern sounded like he'd been hoodwinked. "I suppose it's because you're here in the summer." He lifted a cigarette from his pack and tapped it on the table. "At any rate, it shouldn't make a difference." He hesitated a moment and then looked up. "Do you go to church?"

"No."

"Never?"

"My mother says it's devil worship."

"*What's* devil worship?" Vern looked Stan over, a smile appearing on his face.

"Church."

"What do *you* think about it?"

"People go to church because they don't have any imagination," Stan said.

"Hmm." Vern smiled as he reached for his cigarettes.

"They want somebody else to tell them what they can't figure out for themselves. They want to be with other unimaginative people to keep on doing unimaginative things and . . ."

I started to chuckle. It tickled me to wonder how Vern was going to wiggle out of this one. We had been attending St. Mary's Episcopal Church, though not regularly.

"If you've never been to church, you have no business judging it," Vern said. He held his head down deferentially as he recited a ditty— something like, "Good bread, good meat, good God, let's eat." It was his version of a prayer, which was strange, since we'd heard it from my parents, who were Catholic, and had never recited it before ourselves.

SHOOTING OUT THE LIGHTS

Vern and I often pushed the newspapers and mail to one side of the round oak table before sitting down to dinner, but this time, Vern cleared everything off. We even used linen placemats. I usually whipped up something without much thought—my meals were hit or miss—but this night I arranged the food on the plate so it looked like something you'd see in an ad for a diner: meatloaf, mashed potatoes, buttered green beans, and, as a special treat, Pillsbury biscuits, the kind that were loaded with something resembling butter and peeled off in layers. Stan gobbled the vegetables down and then grabbed for the biscuits, which he tossed in his mouth and swallowed whole.

"Slow down, slow down," Vern said. "This is not a race."

But Stan continued chewing wildly before wiping his mouth with the back of his hand and explaining that he'd never had food like this before.

"You seem to like it," Vern said, sipping his bourbon and water and winking at me.

Stan nodded for a moment. "I'm starving, but . . ." He bent over, clutching his stomach with his hand. "I feel sick."

Vern pushed his small glass of milk closer. "Have a sip."

"I can't drink milk." He pushed it away again. "My mother will kill me."

"What do you mean, your mother will kill you? She's not here. Try it. It'll settle your stomach."

"I can't."

"Why not?"

"Because I've never had it."

"You had a milkshake. That had milk in it." Vern gulped his drink.

"Well, my mother says I should never drink it." Stan rocked forward and back, his arms wrapped around his waist, his mouth quivering like he was about to puke. It was obvious this was no prank. His face, drained of color, nearly touched his plate, and I could hear his stomach rumbling.

"Vern, he's sick."

"All right. Why don't you go upstairs to the bathroom and see if that helps?"

Stan pushed his chair away from the table and rushed up the back steps. Moments later, we heard dramatic grunts coming from the bathroom.

"Oh, God. Maybe you should go up there." I nearly gagged from the thought of vomit. "This is a guy thing, isn't it?"

Vern slowly pushed away from the table and opened the cabinet behind him to dig for a pack of matches. He lit a cigarette and shook out the flame. "You have to admit it was extremely pleasing to hear the gaiety in his voice as he ate your dinner, darling."

I couldn't tell for sure if Vern shared my feeling that Stan was odd. So I talked about him the way I was taught in figure drawing class to give feedback in critiques. I told him what I was seeing—an unusual kid—and then I focused on the positive, saying, "It *was* a good feeling that Stan seemed to like it so much." Nobody had ever shown that much enthusiasm for anything I'd ever prepared for dinner.

"One need only look at these situations with good humor." Vern's voice was tender. I think he genuinely believed what he was saying.

I took my dishes to the sink, flinching with every percussive keck from the upstairs bathroom. "So, I'm curious," I said. "When is he actually leaving?"

No answer.

"Vern? Can we talk about this for a minute? It's day one and he's already sick. If he eats what we eat, he's going to be sick every night. Have you read the literature she sent us?" I was pretty darned sure that, despite being eleven years old, Stan was still drinking breast milk. I was imagining having to drive into Cincinnati to some kind of offbeat hippie breast-milk bank.

"Honey, you know what I know." Vern was focused on a newsletter or brochure from somewhere.

"Okay . . . but did she send you a return ticket?"

No response.

"Vern! Does . . . Stan . . . have . . . a . . . return . . . ticket?"

"For Christsake," he said, slapping the brochure on the table. "*We* paid for the ticket. Two weeks is not long. If you change your routine, you go back to it two weeks later with no harm done." He set his cigarette on the edge of a dirty plate, flicked a small piece of tobacco from his upper lip, and climbed the stairs, pushing down on the handrail as if it were a cane.

He was gone for another half hour, and it sounded like he was helping Stan into bed.

We put Stan in Cassie's old room, mainly because it was across the hall from ours and because Ben's room was set up as a memorial to him. Every arrowhead, geode, or abalone shell Ben had owned was on display beside his books, school projects, and collection of knives. One knife in particular looked antique, like some kind of Boy Scout tool, with a dirty cord wrapped around its handle. His bed was covered with a heavy deep-red-and-black spread. The tiny brass lamp; the bulletin board; the photos, notes, and award certificates; the twelve-inch-long jaw bone with teeth; the giant machete in its sheath—everything in the room reflected Ben's fourteen years of life. It seemed only right to leave it alone until Vern was ready to deal with it. I didn't want to be the one to dismantle it, and from what I could tell, it would take a while for anyone else.

I stretched out in the living room to calm myself, nauseous from the pregnancy, trying to wrestle meaning from what had just happened. The reality of Stanislaus had taken me by surprise. My mind drifted back to the momentous hike Vern and I had taken in Yosemite before we were married.

Vern had reserved a tent with two twin beds in Half Dome Village, and we'd only been there a day when we decided to go for a scenic hike. Vern had pointed to a purple finch, a white-breasted nuthatch, several thrushes and English sparrows, the birds we had in common back in Ohio. I was snapping pictures atop huge granite rocks in the midst of giant sequoias. As I set the camera's timer, I dropped my filter and lens cap several times and made mistakes with various settings. Vern enjoyed my enthusiasm as much as my ineptitude with the camera.

Speaking slowly, he'd said he had a question for me. "I was wondering . . ."

"Yes?"

He'd leaned back on a rock, his legs outstretched, his left hand resting in his lap. "Well, this is out of curiosity."

"What?"

"Well, I'm not quite sure how to say this."

"Just say it." I worried he was going to say something sentimental about the weather or the scenic spot, and I would feel uncomfortable and inarticulate. He combed through his salt-and-pepper hair with his fingers, and then paused. "What is it?"

"Well, if I were to ask you tomorrow, for instance, if I were to say something like, 'Would you marry me,' how would you answer?" He glanced down for a second and then straight at me.

"Um, well . . . I guess I'd say 'yes.'"

"Yippee!" He scooted along the rock and dropped one foot, and I held out my right hand to steady his jump. We stared at each other with big, silly grins and then impulsively hugged. I could feel his lips on the side of my neck. "I love you so much," he said.

I squeezed him again. "I love you too," I said, and it was like the movies. I had electricity shooting through my spine and a sudden flood of images in my head. Just like that, I was engaged. Engaged! It didn't seem like a proposal, and yet images—of Hillsboro, my immediate family, friends, relatives, the church, babies, my job and coworkers—flashed through me, overlapping like a collage. It had been such a shock—me, married to this charming older man!—and yet I'd known it was the right thing to do.

We drank that night to God and guardian angels, to life and death, to youth and age, to talking too much and saying too little, and then we'd pushed our twin beds together and collapsed.

Now, I found myself questioning my decision. *Did I see Vern clearly then? Or only the side of him I wanted to see?*

With Stan asleep, a peaceful quiet settled over the house. Chippie, curled up by Vern's chair, grunted as he dreamed. I listened to the lulling hum of the refrigerator. Vern, wearing his green plaid bathrobe, joined me in the living room with a book and a cigarette. I wiggled in one of our two gold-striped wingback chairs, trying to get comfortable. These chairs were ideal for political discussions because they kept you from falling sideways if you dozed off sitting up. They weren't bad-looking, either. They had been perfect for the monthly meeting of the Hillsboro Esoteric Club, to which Caroline had belonged—after the divorce, she'd moved to Cincinnati—and to which Ann Pence across the street was proposing me as a prospective member. But these were not chairs you would curl up in.

After I moved in, Vern had recognized the need for me to make his nineteenth-century I-house (so named because it was common in rural areas of Indiana, Iowa, and Illinois) my own. I liked its style and I appreciated its Greek Revival flourishes, like the pilasters flanking the front door. But it wasn't the house I would've chosen. It wasn't really "me." And Vern, knowing that, had said again and again, "If you want to paint the rooms or buy new furniture, only say the word."

I think we did paint a few rooms. And Vern was as superstitious as I was and had agreed we should buy a new bed and move out of the room he'd shared with Caroline and into Laura's room when we first got married. But the furniture—his early-American antiques—had beautiful lines, were well crafted, and were in good taste. He owned interesting hardware tools he'd collected over the years and furniture of local historical significance like a dresser with the name Eliza Jane Thompson (aka Mother Thompson of Temperance Crusade fame) etched in a metal plate on the front. So to waste good money on new furniture of lesser quality that wouldn't improve the appearance of the house at all just didn't make sense. It would be like insisting Vern give up the family hardware business. He was the third generation, continuing a business that had worked, one that had served the community and provided income to the family. Why start something new if it wasn't necessary?

That night, though, sitting in the wingback chair, I glanced down at one of the rugs Vern said had been brought back from Iran by his ex-father-in-law, who had been the former president or chancellor of four universities, and I thought, *What am I doing with this stuff? Do these things even look like me?* The furniture, the flooring, the gold drapes and Persian rugs—all had something to do with Caroline. I might as well have been wearing Caroline's clothes. I was pleased with the look of the room, the way I'd moved the furniture around and rearranged the art on the walls, but I hadn't been a part of the decision to acquire any of it. I had stepped into another woman's world and allowed my environment to shape me.

I told myself I was safe in my new life. I had a husband who loved me—one who was not in great shape physically, *But so what?* He could protect me. He was honest and direct, the kind of person who could tell the bank president with a broad smile, "I'm sorry I can't come to your party, Bob. I'm going to be working on my novel, *The Joy of Not Going.*"

I flipped through *The New Yorker*, unable to concentrate, when I noticed Vern about to nod off with a cigarette in his hand.

"Vern!" My response was immediate, visceral.

He jumped. As his hand trembled, a column of ash fell into his lap. He brushed it off, chuckling. It had burned the wool of his plaid bathrobe.

"Why are you laughing?" I knew I was testy, but he was about to set himself on fire. And this was the same way he was dealing with

Stan—*Aw, what the heck, laugh it off*, like we'd meant to buy parsley and instead ended up with cilantro. *Why is he so pleased with this boy?* I just didn't get it.

Even so, I was so close to settling into the feeling of family togetherness, to being more positive, to letting all Vern's decisions from the previous few days go, when Vern stared brazenly into my eyes, set down his book—*Growing Young*, by Ashley Montagu—and said, "That was joyous tonight."

I about swallowed my tongue. Heat spread from my face to my ears to my neck and onto my chest as I turned the pages of *The New Yorker*.

"We need to keep Stan busy," he said. "He has too much energy."

With both hands, I slapped the magazine shut. *Why isn't he seeing Stan's behavior as odd? Why is he not concerned?* All at once, the arguments against Stan's visit boiled up in me. "Vern, you're having breathing problems and I'm pregnant." What about *our* kid, I wanted to shout. Let's talk about *him*.

"I know, darling." His chest swelled as I sat back in my chair. I knew my level of emotion was too much for Vern. He was barely treading water, and I was pushing him under. At least, that's what I thought back then.

"I'm sorry, Vern. I shouldn't have been so loud."

He took a drag from the cigarette pinched between his fingers, and propped his heavy head with his other hand. "Oh, well, what the hell."

"I'm sorry. I'll try to be more positive. You're right. Two weeks isn't long." In that moment, I was safe from further conflict. I didn't have to say one more idiotic word, and the conversation would've ended. But something inside me couldn't stop. No matter what, I could not muzzle my bitterness—so I said, "Can I ask you something, Vern?"

He waited a good seven seconds while he took another puff and smashed the cigarette in a saucer beside him.

Something nagged at me to keep going. I could've said, "Never mind; no big deal," and Vern would've understood. Maybe he would've comforted me. For sure, we would have been in this together. I would've been helping a boy who was missing his father by helping a husband who was missing his son.

His eyes cast downward, revealing a shimmer of sadness, like something shiny rising up through those deep layers of protection. "What is it, darling?"

I cocked my head and squinted. "Is this about Ben? Is this your penance, having Stan stay with us?"

When he didn't say anything, I started digging at him.

"Did you really think today was joyous? What was so joyous?"

Vern reached for his pack of cigarettes, stuffed them in his pocket, and, tightening the belt of his bathrobe, stood. "Good night, honey."

"That's all you can say?"

I flopped back, my hands gripping the arms of the wingback chair, staring at the back of Vern's worn-out bathrobe as he left the room.

But I wasn't thinking of Vern, I was thinking of myself. My angst was not based in fear of my not being able to handle Stan. It had little to do with my confidence in my abilities as a mother, either. My angst was about my own happiness, about whether I could truly experience the unadulterated joy I'd imagined—of being married for the first time, of becoming pregnant, and of sharing the excitement with my husband. Vern had been through all this before. Clearly, he was wounded. Was Stan really a catalyst for my distress, or was Vern using Stan to create distance from me and my joy?

It dawned on me that this wasn't about Stan. I was fighting for my unborn child, and for myself.

CHAPTER 5

In the morning, leaving Vern in our bed, I wandered downstairs, where I found, on a scrap of paper on the kitchen counter, a reminder from Vern to wake him:

Darling,

Please use drastic measures to awaken Rip (Old Rip) Van Winkle as soon as you are up (before dressing or anything else). Suggest #1: Loud yah-yah on radio followed by #2 Water treatment, teaspoons of cold water followed by repeated tablespoons and lastly ½ cupfuls. In administering the treatment, wear the ear muffs and apply from five feet away. Remember I love you dearly no matter what's said. I'm not responsible for what's said when I'm being awakened.

Love, Vern (Old Sludge)

I did as I was told, minus the music or water treatment, assuming Vern had an important meeting of some kind. He dressed quickly, too anxious to engage in conversation, and still trying to inject humor, he leaned over the kitchen peninsula and said, "I want to start the day off right, darling, so I'm skipping breakfast." Turns out, he was having an "emergency"—code word for a nicotine fit—and wanted to race off to our town's small 7-Eleven-type shop, called Convenience Store, for cigarettes.

Vern could be at his best in the midst of a crisis, and he was cracking himself up. I shot him a warm smile. "What about Stan?" I asked. He was still in bed and hadn't eaten breakfast yet either.

"Oh," he said, "I guess I should take him with me."

Stan appeared in the doorway then, blinking back sleep. With his hand on Stan's head, Vern led the boy toward the hallway.

I gave Vern what he called the Hillsboro nod: one brief head shake—not too big, not too small—to acknowledge his departure. Then I sat at the kitchen table glancing at Caroline's old eyelet curtains, streaked yellow from cigarette smoke despite countless bleach-powered washings. It was the middle of spring, not long after my birthday, and I looked out at nearly dead rhododendrons, their leaves dangling and ready to drop. I knew nothing about gardening. *Am I overwatering?*

In the side yard, thanks to a multiplying family of squirrels, many of the bulbs had disappeared, leaving a muddy mess with only a few dwindling clusters of crocuses and grape hyacinths. I'd thought I might add some new bulbs or shade-loving shrubs, but making changes to the house was a touchy business. Caroline—or someone she had hired—had known how to choose the best fabric or the right kind of bushes and bulbs. I wasn't sure I could make selections that would improve and not ruin the appearance of the house.

What did I know about Caroline? I knew she was a concert pianist. I knew she was a detail person who kept lists. I knew she was an intellectual, the daughter of a famous psychologist and a psychologist herself. And I knew their marriage hadn't been great, even before Ben's death. Caroline had been forced to put Vern into the hospital for treatment on at least two occasions: once on a ski trip, when he was determined to dismantle the plumbing to fix a small leak under the sink, and another time, when he and Ben cut dozens of roses from a neighbor's garden, then planted single roses on the front porches of the homes in town that Vern thought were especially well preserved. I'd heard these stories from Vern, and unflattering rumors about his marriage to Caroline from other people. Mostly I didn't want to hear it.

The thing about marrying someone who's been divorced is that you want to prove to yourself—and everyone else—that you're different, that you aren't cold, rigid, or locked in a need to be right like that old bitch who lived there before you. You're more creative, or attractive, or successful in some way. You're more tolerant, more loving. You tell yourself you're a wee bit better in every area required for a marriage to be successful.

I knew I was doing this, that I needed to make Caroline detestable to feel like less of a replacement wife. She had filed for divorce from Vern—hadn't wanted to stay married to him—and yet I was still living in her shadow. *How does a woman deal with the grief of losing a child? And the guilt?* Vern had said Caroline insisted on going to the New Year's party the night of Ben's death. They'd already arranged to go with Jerry and his wife. Vern hadn't wanted to go. *Did she blame herself for attending the party? Or if it was Vern's gun that killed him, did she blame Vern?*

I hated that there was a gun still sitting in the junk drawer over the liquor cabinet in our kitchen. Was that the gun that had killed Ben? I worried that it had been placed there like one of Vern's hardware tools, just waiting until the day his grief would become unbearable and he'd need to use it.

Vern liked to call me his enchantress, his sweetheart, his *petit chou*. In a letter he wrote to me before we were married, he said, "I'd climb the highest mountain, swim the widest fiord, cross the driest desert to be with you, my love." I ran across an old photograph of Caroline once and noticed that her engagement ring looked an awful lot like the one Vern had asked Limes Jewelry to create especially for me. Did he just happen to like platinum and star sapphires?

There was no way to pretend we were "beginning" our lives, since Vern's life had come to a dead halt after Ben's death. Caroline had moved on. Vern and Caroline's two daughters, ages twenty-three and twenty-one, were on their own. Cassie was working in Syracuse; Laura, living in Cincinnati. I had believed that despite

Vern's immeasurable sorrow, I could kick-start his life again, and everything would be perfect. But Ben was still there, and I was, in some sense, an outsider looking in on a past I wasn't a part of.

To heal grief, maybe it's necessary to have someone or something to push against. Was Vern pushing against me since Caroline wasn't there? If so, as her stand-in, I couldn't push back. I had no history with Ben—hadn't even known him. So where were Vern's guilt, self-blame, and self-loathing supposed to go?

Returning from the Convenience Store, Vern made his way through the squeaky back door and within minutes was slumped, barely breathing, over the kitchen counter. I tried to bend his ear, but he held up his index finger, lifted his albuterol inhaler to his mouth with his other hand, and puffed, his shoulders heaving. I glanced out the window as I waited and caught Stan heaving a heavy stick into our huge oak tree at a squirrel.

I jumped to my feet and pounded the window. "Hey!"

Vern nearly knocked over a chair, rushing to the door. "We don't hurt animals," he shouted. Then he collapsed again at the table, gasping like a fish on a beach.

"I'm worried about you, Vern."

He shut his eyes, shook his inhaler, and gave himself another puff. When he caught his breath, he said something about compassion—that if you chase two rabbits, both will escape.

I kissed him on the neck and waited. Was he saying his health and Stan's visit were the two rabbits? Or was he chasing two rabbits, meaning Stan and me, implying the two of us were too much? I wasn't sure.

"I discovered something interesting this morning," he mused. "Stan has never had candy or chewing gum."

"Never?"

"Not until now." He took several deep breaths and moved closer to the window, eyeing the backyard. He said Stan had stuffed himself at the Convenience Store with candy bars—Snickers, Nestlé's Crunch, whatever he could hold in his hands—until his mouth was so full he was unable to speak. Vern bent over the table, hunting under stacks of various papers.

"What are you looking for?"

He held up an empty pack of cigarettes and gave a throaty laugh. "Fibber Magee's closet."

I had no idea he was referring to a radio show from before I was born.

Vern said Stan had crammed a square of Bubblicious gum into a mouth full of chocolate. He'd barely removed the wrapper. Saliva and long, sticky strings of gum dribbled from his mouth onto the truck's seat and floor, and before Vern could hand him a handkerchief, Stan opened his door, pitched his head out, and drooled onto the pavement. When he pulled his head back inside the truck, he told Vern, "It's sticking to my teeth."

I grimaced. "You're not supposed to eat chocolate at ten o'clock in the morning, you know." I pulled a cup of instant coffee from the microwave and poured in a thin stream of 2 percent milk.

"And you should learn to drink your coffee black," Vern said. "You become a nuisance to people when you need all the accoutrements." He came around the kitchen peninsula and put his arm around me. "I want you to reread the essay by Don Marquis about the good time that is coming."

Vern was always referring to Don Marquis, especially the essay "The Almost Perfect State," which read, in part:

> Between the years of ninety-two and a hundred and two, however, we shall be the ribald, useless, drunken, outcast person we have always wished to be. We shall have a long white beard and long white hair; we shall not walk at all, but recline in a wheel chair and bellow for alcoholic beverages; in the winter we shall sit before the fire with our feet in a bucket of hot water, a decanter of corn whiskey near at hand, and write ribald songs against organized

society; strapped to one arm of our chair will be a forty-five calibre revolver, and we shall shoot out the lights when we want to go to sleep, instead of turning them off; when we want air we shall throw a silver candlestick through the front window and be damned to it; we shall address public meetings (to which we have been invited because of our wisdom) in a vein of jocund malice. We shall . . . but we don't wish to make any one envious of the good time that is coming to us . . . We look forward to a disreputable, vigorous, unhonoured, and disorderly old age.

The first day Vern and I met, sitting in Vern's tiny brown office with its two massive desks facing each other and its wall of smoke-stained comic strips, Vern asked me to copy the Marquis essay. For some ridiculous reason, I decided he wanted a handwriting sample as part of the job interview. Later, I found out he'd asked two other people to copy the same page, and realized it must've been import-ant to him. Why was he bringing this up now? How did any of this relate to Stan? And what was he trying to teach me, if anything?

Vern had described himself as a mischievous teenager. It was the late 1930s then, and he made himself sick smoking horseweed and dried corn silk wrapped in toilet paper. He shot out the glass insula-tors on electrical poles. With another boy, Dick Lukens, he climbed a 130-foot-high, 30-foot-wide standpipe to skinny dip in the town's water supply. The old Detwiler sisters were said to have boiled their water for three months after that.

Stan didn't seem like that kind of boy, but was he? Was he mis-chievous—interested in stretching the boundaries, breaking the rules? Stan was missing basic social skills, but it was impossible to ascertain if his awkwardness was due to his not having experienced other children or if he had something diagnosable that we didn't know about.

I excused myself to use the small powder room off the hallway, and as I glanced at my long, dark hair in the mirror in front of me, thinking of the unusual, but wonderful, husband I was married to,

I considered that Vern might be identifying in some way with Stan.

I unzipped my pants, sat down on the toilet seat, and instantly winced. "Dammit." The seat was soaking wet.

Vern called out, "You okay?"

I didn't answer at first. *Who is doing this? Stan? Vern?* I wasn't a control freak. I hardly flinched when I found mouse droppings under the sink or hair on the wall of the shower. But sitting on a wet toilet seat? Now that was disgusting. I reached under the sink for the isopropyl alcohol, sterilized my bum, and decided to wait for more evidence before I accused anyone.

A few minutes later, Chippie, our doorbell, charged to the back of the house to greet Ruth, arriving to clean. "Oh . . . you," he seemed to grunt, and then he trotted off.

Vern pulled me aside on his way upstairs. "I'd like to offer a suggestion," he said. "I know you have things you want to do. And I don't think Stan has ever watched television. Maybe it would settle him."

I nodded. "Let me think about it," I said, and then I headed to the back door to meet Ruth and waited as she unloaded her purse on the washing machine.

Ruth was a kind, older woman with a round face, chestnut skin, and thick tan glasses she wore on the tip of her nose. For some reason, she mostly laughed when we interacted, which encouraged me to state my opinions. When I asked for her advice, my questions were often veiled attempts at comparisons. I wanted her to tell me how much happier Vern seemed married to me; I wanted specifics. But Ruth said there were things she couldn't tell me. Being my father's daughter, of course, I was dying to find out exactly what those things were. I asked her at least five questions every day as a matter of habit.

Today, she laughed as soon as she saw me.

"Did you see we have a visitor?" I asked.

Together, we looked through the sliding glass family room windows.

"He's here for two weeks, and he's, uh . . ." I held back my feelings. I told her about his diet, which sounded like mostly home-grown vegetables and the bread he ate, called "essene," which had no fat, no sugar, and no salt and was supposed to digest like vegetables.

Ruth shrugged, amused.

"His mother sent us instructions with literature about breast-feeding. I mean *a lot* of literature. I know this sounds off the wall, but at his age, he wouldn't be drinking breast milk, right?" I laughed as the words came out, surprised by my boldness. I was 100 percent sure he *was* drinking breast milk—only breast milk—but I didn't want to sound like *I* was the kooky one.

"What? That doesn't make sense," she said.

"I know, it's weird, Ruth, but his mother is kind of a hippie."

"How old is he?"

"Eleven?"

Ruth snickered. "*Breast* milk?"

Vern introduced me to Ruth the year before he and I became engaged. He had been inviting me over for drinks on his front stoop—or, on rainy days, to his kitchen—with others from the neighborhood who gathered to sing or brainstorm about how to improve Hillsboro.

It was during one of those nights that I learned he had purchased Ayres Drugstore when it closed, hoping he could run it from the hardware store to keep it operational as a drug store. Ayres was by far my favorite Hillsboro building—built in French Second Empire style, with a slate mansard roof and two glass show globes hanging from solid brass brackets in its front window. Its handsome walnut shelves were loaded with apothecary jars, hand-blown with ground glass stoppers and hand-printed glass labels. It had been the oldest pharmacy in continuous operation west of the Alleghenies. When Vern complained that it wasn't working, that he found it impossible to operate two distinctly different businesses, I had gushed to him about Ayres, about how exciting it would be to see the building turned into a museum.

I could hardly believe it when he hired me to fix it up. Together, Ruth and I sorted and scrubbed for days. And the relics were end-less. Antique medical devices, cocaine-imbued remedies once peddled by snake oil salesmen—the place was loaded with every antique pharmaceutical gadget imaginable.

When I reached for a veterinary medication for goats and the label on the bottle read, "Teat Salve," I thought it looked interesting but had no idea what it was.

"Teat? What's teat?" I asked Ruth.

She scowled. "You know."

"No . . . I don't. What is it?"

"You ask Mr. Fairley." I could tell she didn't believe me. She lifted a bucket of soapy water and was about to pour it down the drain when I latched on to her forearm.

"Tell me. What is it? I've never heard of it. Teat? What's teat?" Suddenly, it hit me. "Oh, you mean like . . ." I whispered as if some-one were listening. "*Tit*? Teat is a *tit*?"

Ruth nearly fell over in hysterics. I could only imagine what she was thinking—*She sure is naive*—but what did I know? I'd never heard of bag balm, either. I'd never been close to an udder in my life. When *I* was a kid, milk had arrived at the back door in glass bottles.

I realized the idea that Stan might be drinking breast milk at age eleven seemed far-fetched—so, as soon as the words came out of my mouth, I backpedaled. Shaking my head and following Ruth into the kitchen, I said, "Maybe I'm getting carried away."

When we passed the living room, we saw Vern clicking the television dial and Stan on his knees on the floor, one foot from the television screen.

"Say hello to Ruth," Vern said.

"Hi, Ruth," Stan mumbled.

"You will need to look at Mrs. Captain when you speak to her," Vern said.

"Hi, Ruth." Stan whipped his head around as if it were a rubber band, then snapped back toward the screen.

Ruth had a playful look on her face. "We won't need to worry about him for the rest of the day."

In the kitchen, Ruth fixed her gaze on me in a way that made me nervous. I followed her eyes to my stomach, and we stood there with silly grins, not speaking. I don't know how she knew I was pregnant, but I did know that no amount of argument or new detail would change the way she thought, so I gave up trying.

She grinned as she reached out to hug me. "I won't tell. Congratulations!"

I curled up on the hard blue-and-ivory-striped loveseat that divided the living room and nodded off while Stan knelt in front of me, five feet from the TV. When I woke, he was still there, rocking on his knees.

I staggered to the bathroom, dazed and nauseous. The door to the powder room was ajar, and I was too tired to bother with the light, but there was something sparkling on the toilet seat and floor.

I flicked the light switch and hollered, "Stanislaus!"

He appeared out of nowhere.

"Do you see this?" My voice quavered.

"Yes, ma'am."

"Are you forgetting to pick up the seat?"

He looked down, stubbing the linoleum tile with his shoe, his hands in his pockets. "I didn't do it."

"Well, okay." I shook my head. "Next time, um, pick up the seat, okay?" I wasn't in any mood to argue.

Ruth came in from the kitchen and peered over my shoulder. She watched with a straight face as Stan returned to the living room and plopped back down on his knees, his wispy blond hair lifting as he rocked two feet from the TV screen. Then she stepped past me and wiped the powder room countertop with a worn cloth diaper, after which she soaked up the mess on the toilet and floor.

My body ached. I crossed my arms and put my head down on the kitchen table. If Stan intentionally wet the seat, he would've protested loudly, but he hadn't. He seemed calm.

Ruth rinsed the cloth and wrung it out in the sink. She shook her head as she took a few steps toward me. Then, in a low voice she said, "This is not normal. Have you ever thought . . ." She hesitated. "No."

"What?"

"Well, maybe he goes outside."

I squinted as I stared back at her. I couldn't imagine they were so poor that they didn't have working toilets. What else hadn't Vern told me about this boy?

Ruth said when she'd first arrived, she'd spotted Stan up against a tree in the yard. She hadn't thought anything of it.

That morning, he'd drunk a lot of water. Was he drinking too much and waiting too long? "We should get a timer," I said, "so every few hours we can remind him to use the bathroom."

Ruth's infectious laugh got me started, and I couldn't stop. It was so hot her glasses slid off her nose, and she caught them in her hand. I wasn't sure if she was laughing at Stan or our situation.

Stan had only been with us a few short days, but it felt like weeks. When Vern arrived home from work that evening, he tossed a stack of mail on the counter. I was at the stove, marinating my woes. He grabbed me by the front of the shirt, pulled me toward him, and kissed me. I glanced down, noticed Stan's mother's unmistakable handwriting, and shrank.

"Where's Chippie?" His normal habit was to kiss me and then pet the dog.

Stan tromped into the kitchen. "Can I play with him? With Chippie?" His long wooden face was matter-of-fact.

Vern placed his hand on my waist. "Darling, do you mind?"

I had barely shrugged when Stan scrambled toward the open kitchen door. Vern latched on to his arm. "Don't forget, Stan, Chip is an old dog, perhaps seventy in dog years. Try to be gentle."

"Yessir," he said, and he was gone.

Vern ripped open the thick yellow envelope from Ruthann and shook the contents onto the counter. A couple of newspaper articles and a long handwritten letter fell out. I stood behind Vern, reading the new La Leche League literature over his shoulder, thinking of my own child, wondering if I might learn something, since I planned to breastfeed. He unfolded a *New York Times* article. "Mother's milk is the world's original and best fast food," he read, "a complex recipe containing more than a hundred nutrients, many of which—"

"Okay, that's enough." What bothered me was Vern's apparent loose arrangement with Stan's mother. Two weeks and "about two weeks" were different animals. From the quantity of stodgy literature before us, I was getting vibes she was planning on a much longer stay. *What is the agreement?* I didn't understand why she was sending us this stuff, anyway. Hadn't Vern told her I was pregnant?

Vern looked unsure. "I *may* have told her, darling."

"You *may* have?"

I supposed Vern might've been relieved that there was a possibility that Stan was no longer breastfeeding, that she was sending this literature to me, but it seemed more a case of Vern's wanting to shut down the conversation than anything else. I could feel my anger welling up again. *If Stan isn't breastfeeding, then what? Is this a religious conviction of hers?* To an outside observer, Ruthann's bombarding us with literature might've seemed harmless, even thoughtful. So why was I so hooked? Was she jangling a discordant bell in my brain?

I started ranting and couldn't stop. "She needs our help, yeah, okay. Sure. What about the help *we* need? Don't you have jobs you want me to do? Have you thought of the baby? Have you?"

"Honey . . ." Vern shook his head as I continued peppering him with rhetorical questions. "Your pregnancy would only elicit a passing thought. It wouldn't make a whit of difference to her." Vern slid open the liquor cabinet, grabbed the nearest bottle by the neck, and poured himself a drink.

"So you're telling me this literature is not aimed at me? At my pregnancy? Then who? Is she telling us she wants Stan drinking only breast milk?"

Vern didn't answer.

"Fine, Vern. It doesn't matter." I turned off the stove and tossed—slammed—a potholder onto the counter. "The damage is done. Besides, this is what *you* need, right? This is a favor for *you*, not for Stan or his mother. I keep forgetting." For a moment, I thought I understood Caroline. Maybe she left him because she grew tired of his stubbornness. He had become so unyielding, so uncommunicative. I wanted a reset.

I leaned over to kiss him, but he backed away from my sarcasm.

"I gave at the office," he said, trying to be funny. He sipped from his drink, grabbed his cigarettes, and headed toward the front door. "Come on, we'd better check on Stan."

CHAPTER 6

Our neighbor Ann's dog, Joey, was barking in back. We found Ann in her front yard and stood with her on the sidewalk, making small talk, as she watered her pachysandra and cotoneasters.

"We've come for our house guest," Vern said, chuckling. "It sounds as if he's met Joey."

Ann had large brown eyes and wavy dark brown hair, cut stylishly so that every strand fell in place. She had the look you'd find in *Vogue*: olive skin, dark eyebrows, and perfect cupid's bow lips. The kind of person who was interested in everybody, she always made time for meaningful connections with other people. No matter what the occasion, Ann's cheerful voice was sprinkled with laughter. It was as if she carried a device in her pocket, and with a single flick she could bring the sun out from behind the clouds.

Ann had told us she was studying to be a substance abuse counselor. When she complimented Vern—"Do you feel as healthy as you look?"—I could've sworn she was practicing on him. She implied it was my nurturing that had given Vern his rosy cheeks, and I took it as a compliment.

"You've only been married, what, three months?" she asked. "How's it going?"

"Yep. Three and a half months." I tried to sound upbeat. Ann was a friend of Caroline's. I didn't want the whole world, and especially Vern's ex-wife, to know we were struggling so early into our marriage.

As Chippie lunged at Stan's dirty shoelaces, Ann stepped back to avoid a collision, and I let out a sharp squeal. The thought came to me . . . Ann's reactions were calmer, more mature than mine. It bothered me that she was so relaxed. I think I knew my anxiety was my own doing and that if I wanted to feel like a grown woman, I needed to overcome it.

Vern held out his cigarette pack and offered Ann one. Though she was a smoker herself, as soon as she inhaled, she doubled over, coughing. "You really should switch to the filters," she said. She and Vern had gone on several failed smoking-cessation trips. They'd gone on one to Springfield, Ohio, with a group in a van, dense smoke billowing out of its windows as they psyched up in the parking lot before the appointments. They'd returned with a treatment some masochist had dreamed up—staples in their ears—and joked about the metallic odor of blood running down their necks as they massaged the staple with every craving.

I stood there, trying to appear comfortable despite the fact that I was pregnant and standing in the middle of a smoke cloud. Smoking was something I chose to ignore. It's laughable when I think of how much control I believed I possessed back then, as if I alone could make Vern happy enough to just quit smoking.

"He's accustomed to a lifestyle reminiscent of the Amish," Vern said, changing the subject.

Ann blew a column of smoke up over her head. "I can't imagine what an Amish boy would think after a couple of weeks with the Fairley family."

I squirmed, thinking I needed to explain myself, since at the moment Stan seemed to be behaving like any other kid. "He's not *normal*," I said.

Ann laughed. "Well, I noticed he has a lot of energy." She said something about how kind and thoughtful we were to take him, which immediately triggered my guilt.

Thinking I needed to prove how weird he was to justify my

frustration, I told her how much Stan had missed—that he'd never had gum, candy, meat, eggs, dairy—and added, "He's never been to school. And he wets the seat. Did I tell you, Vern?"

"Oh, for Christsake, honey." He coughed and spit in a handkerchief as Ann burst out laughing. I knew I wasn't convincing her of anything except the friction in the air.

When Stan appeared around the corner, Vern took on a look of pride, as if he were showing off our new baby. The thought crossed my mind . . . *Is this what happened to Ben? Was he doing things he shouldn't, with everyone chuckling and looking the other way? What will become of my own child? Will I always be the bad guy, jumping in to say no?*

We heard one of the dogs yelp. "You hear that?" I glanced back at Vern, who seemed amused. Chippie rounded the corner too, following Stan—and instinctively, I headed toward them.

Chippie dropped down on his hind legs, panting, his tiny tongue hanging out. I was reminded of my sister's cat, who once arrived home with his eyeball dangling from its socket after spending all night out in the neighborhood. He had panted and dropped down on his hind legs in the same way.

It was more than a feeling in my gut. Stan had tormented that dog. I knew it.

"Why did Chippie squeal?" Vern asked him.

Stan looked surprised by the question. "*I* didn't do it."

"Well." Ann laughed sarcastically. "That solves that."

Stan disappeared again, and we moved on to other topics. But my mind wandered. I couldn't help but think of earlier, when Stan threw that stick into our tree. Was he some kind of animal abuser?

We spoke briefly about the pile of literature that had arrived with Stan, and Ann's lighthearted laughter seemed as dismissive as Vern's. To me, Ann and Vern were a world away, carefree and happy, collecting and handing over compliments like they were fireflies.

"Do you like to play video games?" Ann asked Stan when he approached for a moment. She and her husband, David, had opened a video arcade on West Main Street. She took a long drag, licked her upper lip, then blew the smoke to one side as she waited for a response. "Do you have any favorites?"

Stan was staring up at the trees.

"No, Annie, he doesn't," Vern said. "He helps his mother on the farm."

Stan rocked to an invisible rhythm as he glanced down the tree-lined street toward town.

"So, Stan, I'd like to invite you to the Wigwam," Ann said. "It's a fun place with video games. I also want you to feel free to drop by the house any time if you want to talk, need a break, or anything, okay? Even if you just want to visit Joey, that's fine. Just come over."

I was grateful for the offer, but I also felt alienated. I hoped Ann would find in short order that Stan was nothing like her own two children.

It wasn't the first time I'd heard of the Wigwam, but the name made me cringe. *Isn't that poking fun?* We lived in an area of Ohio famous for its Native American history—Fort Hill, Fort Ancient, the mound builders. The name "Wigwam" sounded all wrong, and I'd mentioned this to Vern before. But he'd pointed to our local high school's mascot: the Indian. Maybe I was being too uptight. The marriage. The pregnancy. The stress of Stan. I needed to relax.

"Lighten up, honey," Vern said. "You're taking things too seriously."

But I couldn't let it go. Stan was off chasing Chippie, and I was chasing the negative thoughts popping into my head. I pictured my visit to Atlantic City with my parents when I was young and how my father loved the ringing bells, flashing lights, and ghastly clatter and clank of the arcade. I had found it so unpleasant that I'd spent the day with my index fingers plugging my ears.

"Would all that stimulation of video games be good for him?" I asked. "He's only eleven, you know."

Ann waved her hand, communicating that I was being silly.

"What is it? What are you worried about?" Vern asked. He took one last drag and stubbed his cigarette on the sidewalk.

"It makes me uncomfortable, is all."

"Don't you worry one bit. Send him over," Ann said without hesitation. "I'll keep an eye on him."

That night at dinner, Vern quizzed Stan about his schooling. "If you haven't been to school, who teaches you?"

"My mother takes me to Clinton, Connecticut," he said.

"Where you meet with a tutor?"

Stan nodded. "And my father sometimes teaches me too. Taught me," he corrected himself.

Years later, I would learn that when Stan was nine, his father had helped him memorize and recite Thomas Paine's poem "Contentment" for a declamation contest at the Madison Library. Stan had won an award and gotten his smiling mug in the newspaper.

He leapt up from the table, and Vern followed him.

When Vern returned, he pulled me aside to say that he had spoken privately to Stan. "It's taken care of," he said. "I was strong with him, and he assured me there would be no more messes."

Stan rolled into the kitchen. I knew he'd overheard some of Vern's words, so I asked him directly if he'd grown up with indoor plumbing.

"Is this necessary?" Vern asked. "Let's assume he has indoor plumbing." He wiped the corners of his lips with his napkin and tossed the napkin in the trash.

Stan glanced at me sideways. "We do, but it never works. Usually, we go outside."

"Even in the middle of winter?" Vern looked surprised.

"Yes, sir, you get used to it."

I couldn't let it drop. "You go outside? You go in the garden? Is that what you mean by organic?"

"Honey, that's enough!" Vern said.

It wasn't enough. I knew I was on the right track. I tossed my plate in the sink with a clatter and exited the room.

Within a week, I had trouble being within ten feet of Stan. His movements had slowed like a bee trapped in a jar. I knew keeping him inside wasn't good for him—but at the same time, I was afraid to let him out.

I wondered if Stan's father had been sick long. Had he been fighting the lawsuit up until his death? How many years had he known Vern? Had Vern even been in contact with him before he died? I had so many unanswered questions, but any attempt I made to understand seemed to upset Vern. My back and shoulders ached.

Vern must've been exhausted too, because he set Stan up in front of the television for a second round a short while later, then came back into the kitchen.

"We must let this be a learning experience," Vern whispered. I figured he was referring to *us* and our making rash decisions without consulting each other. "We must introduce him to the life of the average eleven-year-old."

"Why?" I asked.

Vern wore a silly grin. "Yours not to question why. Yours but—"

"I know, I know. 'Yours but to do or die.' You're not listening." Vern had a habit of quoting *The Charge of the Light Brigade*, changing the words to suit the situation. He had finished his drink and hadn't eaten enough to absorb all the alcohol. I wondered if he was always this evasive, and I hadn't noticed before the pregnancy because I'd been drinking the whiskey sours with him. It seemed now that we were speaking two different languages.

Vern straightened. "The boy has missed so much. Without his father . . ."

"No, Vern. Stan *had* a father." I let my words ping-pong off the walls for a moment; then I reminded him my parents were rarely around when I was a kid, and I'd turned out all right.

He poured himself another bourbon and water and then sat at the round table, staring out the window, lost in thought.

I said it again. "We were missing our father *and* our mother."

"But only once in a while, right?"

"No. Every month they were gone for a week or two. Every month of every year." This seemed to be news to Vern, and I wondered if he was thinking less of me. Or less of my parents. Hadn't I mentioned this? Why was he forgetting? Now I wished this had been one of the secrets I had kept to myself. But instead of dwelling on that, I pitched my shoulders back and reminded him that it wasn't his job to make up for what Stan was going to miss without his father around.

He sipped his drink as we watched one of our two mourning doves, perched on a nearby branch. Then he handed me a tissue. "I'm sorry, honey. I didn't know it was so hard for you."

It was tragic to think of all that Stan had experienced by age eleven. The idea was crushing. But our *own* situation was complicated as well. I'd never been married before. Or had a child. I was such a kid myself. I hadn't experienced any of the heartbreak that Vern had experienced: He'd lost his mother, his father had died two years earlier, and his only sibling, a sister, had died of suicide. He'd also lost his son and his first marriage and now was coping with his own health issues—bipolar disorder and COPD (Chronic Obstructive Pulmonary Disease)—with a new marriage and a baby on the way, despite being older than my own father. And those were the highlights.

Recently, I'd found a picture of Vern's mother. Taken in 1948, when Vern was twenty-three and she was fifty-five, before the weight of life's battles had taken its toll, it was a beautiful studio image. Her wavy gray hair, streaked with silver on one side, was worn up, loosely, with every stray hair flowing. Tucked in behind the picture, I'd discovered a note in her handwriting that ended with "Just couldn't face one more thing out in the open." I'd asked Vern what it meant, and he'd said he didn't know.

"How can you not know?" I'd asked. "She must've been ashamed of something. What was it?"

"Haven't you heard the prayer? 'Lord, help us to remember what we ought not to forget, and to forget what we ought not to remember.'" Vern's shoulders had dropped, and he had spoken so quietly I could barely hear him. "I wish you could have a drink, darling, so you wouldn't worry so much." He pulled a newspaper in front of him and began to read. After a few minutes, he looked up. "About Mother . . . Is there a need to know?"

I rubbed my stomach now, as a dove flitted past our bay window. Why couldn't I behave like one of them, gliding back and forth, so present, only concerned with the necessities of life? *Yes*, there was a need to know. I didn't know what in the hell I was doing! Could I expect a normal pregnancy? What about all the drugs Vern was taking? Lanoxin for the heart, Lasix for the fluid retention, ranitidine for heartburn, lithium for bipolar disorder—all this mixed with drinking and smoking. Would they damage the baby? And what about the hardware business falling on hard times? How long could we keep it going?

I barely had time to consider my own fears with Stan darting through the house like a rabid bat.

"Do you honestly think this is *good* for him?" I asked. "I mean, do you think he wants all this change in his life?"

"Stan? Hell, yes. He's begging for it. Listen to him." We paused a moment, and even with the door closed, we heard joyful cries above the sound of the TV across the hall. "He's happy to be here. He's like a damn three-year-old."

It really did seem that Stan was a substitute for Ben. But I wanted to believe Vern would come through and support me if the stress of this visit became too much.

As Vern stirred cherry juice into his drink, I pushed away from the table, muttering to myself, "No milk, no candy, no TV, no school, no skating, no swings, no softball . . ."

"Never mind," Vern said softly. "I'm going to call the old rip tomorrow and tell her that as long as he's here, he's going to live like we do. Otherwise, he returns to Connecticut early."

CHAPTER 7

On Stan's tenth day with us, Vern received a rambling missive from Ruthann about the lawsuit involving her property. According to her, at the time of her husband's death, he had been fighting with his brother, John, over their mother's inheritance. When it looked to John like he was never going to receive his share of his mother's inheritance because Stan's family was living on the property with no way to pay him, John sold his share to a man named Lohmann, a local developer. Ruthann and Lohmann had been trying to reach an agreement to divide the property in a way that would give her the house, a small amount of land, and access to the Lieutenant River, but she didn't trust Lohmann. She said Lohmann had claimed he would donate the land to the Old Lyme Conservation Trust, where he was a member, but there was no guarantee that would happen. She wanted the land retained for agriculture and was positive it would be developed for housing if Lohmann had anything to do with it.

After reading this, Vern either lost his nerve to call her—probably imagining a long-winded, angry rant—or maybe he believed it wouldn't matter, because the two weeks were almost over, and Stan would be home in Connecticut in a few days anyway.

Stan seemed more relaxed now, which was good, but it bothered my conscience that we were allowing him to sit transfixed in front of the television, watching silly reruns, for long hours every day. I wasn't monitoring his toothbrushing or bathing. I wasn't reading books to him at night. I wasn't taking him to the Colony

Theater or any kind of playground. I considered driving him to Serpent Mound to let him climb the lookout tower and see the Native American serpent, or Fort Hill, where he could learn about the Hopewell culture. I even considered Rocky Fork Lake, where he could swim safely without my help (I wasn't about to wear a bathing suit right now). But I was nauseous and tired, my legs heavy. I thought if I spent all day horizontal, with saltines and ginger ale on the bedside table, maybe Vern would pay attention to what I was saying about Stan.

As a compromising gesture, I gave in to expediency. Which meant *Happy Days*, *Cheers*, *Dallas*, and *Little House on the Prairie*.

I told Ruth that every time I complained to Vern, I felt a hot wave of shame. He was generous to take on Stanislaus. And it wasn't Stan's fault he was stuck with us. Ruth stopped cleaning for a moment, dried her hands, and listened. I told her my younger sister had taken care of my siblings when I was busy swimming, and together we had done what we wanted. Maybe I was being selfish in this parental role, doing a half-assed job, because I was modeling the way I'd avoided responsibility as the oldest when I was a kid. I was resenting it so much.

Her smile told me I should stop worrying. "If he can't watch TV at home, this is good for him. He's learning *something*."

She added that I needed to get out myself. For fresh air. She suggested that I take him to lunch.

"Where?" Hillsboro had the Wooden Spoon—too fancy; The Koffee Kup—too many people I might know; Magee's—would he sit politely on one of those stools?

"What about McDonald's?"

"McDonald's?" It sounded weird for a field trip. A kind of shock therapy for a kid growing up on raw vegetables and breast milk. But maybe Stan *would* enjoy it. I had a flicker of a thought that Ruth might also need a break. Maybe she was tired of hearing the television, with its volume turned up full blast, or the hooting and hollering, or the muddy shoes running through the house. I also speculated that she might be tired of what Vern called my mulligan stew of questions. *Why not?* I thought. *What do we have to lose?*

I took Stan through the drive-thru and we heard the usual, "Welcome to McDonald's, may I take your order?"

Stan nearly jumped into my lap. "They bring it to you?" He leaned over me, reading every word on the sign. "Oh, okay." He sat at attention as we drove around to pick it up.

That day, I tried to form an attachment. It seemed as if he *was* my child. As his foot tapped the floor and the seat springs squeaked, I felt a mother's pride. Stan, with his inquisitive mind, his enthusiasm, was adorable. It tickled me that he didn't want a happy meal. All he wanted was a plain burger—no cheese, no pickles—and fries. *Hey, maybe he'll be a drummer*, I thought as we ate our burgers and he continued tapping his foot, and despite the traffic rushing by us on North High Street, I felt both in sync with his rhythm and happy to be out of the house and introducing him to something new.

Hearing Stan's loud blast of enthusiasm as he burst through the back door of the house after we returned home, I felt I'd scored points.

"How was lunch?" Ruth asked. "Did you have a good time?"

Stan pulled his stained white T-shirt away from his chest and began listing the problems. "McDonald's is horsemeat," he said.

He repeated that several times, and each time, we erupted in laughter. He sounded serious, as if he were working for the USDA or the state meat inspector.

"It's not *horse*meat," I finally said. "It isn't healthy—you wouldn't want McDonald's every day—but it *is* beef."

He was daring me to fight. "My mother said they don't tell you what's in it."

"Well, she's *wrong*," I blurted, too strongly, though I actually thought she *might* be right. This was a disagreement between his mother and me—the many things she was refusing to expose him to. But I decided to hold my tongue and not add to his confusion. I would save *that* conversation for Vern. He could argue with Stan's mother over beef or horsemeat. With luck, she'd be passionate enough about his diet that she'd insist he return home.

I placed my hand on Stan's shoulder. "You didn't have to eat it."

"I know." He held his arms around his waist, scratching at his elbows. The way he rocked, it was as if he were nodding in agreement. His mother had educated him about the dangers of fast food. He hadn't wanted the plastic toys, either. Yet he had popped the burger into his maw faster than I could pull into a parking space.

Stan rocked from one foot to the other, a maniacal look in his eye. "Pickles are poisonous."

I was thinking about my pregnancy. I was supposed to be craving pickles, but so far I wasn't longing for anything except maybe a drive from Hillsboro to the Cincinnati Airport with Stan in the backseat.

"My mother says they use rotten tomatoes for ketchup and white flour for bread."

"Okay, so what? You liked it, though, right?"

He nodded enthusiastically, lifting his heels off the floor. "I loved it."

Ruth seemed to wink at me, and for a split second, I tasted relief. Stan would be going home in a few days, and he could add McDonald's to the list of new experiences he'd had during his time with us.

"Did you notice the bike?" On our way into the house, we had passed a rusty red Schwinn bicycle leaning against the porch. Vern had asked Archie Whiting, one of his delivery guys, to go out to The Point, our summer cottage out on Cave Road, to get Ben's old bike out of storage. I suggested to Stan that he ride around the neighborhood to burn off some energy. In seconds, he was bounding out the door and onto the red bike, which he rode off on at top speed.

I sat in our steamy kitchen at our round pedestal table, thinking about Ruth and how she spent so much time with this white family and not her own kids or grandkids. It wasn't full time the way it was for us with Stan, but how did she feel about taking care of another family? She seemed to keep a healthy distance from us. I considered that maybe I should try her detached approach to maintain my sanity. Maybe I was taking on more responsibility with Stan than I needed to.

As Ruth put away the dishes, beads of sweat running down her cheeks, I asked about her family. "How's Paul? How are the grandkids?"

She talked up her grandson, Michael, who was six and already interested in football. I told her about my younger brother, Rick, who'd been in Ben's high school class and played football, and my mind wandered to the pig roast. Had word gotten out? If anyone knew about it, Ruth would. "Did you hear about the wild party my brother had out at my parents' house?"

"No," she said. "Why?"

"Oh, nothing." As we talked, I started to feel weak and thought I might need to lie down. I uncrossed my legs, touched my knee to the underside of the table, and felt something smoosh. It was soft and gooey—a piece of stringy bubble gum, now stuck to my knee.

"Dammit!" I peered under the table. Wads pocked the wood like mud dauber nests on an old barn ceiling. "Where is the little brat?" I muttered.

Ruth pushed up the bridge of her thick glasses and twisted her head to look. With a sharp knife, she scraped at the gum as I held either side of the fabric of my pants. Then, together we examined the underside of every hard surface—the coffee table, the dining room table, end tables, and chairs—in the downstairs rooms. There was a combination of fresh and old chewing gum on all of it.

In the middle of West South Street, I cupped my hands to form a megaphone and screamed Stan's name in every direction, my hands shaking. I was sure the whole neighborhood heard me. Ann's twelve-year-old daughter, Nina, came to their front door with the same winning smile as her mother's. "He's with Mom up at the Wigwam. You want me to call her?"

I shook my head no. I didn't know why Ann hadn't mentioned taking Stan with her. *Didn't she know the idea made me uncomfortable? Why didn't she warn me?*

I returned to the house, weeping, and called Vern at the hardware store. "There's chewing gum on everything," I sputtered. "He's at the Wigwam."

"Do I need to come home?" Vern sounded indifferent.

I was blubbering. "No, no, I'm okay."

"Honey, you're worrying unnecessarily." Vern's voice was dragging, but I let his soothing words wash over me. "If Stan is up there with Ann, he's fine. I'll be home early, and we can speak to him."

"I'm sorry," I said. The sound of Vern's voice alone helped calm me.

He suggested I pull back and let Ruth handle him, but I detected a somberness, as if he were carrying a weight—my weight—that was far too heavy for his fragile health. Vern had claimed he'd competed in tennis when he was younger, that he was quick on his feet and acrobatic, but now his only speed was with the occasional quip. Between the chronic bronchitis, COPD, and manic episodes that had landed him in the hospital, I had no idea what symptoms might indicate a problem. What did bipolar disorder even look like? *I* was the athlete. I was the one capable of chasing after Stan, staying up late and waking up early. Yet I was unloading on Vern.

Perspiration covered Ruth's bronze face. She grabbed her loose-knit shirt under her heavy breasts and shook it. "You need to rest," she said. "This isn't good for the baby."

I realized she was right. I was the one who needed to change. If I truly wanted to feel connected to Vern, to help him, to make his life happier, and at the same time stand on my own two feet, I needed to stop calling him at every whipstitch. I needed to let go of things like chewing gum on furniture. Stan would be going home soon, and I would be able to rest when he did. In the meantime, I needed to back off for the health of the baby.

Or was I giving in?

For several moments, I stared fixedly at Ruth as she wiped off the counter. Then I said, "He's down at the Wigwam with Ann Pence."

She raised her eyebrows as she adjusted her thick glasses. "He rode down by himself?"

"I don't know. Maybe Ann drove him."

"He's trouble," she said. "It's not his fault, but he's trouble." She nodded as she folded several towels and placed them into a nearby drawer.

My mind went right to Ben. "I'm curious . . . Vern's kids . . . were *they* trouble?"

Ruth turned away for a moment as though she hadn't heard me.

"Were they?" I pressed.

She laughed. "Sometimes."

"Like what? Like smoking weed?"

"Girl." Her laughter was shaky. "You'll get me in trouble." She lifted a stack of dishes and placed them in an upper cabinet as she told me about how Vern's daughter, Laura, never got over the murder of her friend, Robin Gossett. I'd heard about Robin. He'd been on the track team—a pole vaulter—with my brother, Rick, and Rick had thought he was a nice guy. Robin's body had been found two years earlier in a shallow grave, the victim of an unsolved shooting.

"Those kids, they . . ."

"What?"

She didn't want to say. She changed tack. "Ben was smart. But stubborn." She chuckled. "Like his father." She said her husband had called the night of Ben's death, that he'd lingered on the phone because he'd thought Ben might be up to no good. She said he'd driven by the house to check on him.

"And everything was okay?"

"Far as he could tell."

We sat in the quiet of the kitchen a long while. I wondered if Ruth was embellishing her story about Paul's being the last one to talk to Benji—she called him Benji—before he died. Ruth said again that Ben was her "baby," that she had started to work for Vern and Caroline when Ben was an infant.

As she spoke, I felt a twinge of jealousy. Would she feel the same way about my child? I hoped not. The whole idea of someone else taking care of my kids when I was perfectly capable of doing that rubbed me the wrong way. For a split second, I thought of Ben's room and how much I wanted to get rid of all his stuff.

"We should clean out his room, right?" I asked. It was beginning to smell musty, and I'd noticed from the dust line that Ruth wiped around the objects on Ben's shelf instead of picking them up and dusting under them. His room was looking more and more like a museum with no visitors.

Ruth didn't respond, though I knew she'd heard me.

"Ruth? Don't you think it's time? I mean, with the baby's coming and everything?"

She answered with a reluctant nod. There were jobs Ruth refused to do. She didn't do windows, inside or out. She didn't do car interiors. She didn't clean woodwork or basements or porches or sidewalks. And as far as I could tell, she didn't clean Ben's room.

She had cleaned Ben's room for years before he died. She'd washed his dirty clothes, vacuumed his cookie crumbs, organized his books and toys on a shelf. I knew she didn't want to touch his things.

I trudged up the stairs and stood at the entrance to Ben's room. I imagined the twin bed gone, the bookshelf removed, his important keepsakes in storage. I looked closely at the oak dresser. Its drawers had begun to show tiny pinholes and piles of sawdust from invading powder post beetles. Ben's papers were yellowing, his photographs sticking together. Four years had passed, and the items before me had gone mostly untouched for all that time. The room was decaying.

It would be easiest for me to continue to pretend the room wasn't there, to leave it alone and wait for Vern or Ruth—someone—to recover enough to deal with it. It was a decision not to decide. But not to decide *was* to decide.

I told myself Stan was the obstacle. Once he was gone, I'd deal with Ben's room. It seemed I was the only one who could.

CHAPTER 8

A **thundercloud drifted in with Vern** as he arrived home from work. By then, I'd calmed down. I'd thrown together a meatloaf and was mashing potatoes. Stan was still MIA—presumably with Ann.

"Mother's furniture never had chewing gum," Vern said, implying he knew all about it, which I doubted.

"Some of it did." I explained that we'd found old and new gum.

"The girls and their friends are too old."

I was nodding in agreement.

But then he said, "Who in the hell even chews gum? You chew it; who else?"

What the hell, I thought. What was going on with Vern? I didn't want to rehash the gum details, but . . . *I call frantic and upset and he comes home—what, angry? Aren't husbands supposed to support and care for their wives?* My father was of Vern's generation. He would've been kissing Mom, pinching her, making lewd comments about how he was going to make her feel better later. Anything to get her giggling and off topic. But not Vern. He seemed to be irritated with me.

While he poured himself a drink, I stood stone-still, watching him and wondering. Was this because of our age difference? Because he'd mellowed in his old age and couldn't stand my emotional response?

He dropped his cigarette into a plate of soft butter. "Where is the little rascal, anyway?"

Stan appeared out of nowhere, more agitated than I'd ever seen him. His head jerked from one side to another with the slightest sound from outside the house. "I scored high points and got free tokens," he said breathlessly. "And then I played air hockey and won again and got even more free tokens." He shifted from side to side.

"Stan, stop for a moment, please," Vern said.

Stan stopped suddenly, then started up again, rocking like a metronome.

"First of all, how did you get back here?"

"Mrs. Pence."

"Okay, that's fine. I don't want you at the Wigwam unless Mr. or Mrs. Pence is there."

"Yes, sir."

"There's something else, Stan." Vern started to cough, and we waited until he caught his breath. We stood in the middle of the kitchen, the three of us facing each other, three points in an equilateral triangle. "Someone has been placing chewing gum on the furniture. Do you know anything about that?"

"No, sir," he said, scratching his nose.

"You understand you must place gum in a proper receptacle, though, right? These are antiques, and gum ruins the finish."

"Yes, sir."

"Also, you needn't say 'yes, sir.' Yes will suffice." Vern began to gasp as he hunted for his inhaler.

Stan slid the nearest chair under the table. "Yes, sir . . . Um, sorry. Can I go outside?"

Vern drew a deep, bottomless breath. "If it's all right with Kim."

I was too irritated to respond. *Come on, Vern. Is that the best you can do? "If it's all right with Kim?"* Dammit.

Stan read my lack of reaction as permission. He darted for the door.

"Stay close to the house, Stan," Vern tried to shout, "so we can call you when dinner's ready." His voice sounded so weak I questioned if he should be in the hospital. He shook his bronchodilator, took a few whiffs, and within minutes was breathing freely again.

One more week, I told myself. *One more freaking week until Memorial Day, and then we can celebrate.*

A week had passed; it was Memorial Day weekend, the weekend Stan was supposed to return to Connecticut. Vern had been complaining that he hadn't taken out enough of the right kind of advertising for his hardware stores and nobody seemed to know about the holiday weekend sales. He was grumbling and I was about to call Stan to dinner when the phone rang.

Vern answered.

Judging by his sudden good cheer, I thought the caller might be an old buddy of his, or maybe one of his daughters checking on us. "It's been glorious," he said. "Yes, yes, uh-huh. Yes."

Then the phone call took a weird turn. Vern said, "Oh, law"— and then, dead silence. He sat back down, rested his elbow on the table, and pushed his dinner plate to one side. He hunted for his cigarettes under a stack of newspapers. He located them, shoved a cig in his mouth, flicked his lighter, and puffed.

"Uh-hunh, uh-hunh . . ." He hardly said a word. It clearly wasn't family. It wasn't even a close friend.

Suddenly it slapped me. Stan's *mother*!

The kitchen filled with smoke—or maybe that's the way I want to remember it. To think Vern was on the phone a long time, listening to Ruthann and responding with kindness.

He nodded, then coughed—the thick, viscous kind of cough that stopped conversations.

Come on, Vern, say it, I thought. I could hear resignation in his tone. *We agreed on two weeks. That's it. This is your moment to stand up for your wife. To speak for your unborn child. This is your chance to say enough is enough.*

When it came to money, Vern had been setting limits for years by calling loaned money a "gift." He'd told me he didn't mind friends asking to borrow money. "When you call it a gift, they never ask again."

So what was the deal with Stan? Why hadn't Vern told Stan's mother, "Two weeks—our gift"? I mean, good grief. Stan had a much older brother, Sam. Couldn't he do some babysitting? For the life of me, I couldn't figure out what we were doing with this kid.

I removed my plate and silverware, wanting to send a message to Vern that I wouldn't be joining them for dinner. I climbed the stairs and listened from the hallway, hoping my absence would end the conversation. But when the phone call ended, there was an ear-splitting silence.

I heard Stan shuffle into the kitchen from the living room.

Vern's question struck me like a sledgehammer. "How would you like to stay another two weeks, Stan?"

I felt an awful ache, an unbearable pressure in the pit of my stomach. With that simple, innocuous question, I was eleven years old again—the oldest of five, alone and unsure, in charge of my younger siblings—at the beginning of seven years of abandonment.

I wanted to scream and shout at Stan's mother, "You don't *do* this to a child! You don't leave your kid at eleven years old, no matter what your marital situation is! You don't do it if you're financially strapped. You don't do it if you're having an affair. You just don't *do* it!"

Stan's mother was the adult. Stan was the child, the victim. It wasn't *his* fault he was marooned with us. Though I felt enormous empathy, I dreaded the lie I would have to tell about how happy I was to have him with us for two more weeks. Or the lie about how much fun it would be for him. Kids know when they're lied to. They don't always know why, but they know. I had a sixth sense when it came to my parents. Stan was sure to have a sixth sense when it came to his mother.

From upstairs, with my head hung over the landing, I listened to Vern fix himself a drink—the rattle of his hand in the ice, the ping of a single cube in a glass, the plip-plip-ploop of bourbon. After a pause, I heard him tell Stan, "I want a navigational fix on you at all times. I don't mind if you go with Mrs. Pence to the Wigwam, but you must let me know."

And with that comment, suddenly I was doing a one-eighty. The Wigwam? Well . . . what the hell. It wasn't a great idea, not particularly wholesome, but TV wasn't either, so yeah, okay . . . sure. Why not? I'd grown up on TV, lots of it, and I'd turned out okay. Another thought struck me: How did Vern expect to have his so-called navigational fix, anyway? What he'd meant to say, clearly, was that Stan should make sure *I* had the navigational fix—that he must let *me* know where he was at all times.

I'd been craning my neck, listening to every word, and I'd had enough. I was about to slam the door and change into a nightgown when Vern said, "And one more thing, Stan. Be sure to thank Kim for this dinner."

"Where is she?" he asked.

Vern cleared his throat. I could hear the harsh crunch of plates sliding across the table. "Where is she *now*? Is that what you're asking?"

"Yes."

"Kim's not feeling well," he said.

A wave of guilt rushed through me. I didn't want to adopt Vern's style of avoidance as a solution. *Not feeling well?* That was for damn sure.

I staggered into our room and dropped my clothes in a heap on the floor. I grabbed my soft cotton nightgown from under my pillow and slipped it over my head. In a daze, I pulled back the covers and sat down on the clean sheets. The walls, a cool blue, pressed in on four sides, like a vise pressing in on my future. But I could see Vern's struggle. I saw it in his patience, in his optimistic interpretation of Stan's behavior, and in his genuine smile when he didn't think I was looking. No matter how Stan behaved, it was obvious he brightened Vern's life.

When I listened to him tucking Stan into bed that night, sounding so sweet, I felt a wave of regret. "I'm sorry, I'm so sorry," I said when he found me awake. "Maybe it's the pregnancy." I wanted to find a reason for my anger.

Vern sat on the edge of the bed and placed his hand on my trembling leg. "This was my anniversary," he said.

"To Caroline?"

Vern chuckled. "Let's call her Brand X."

"So you've been thinking about her? About your first family?"

"I haven't felt well. I'm sorry, darling," he said. "You know I love you more than anything in the world. It'll all work out. I promise." He leaned over and hugged me so long I was afraid he might nod off on top of me.

I hope so, I thought. I wanted to believe him.

That night, I leaned toward Vern and thought of all I was grateful for. I loved that he cared so much, that he seemed to be a good father. That he spoke regularly with his daughters and brainstormed about ways to get them to visit more often and be more a part of our lives. I couldn't help but wonder if his deteriorating health and fear of not being able to see our own child reach age eleven was partially motivating him with Stan. Maybe Stan wasn't giving me practice as a mother as much as he was giving me practice observing Vern as a father.

I was snuggling into this thought, running the day's events over and over in my mind, when suddenly I was jolted awake by the acrid smell of smoke.

I shot up in bed, wondering if I was having a vivid nightmare in all the turmoil, or if Vern had left a cigarette burning in the kitchen. I flung my blue flannel robe through my arms and followed the smoke to the hallway. Where was it coming from?

I paused on the landing and sniffed. *Stan's room?*

I pushed open the door. Light flickered around tall, dark shadows. "Vern!" I shouted. "Vern!"

Vern rushed in behind me with no teeth, wearing his saggy white Jockey underwear and T-shirt. Three candles, pooling in the center of one of Vern's mother's fancy Haviland Limoges dinner plates, had poured onto the top of the dresser, and tall flames were piercing the air. Two feet from the flames, Stan hid behind a sheer white curtain.

I grabbed the nearest blanket, slung over Vern's grandfather's antique rocker. Stan frantically blew at the flames, splashing liquid wax in every direction. The flames grew larger and Vern jumped back. Like a wrangler, I tossed the blanket over the fire, suffocating it.

As smoke seeped from the blanket's edges, Vern and I shouted at Stan, in stereo, "What is this? What in the hell are you doing?"

The seared blanket was no great loss; its rayon binding was tattered and frayed. But the cherry dresser—only showing light usage over sixty years—was now permanently damaged. And so were my nerves.

I recalled my father and younger siblings diving into our turquoise Chevy and shouting out directions—right, left, left again—on our way to a fire. We'd join a crowd of onlookers, and Dad would put us on his shoulders or we'd crane our necks from the sidewalk as smoke poured out of windows and roofs.

It was my mother who pointed out the suffering connected to fires, that people go to jail for setting them. "They take pictures at those fires, Dick," she said. "If you aren't careful, they're liable to think you set them."

I'd thought my mother was spoiling our fun. Now, standing in my house, shuddering, I understood.

When the smoke died down, Vern rubbed his fingers over the top of the dresser. For once, he seemed more frustrated than I was. I figured it was his turn to speak to Stan. I tightened my robe and tiptoed out.

When Vern returned, he was gasping, his neck deep red, his complexion grayish. He spent a long time leaning against his military dresser, his back to me, as he propped his lungs with his shoulders up, his weight on his elbows. I could feel my anger growing. I didn't care what had caused Stan's behavior. His father's passing? His mother's take no prisoners approach? Did it matter? This was too much for Vern.

"The little urchin was on his way to the video arcade," he said.

"At midnight?" I wasn't sure it was even open at that hour.

"Yep. He was dressed to go out. His trouser pocket was filled with those damn video tokens." Vern smashed his cigarette in an overflowing ashtray and climbed into bed with me.

I rolled away from him, and Vern cuddled up close, nibbling at my neck and embracing me from behind. Weren't pregnant women supposed to be more attractive—their skin softer, their complexion clearer? I felt like hell. I was wearing loose, frumpy clothes and resembling my mother more and more by the day. I wasn't taking care of myself. I squeezed the cotton sheet in my fist and pulled it up under my chin. I did feel some relief that Vern finally seemed to see what I was telling him, but something told me this wouldn't last long.

"I'm overwhelmed," I said. I didn't feel right about Stan's spending so much time playing video games and watching TV, but I was too tired to search out other kids his age or to plan anything that took energy. "I love you, Vern, and I'm trying hard, but what are we supposed to do?"

"We can move to The Point," he said without hesitation. "We should pack up our things and move this weekend. It's our only hope."

CHAPTER 9

The moment we pulled into the driveway on Cave Road in the blue Nissan hatchback, my whole body felt lighter. Vern and I unloaded the wallpaper books I'd picked up from Tissot's and the clothes and kitchen supplies as Stan tore down the driveway and around the property, exploring. I have to admit, I felt a moment of joy right then, the kind of pride you feel when you do something for your child and you sense his excitement.

Within a short while, Stan was hanging over the creek, pulling sticks from high tree limbs, kicking through the tall grass, poking long branches into the wet ground, and throwing rocks at dragonflies, creating loud splashes as his missiles landed in the water. His actions were innocent enough. But I couldn't get the fire out of my mind. I kept tossing around the details of that night. *Was he trying to run away and afraid to turn on the overhead light? Afraid he'd wake us? Where did he think he was going? Back to Connecticut? Or is he some kind of child arsonist?*

I tried to block the thought darts shooting through my head and focus on the natural beauty of the place. I'd forgotten how soothing it was to hear the swoosh of water falling on rock or catch a whiff of wild phlox and asters wafting through the damp air. I loved the crumbling outdoor cobblestone fireplace, the old privy, and the stone wall. The paw-paws and buckeyes, the hemlocks and sycamores. I loved the screened-in porch, the way it overlooked the old footbridge with the cast-iron street lamp. I loved the front porch, too, with its decorative iron fretwork, salvaged from an 1870s

Italianate house. The old furnace pumped out heat that smelled of kerosene in the winter. On sweltering summer days, we opened the windows and felt the cool breeze rising up from the creek. With its cold concrete floors and old furniture, I wouldn't say the place was cozy—but the setting was bucolic, the kind you might expect to find in Upstate New York or Western Massachusetts.

By the end of the week, the decision to move to The Point seemed the right one. I wasn't ready to admit this to Vern, however. I liked having Vern in a position of problem-solving, and I feared that admitting the move was a good one could put us right back where we had been before—with all the responsibility on me.

One night, Vern stopped for groceries on his thirteen-mile drive home. I had spent the morning poring over wallpaper samples for the nursery, then hunting for Stan so I could feed him some lunch. I had that empty feeling you get when you haven't accomplished much and the day's almost over.

Vern arrived singing the song from *South Pacific* about finding her and never letting go. He removed his button-down Brooks Brothers shirt and hung it over the back of a green-painted chair. His voice, with its lilting cadence, sounded sweet even though I knew he was buttering me up. It tickled me when he referred to the moment as enchanted.

He handed me a pack of chicken breasts and a pan of goetta, a type of meat-and-grain sausage in a loaf pan, from a friend. He said something corny about coconut milk, frangipani essence, and palm fronds, and I playfully pinched his waist as he kissed me.

I served a simple meal of corn, zucchini, and sliced tomatoes with grilled chicken. Stan wiped corn kernels off his cheek as Chippie lapped them up by his feet.

Vern said that day at work he'd told people about my pregnancy. Some of our friends had made jokes as they'd considered what name we would give the baby.

"Why does everyone use nicknames?" Stan asked when he heard Vern used to be called "Brother."

"Your father went by a nickname, didn't he?" Vern asked.

"Popseed," Stan said. "I called him Popseed, and they used to call me Stasiu."

Vern nodded. "They're terms of endearment. Kim has had some nicknames too, haven't you?" This was Vern's way of poking me in the ribs to get me involved in the conversation.

I went down the list: "Sneaky Pete, Kimmybuster, Butch, Piggy . . ."

"They called you 'Piggy'?" Stan burst out laughing. "Why would they call you Piggy?"

"An old swimming coach started it."

Stan seemed happy, and Vern gobbled up every ounce of his enthusiasm. As he poured on the charm, I grew even quieter.

Stan bounced on the metal bench, scraping the floor. Vern clasped him by the wrist. "Sit still for a moment, will you? Bouncing is fine, but leave the bench where it is."

Stan shot Vern an evil eye, which Vern didn't notice. Then, like the wind, he shot off to ride Ben's bike.

For several hours, we lingered on the porch in a fragile calm, watching Stan zoom around. At one point, when Stan hollered something, Vern glanced up from his book with a loving smile. "Don't you enjoy him at all?"

I thought for a moment about how to answer. *Enjoy him? Well, um, not at this moment. Not while newly married and pregnant.* "I need a break, Vern, that's all. He's a nice kid. I love The Point. But he's too much. I get nothing done. I can't relax. I'm nauseous. I'm sticky and uncomfortable, and there's something wrong with the shower in the house."

"Why can't you shower under the waterfall? You worried about Father Gude?"

Our local priest (whose name was pronounced "Goody") was tall, thin as a pipe cleaner, and maybe twenty years older than Vern but in better health. He first appeared in our driveway one night shortly after Vern and I began going to The Point.

"Honey," Vern shouted. "I want you to meet someone."

For a moment, Vern and Father Gude spoke about their age, complimenting each other on their good looks. Vern was reminded of a quote: "Youth is the anticipation of joys that probably will never come. Age is the pleasant retrospect of the joys that did come, after all."

Father Gude seemed pleased to meet me. More than likely, he noticed the long crease between my eyebrows that the Chinese call a hanging blade. I'd always considered it the result of Catholic guilt, and I'm sure he'd seen a lot of them. Turned out he was a retired priest from St. Clare's in College Hill, a suburb of Cincinnati, and someone in his family owned a small cabin up the road. He said he drove the two hours every summer for solace.

According to Vern, when Vern's father lived across the creek, kids would show up in the middle of the night to skinny dip in the natural pool below. His father would hit the master switch and light up the place to get them scrambling like mice on the kitchen floor.

"Your father was a good man, though," Father Gude had said. "When it was me down there, I'd call up, 'It's me, George Gude!' and your father would turn off the lights."

Vern had suggested we come up with a signal so we wouldn't accidently run into a naked Father Gude, or he into us. I had found a red bandana in one of the dresser drawers, and it seemed to be working. The bandana tied to the metal railing signaled, *Someone's showering.* The bandana on the ground meant, *The coast is clear.*

Father Gude struck me as a peaceful soul with nothing to prove. Though I had grown up as a "bad Catholic," not attending parochial school and barely following the church rules, I viewed Father Gude's presence as a kind of insurance for our souls. It was comforting to know I could run down the road and get extra spiritual help if the stress of Stan became intolerable. I had nothing to worry about with Father Gude.

"No, no, no!" I scowled. "Father Gude is no problem at all."

"Then what?"

"You honestly think I can shower with Stan here?"

"Can't you wear your bathing suit?"

"Vern, you're not being reasonable. Do you realize I have to watch him constantly?" I tried to explain the way Stan slunk around the bushes like a creeper. "You know, he was in the garage yesterday. I worry that if I don't pay attention, he'll hurt himself."

Whenever I used words that sounded downbeat or negative, Vern immediately stiffened. He either lit a cigarette, poured an alcoholic drink, or used his inhaler, which forced a cough. Today, he puffed his inhaler as the radio blared a scratchy rendition of Bartok's Violin Concerto No. 2.

"He really is a good kid, you know." Vern was trying to convince himself.

"Yeah, I know," I mumbled. "Can we turn off the music? Or at least turn it down? I can't think."

Without waiting for a response, I leapt up from the metal bench and turned the volume down. When I returned with a loud sigh, Vern pretended he didn't notice.

We watched Stan's constant movement through the dark screen, the mesh metal table between us littered with dirty dishes. We might as well have been watching the blades of a fan rotate, yet it was anything but soothing.

Vern leaned over, his tobacco-stained fingers clutching his chin. "You know, darling, I'm afraid we might be hosting Stan even longer than a month." He puffed his Pall Mall as he glanced down at the bridge.

My gut clenched. "Wait, what? Did you tell Stan's mother we would take him for the entire *summer*? Is that what you're saying?"

"No, honey."

"Are you sure?"

"Of course I'm sure."

"Then what?"

"Just a moment." Vern pushed back from the table, set his cigarette on a dirty plate, and trudged out to the truck to retrieve a shopping bag he'd left in the front seat. I helped him stack the dirty dishes on one side of the table so he could show me his brand-new pile of correspondence, which he spread out like a deck of cards.

"I didn't want to upset you," he said.

"What *is* this?" I asked.

He was holding another stack of old issues of *American Agricultural Conservation Gardens*, a newsletter that promoted buying fresh fruits and vegetables without preservatives. On top were a couple of newspaper articles about the auction scheduled to liquidate Stan's family's property and more details about the controversy his mother was having with the developer.

"What's this about the judge ordering a liquidation of the property?" Ruthann's last letter had seemed somewhat hopeful. Now she said a judge was forcing the sale of the whole property.

"She and the developer can't agree on the property lines."

"You think this is true? I mean, she's not making this up as a ruse to keep him with us longer?" I frowned as I thought of all the excuses my parents used to give us.

"No, honey. She has her hands full."

I lifted one article off the table. It was from the previous year and said Ruthann had run as a write-in candidate for the office of selectman of Old Lyme. "Did you read this?" I asked, incredulous. I waited for Vern's full attention. "Coxe, who supports a return to a simple agricultural society, is also waging an unusual campaign. She began last month by marching into a town meeting dragging a red wagon filled with hay and a forty-pound watermelon. A newcomer to politics, Coxe, at Thursday's debate, delivered a 'getting to know you' speech including a musical rendition of the song of that title from *The King and I*. Steady religious beliefs, a 'cash and carry philosophy,' and positive energy are assets Coxe said she would use to help preserve the town's fragile environment."

Vern chuckled as I read, but he didn't seem all that surprised. I was finally getting what Vern meant when he called her a strange bird; unless I was mistaken and Old Lyme was an equally strange town, Ruthann Coxe wasn't the kind of woman capable of accomplishing her goals. I rubbed my stomach and thought of the baby. I was eating well and doing my best to fix healthy foods for all of us, while Stan's mother railed against grocery stores, touting her farm-to-table ethic. I was in disbelief that in the midst of her legal battle, she was sending us literature implying we weren't giving Stan good food. Since Stan hadn't made any phone calls home, it miffed me that she was jumping to conclusions. Was she proselytizing to me because Vern had mentioned my pregnancy?

"Hell, you can't even buy anything organic in Hillsboro, can you?" Vern said. It was his way of supporting me. "Regardless," he continued, "we should keep Stan for as long as his mother needs our help. He seems calmer and less excitable than when he first arrived, don't you think?"

"No."

"Well, you're getting used to his idiosyncrasies, aren't you?"

"No, I am not." I glared at Vern. He seemed to have already made his decision. I scooted the metal bench back and lifted one leg over to get out from under the table.

Vern looked confused, or maybe surprised. I think he wanted to believe my love of The Point included my love of having Stan with us, that I was gradually adjusting to him.

"Vern, I'm barely tolerating him. He doesn't seem calmer, or happier, at all. His bike riding is no different from TV. He's escaping into it. Why can't you see he's not happy?"

Vern pulled a fresh cigarette from behind his ear and lit it. "He's happier now. Look at him."

I peered through the screen as Stan accelerated down the hill, dodging Chippie and shouting, "Watch me go! Count how long it takes." He was small for the bike and mostly stood on its pedals as he shaved off seconds with every loop.

Vern glanced down at his wristwatch, then hollered, "Six minutes, thirty-two seconds."

I felt guilty watching Stan's delicate frame sail past us—as if I had a responsibility to him. But the responsibility was, ultimately, Vern's. Was it really my duty to take care of this kid? I wasn't doing anything for Stan other than fixing his meals, washing his clothes, and telling him "no." Why couldn't I enjoy him as much as Vern could? Was this about our age difference? Vern's feeling of limited time? Or more of my lingering resentment from my childhood because we kids had always had to do all the work?

Ruthann's literature lay scattered before us. In the mix was a photograph of Sam Senior that showed Stan's resemblance to him—the light hair and long face. *What is it?* I wondered. *Does Vern owe this guy in some way?*

Vern stepped into one of his teaching moments. "What is this life if, full of care, we have no time to stand and stare."

I turned and stared directly at him, but he ignored me. For the moment, the only hint of Stan was the sound of bike wheels and Chippie's bark as he glided past.

I bolted up and stood near the door. "You know what?"

"What?" Vern barely moved as he continued to peer through the porch screen.

"I don't need this right now. I'm not enjoying this at all."

"Darling . . . Must I tell you how much I miss being charmed by your cheerful countenance?" There was a hint of sadness in his expression.

"Vern . . ."

He launched into a story from his childhood, and I listened with my head cocked. Apparently he and his friends had pitched a tent at The Point, then gone for a swim. When they returned to the tent, they saw a turkey buzzard entering and decided maybe it would be fun to trap the buzzard. They sneaked up and shut the tent's flap and soon thereafter noticed a horrible stench. "That's when we learned the way buzzards protect themselves—by vomiting their guts out."

It was usually fun to imagine Vern and his friend, Stu, coming up with screwy solutions for the problems presented by their irrational ideas, like the characters from *Spanky and Our Gang*, but today I wasn't in the mood. "Where were your parents?"

"I expect Mother was there. She allowed us to experiment." Vern said his mother was a follower of John Dewey, that she believed children should learn through experience. "We couldn't get near the damn thing," he said. "And once it was gone, we had to burn the tent." He let out a soft, good-humored laugh.

As Vern kept watching Stan, I leaned into the doorjamb and watched Vern.

He'd told me once that when his father was on the Board of Trustees of Miami University in Ohio, it had been against the school's rules to drive a car on campus. Vern, wanting to test the rules, had driven a red convertible through campus, for which he'd received a twenty-dollar fine and promptly gotten suspended.

Stan must have reminded Vern of an earlier time in Hillsboro, when kids were kids and could pretend to be pirates or bank robbers . . . or firefighters. Vern had grown up before every American family owned a television. He'd eaten organic foods before they were called "organic." I'm sure he wanted for Stan the kind of experience he remembered from his own past. He saw value in what he considered Stan's rebellion—rebellion, after all, creates artists and inventors—but I wanted him to transfer some of that positive outlook to *our* child, too.

SHOOTING OUT THE LIGHTS

It was getting darker, and Father Gude appeared at the back porch, a towel under his arm. "How do?" Vern said, jumping up from his seat. "Just a moment. Honey, can you get Stan?"

For a split second, I was reminded of my father. I could hear his voice with the younger boys. "Beej, the baby's crying. He needs a diaper change."

Vern could've called Stan himself, but I went to the front porch and shrieked his name. Stan soon appeared at the end of the driveway and rode straight for the front door. He thrust his bike against the front yews as Father Gude adjusted the bandana. Vern introduced him to the priest. Stan delivered a quick hello and sprinted off, apparently to hide.

Father Gude seemed calmly amused. I waved as he climbed down into the pool.

"Feel free to use the shampoo," I shouted. I had tucked a bottle and bar of soap into a waist-high hole in the rock.

When Stan stepped into the house minutes later—shaking his caked-on dirt onto the concrete floor of the living room, which Chippie promptly trotted through—I shook my head.

"Stan!" Vern called from the back porch. "Before you get ready for bed, there's something we should discuss."

Stan dutifully made his way back to where Vern was waiting for him. "What?" He looked up, a half-smile on his lips.

I was beginning to detect his nuanced gestures. Stan undoubtedly thought this was "the talk." He'd seen his mother's large package. He was aware Vern and I had been gabbing a long time. He thought he was going home. At least, that was my impression.

Vern asked him to have a seat, and Stan happily sprawled on the couch, breathing heavily, exaggerating his breath. Vern looked proud; he had the face of someone about to present an award. "You seem to be enjoying this place," he said.

Stan nodded.

"I want you to think about staying here another month," Vern went on—and Stan went from warm to ice cold. "We don't have to debate this right now," Vern said. "Maybe tomorrow. But I'd like you to consider it."

Stan hardly flinched. He looked to one side as his movements slowed.

According to Vern, Stan took the news of a longer visit well. When we were ready for bed, Vern turned out our bedroom light and opened the windows, and for a moment all that could be heard was the ping of moths hitting the screen. I wondered if my husband's drinking had given him his cheery disposition; for my part, Stan's blunted reaction was worrying.

"Why didn't you tell him you already agreed to let him stay?" I asked.

"I thought he might enjoy the surprise."

"The surprise? Seriously?" I grumbled, thinking, *Some people don't care for surprises.*

With the bed shoved against the wall, and with barely enough room to open and shut the door, we were squeezed in tightly, yet we were poles apart. To Vern, this was any other day. He had blithely announced the possibility of an extended visit as if he were reminding Stan of an upcoming holiday. To me, in contrast, it was worse than cluster headaches. I couldn't sleep.

I lay close to Vern, listening to the whoosh of water slapping rock, tossing from side to side, trying to get comfortable, and thinking about Stan. He had been abandoned by his father, then his mother, and now, for multiple reasons, he was being abandoned by us. I wanted to believe that The Point was an adventure for him and was presenting him with new opportunities for healing, but the truth was that we were leaving this boy to his own devices. Was that what he really needed? I knew what it felt like.

When I was ten, my mother and father twisted my arm about

participating in competitive swimming over the winter. They insisted my younger siblings and I join the team, which meant we had no free time at all because swimming practice and homework were so all-consuming. When I complained and asked my mother why she was forcing us to do something we didn't like, she'd said, "We don't want you kids becoming juvenile delinquents." I couldn't believe it. *Juvenile delinquents?* I thought at the time. *Hardly.* But looking back, swimming *had* kept us out of trouble. Maybe we hadn't needed a sport that absorbed every waking moment—but I did feel grateful we'd had something. Stan needed something too.

Maybe what he needed most was more one-on-one time, the careful attention that showed he was valued and loved. It had only been a year since his father had died. *Why doesn't she care enough to help him deal with such enormous grief?* Sending him off to us was doubling the trauma. Or was this my own guilt rearing its ugly head? Like television or video games, or competitive swimming when I was a kid, The Point had become an escape for Vern and me. Another way to send Stan off on his own.

Soon after I dropped off, a rattling metallic sound peeled my eyes wide open. It sounded like a raccoon in a loose gutter. The sound stopped for a moment and then started again. Half-awake, I noticed the unmistakable smell of smoke.

I sprang up and swung my legs around, let my feet drop to the floor. *Is he setting something else on fire?*

I rushed into Stan's room. At the foot of his bed, a smoldering blanket spewed a billowing black cloud. I smelled burning plastic.

"What's going on?" I barked. I coughed into my cupped hand, then flailed my arms at the smoke. Stan was standing on the far end of the bed—I could hardly see him—and was pressed against the wall, bouncing on the bedsprings and holding a lit candle. He had tried to ignite his blanket.

As I watched him bounce, he blew out the candle, spewing hot wax all over the bed. I sprang back, flipped a comforter up over the smoldering blanket, and reached out to open his window. The wool blanket had a charred black stain; its satin edge was shriveled. The whole room reeked, and the fumes caught me in the back of the throat.

Vern rushed in behind me but didn't say anything.

"There was something in the shadows." Stan pointed to the corner between the open side door to a connecting room and an antique walnut wardrobe that was so dry it looked like firewood.

I switched on the overhead light, closed the door cautiously, and peeked into the corner beside the wardrobe. "Nothing there," I said, softening. "What did you see?"

Stan took in a deep breath, his ribs clearly visible.

"Answer me, Stan. What happened here?" I pointed to the charred area at the foot of his bed and began to cough again.

"I don't know."

"You don't *know*? Where'd you get the candle and matches?" I wasn't so oblivious that I wouldn't have noticed a candle stashed under his shirt. He must've gone to extra lengths to hide them. I couldn't figure out how he got them past me.

Vern peered over my shoulder. Stan started to turn away, but there was no place for him to go.

"*Tell* me. Where did you get the candle?" I waited for him, scowling, still calm. Then it hit me . . . "Do you have electricity in Connecticut?" It seemed a personal question. An insensitive one.

"Well . . . yes." Stan hesitated.

"You do? You have electricity?"

He nodded. It was a weird moment, an awkward moment, as if I were asking if he had money in the bank.

"Do you light candles in Connecticut?"

"Yes, ma'am."

"Why?"

Stan didn't answer. Vern shifted from one foot to the other, uncomfortable with the veiled blaming in my question. "Is it necessary that we get to the bottom of this right now?" he asked. "Is there a need to know?"

Uh, yes, I thought. There *is* a need to know. This was the second time it had happened. Did Vern know something that he wasn't saying? I brushed past him, gathered a few newspapers in the kitchen, then returned to the room and waved what I could of the remaining smoke through the open window.

I leaned into Vern. "We can't ignore this," I said softly in his ear. "He tried to set the comforter on fire!"

But it was the same thing all over again. Vern—without his teeth, standing in his white Jockey underpants and T-shirt—stepped toward Stan. He spoke tenderly to him, trying to show sympathy.

"I see things in the dark," Stan said.

"That's easy. Let's leave the light on in the hallway." Vern reached his arm around and flipped the switch. "How's that? Better?"

"Thank you, sir," Stan said. He handed me the candle and dropped back into his bed as Vern turned out the overhead light. I wish I could say he looked sorry, or afraid, or even sweet, but I didn't believe him. We were being manipulated. I left the splattered wax for the next day.

"It was a raggedy old bedspread anyway," Vern whispered as we returned to the bedroom. "It's an old camp bed."

"I don't care," I said. "That's not the point."

Vern sat down beside me on the bed and placed his hand on my thigh to communicate his approval of the way I'd handled the situation. But I didn't want his approval. I wanted his outrage. Why was Stan seeing things in the dark? Was this something new for him? Where did he sleep at home? Did he have his own bed, his own room? If he was drinking breast milk, was he sleeping in his mother's bed? *I need a counselor myself* was all I could think, along with *Where's Father Gude when you need him?*

Under the covers, my body curled away from Vern. I rubbed

my stomach as if I were rubbing my baby's head. I was seething. It wasn't the dealing with dripping wax and chewing gum that was killing me anymore. Instead, it was an invisible wall in our marriage—with bricks made of Vern's obstinate refusal to see any problem, and mortar made of my refusal to see any good.

CHAPTER 10

If it hadn't been for the second fire, it would've been an ordinary day. Vern smoked at the kitchen table, composing a list of chores, as I sat on the old camp sofa out on the porch, chomping saltines with my feet up. In a repeat from the night before, Stan rode Ben's bike at top speed around the circular drive. Every three or four minutes, as Stan rounded the bend, Chippie would bark and then scamper away, staring like an old man.

Nothing could satiate Stan's craving for speed. Instead of breathing in the fresh air and considering the environment a positive one for myself and the baby, I could only concentrate on how my brain felt squeezed by his constant movement, around and around, like a hamster on a wheel.

Vern joined me on the porch sofa. "Your parents mentioned Rick and Carlos need a job. What do you think about getting them out here?"

I rolled my eyes. It killed me that I'd reached out to my parents for help and instead would be helping *them* by hiring the boys. But Rick and Carlos were undoubtedly aching for an excuse to escape my parents' demands.

"Sure, it's fine," I said. "What about Stanislaus? You want to hire them as babysitters?"

Vern took a long time to answer. I knew he was off on another tangent. "Stan seems to get more revved up out here rather than less. Unlike me."

"He's not like *you* because he's not your *son*."

"I know," he said, sadly. "You keep repeating yourself."

I considered that maybe I'd lost my compassion as I tossed the pack of saltines on the coffee table and stood up. "You don't seem anxious to send him to his mother. That's where he belongs, you know."

Vern's eyes looked baggy and unfocused. "I'm afraid his mother will ask us to put him in school."

"Oh, for Godsake. That's almost three months away. Don't even think about it." I headed for the door.

"We must prepare ourselves," Vern piped up.

"No, Vern." I raised my voice above Chippie's bark. "What are you talking about? You'll have to tell her no."

Vern loosened his shoelaces and pressed his thumb into one of his swollen ankles. "She should have called by now to arrange his return."

"Then call *her*. What's the problem?"

Vern ignored me. "Ruthann's letter said the court ordered that their farm be sold on July 10. We may have to keep him at least that long." He lit a cigarette and began coughing. Then he said, "He acts out because he doesn't want to go home."

"Are you kidding me, Vern?" I half shouted.

"Look at him out there," he said. "He's enjoying this place."

I glanced through the screen. Stan soared down the asphalt pavement, his shirt billowing in back, and zig-zagged across the bridge on Ben's bike. *Is this what all couples go through in their first year of marriage?* I kept thinking. I wanted to run. I wanted to sleep. I wanted to do whatever was necessary to shake some sense into Vern.

"Honey, I'm enjoying his enthusiasm," he said.

"But you are only focused on Stan."

Today, I would be more direct: *What about me? What about our child?* Back then, I didn't know how.

"Look," he said. "I know what you think. But Stan is not a Ben substitute. I regret not making an effort to contact Stan's father." He went on to explain that he'd known Stan's father, an attorney, had moved the family into his mother's house. "I knew they needed help and I did nothing," he said.

"So?" I shook my head. "We all have regrets."

Vern dropped his head, weary from arguing. Then he said, "I thought you would understand, being a preservationist." He reached his tobacco-stained fingers in my direction, and I could feel him sucking the will out of me. "She's fighting a developer who is trying to take over her family farm. For Godsake, I thought you'd concur."

I had been trying to be generous to Vern, but this was too much. What was wrong with him? Was he seriously going to use the preservation defense to manipulate me?

We had conversed incessantly about the Scott House, the keystone of West Main Street that had been on the Underground Railroad and was said to have had a tunnel to a house across the street purportedly used by escaped slaves. We had discussed the deteriorating Parker Hotel. The Mother Thompson House. The hardware store. The East Main Street Historic District. I'd felt great pride in digging up the history of those buildings for my job. And now he was bringing that into our discussion. Preservation? I thought it was one of the things he loved most about me—my interest in saving those old buildings. And now he was . . . what? Calling my bluff to force me to back off with Stan? This was too personal. Too close to home.

As Stan flashed by us again, the dog barked, sparrows darted into the air, and the wind whipped dust onto the porch. Vern lifted a napkin from the table, hacked up a glob of something thick and glutinous, then wiped his mouth and folded it into his napkin. "About Stan . . ."

I stood up. I was beginning to think the problem wasn't really about Stan but between the two of us. I wanted a break. Help by way of the Wigwam. Maybe in some dark space in my brain, I thought Ann might intervene with Vern, since I was getting nowhere.

I left to use the bathroom and, not thinking, forgot to check—and sat down on a soaking wet seat. "Arghhh!" I shouted.

My thoughts went right to my parents, though I knew they would be no help. Maybe it was Vern's stubbornness in the face of my unhappiness that reminded me of Dad. I recalled the times when I sat in our basement stall as a girl, my shorts at my ankles, not yet tall enough for my bare feet to touch the cement, and Dad would stand outside the bathroom door, monitoring my bathroom activity. The reason, he said, was that we had a cistern that collected rainwater and it was expensive hiring a service to deliver water, so it was important that we not run out. But even after we moved to the new house with city water, Dad would want to know whether it was number one or number two.

"Go away," I'd shout, and he'd continue to stand there, listening.

I hadn't seen Dad in a while, and as I looked down at my bare feet, firmly planted on the concrete, I suddenly saw not the similarities but only the differences between him and Vern. There was no restraining Dad on a fact-finding mission, while Vern was closed up, rarely openly inquisitive. I never had to tell him about ex-boyfriends because he didn't want to know. This worked well for me in the beginning of our relationship. I found it attractive that he wasn't judging me by mistakes in my past. I had always assumed Vern's need to not know was his full tank of heartache, his not wanting to stir the sentiment in me for fear his own would overflow. His heartache was the reason I excused his drinking, his smoking, his rules for what he considered appropriate behavior. I didn't want to be the cause of Vern's meltdown.

But as I thought of it, I realized Vern *was* melting down. Despite what he said, his loyalty to Stan was clearly a loyalty to Ben. Putting Stan's needs above his own, not tolerating any negative comments when it came to the boy, constantly seeking out ways to keep him and help him—he was treating him as if he *were* Ben, as if he could magically undo the past by doing things "right" this time.

And my cooperation was enabling him to keep Stan longer.

I resolved right then that I would no longer make excuses for Vern. His gasping and hacking sounded much worse than a simple cold. I didn't know yet that swollen ankles were a sign that fluid was accumulating in his lungs, but I knew it signaled *something* wasn't right, and his distended belly and labored breathing terrified me. With our attention focused on Stan, I'd missed how quickly my husband's health had deteriorated in the last month.

I removed my shorts and oversize blouse, dropped them in a heap on the floor, and turned the warm faucet until water dribbled out of the shower. Then I stepped in, washed off the day's grime, and soaked up whatever I could of the water's warmth.

Later that evening, I felt better but still frustrated. I broke my habit of ignoring the smoking and suggested to Vern that he try to quit.

Vern took a long drag on his cigarette and blew the smoke in front of him. "I've mentioned this before," he said. "It's counterintuitive, but it truly feels better to smoke."

In some way, I understood. It was a habit, after all, and I understood habits. I'd stretched my mouth compulsively as a kid, and beginning when I was twelve, one of my swimming coaches had forced me to focus on my weight to an obsessive degree. Daily weigh-ins and regular lectures had turned normal eating into nibbling around the edges, and food in general became something to be measured and analyzed—a habit I still had. Vern's chronic smoking had become as much a part of him as a stutter.

He launched into a long theoretical monologue about vices, personalities, and the ways we cope. "The Point suits Stan's hyperactivity," he said. "He needn't present a problem if we set limits."

I assumed he meant setting limits on Stan's activity, requiring reading or quiet time of some sort, but I didn't ask for clarification. Instead, I filled in the backstory myself: I assumed Ben had died because Vern hadn't set limits, and now here he was again, not set-ting limits and claiming that was what we had to do.

I'd learned with Vern that silence was power, that I could com-municate more effectively when we disagreed if I held my tongue. So I sat, quietly, waving away the smoke. I listened to a woodpecker hammering for grubs. I focused on the water rushing over the dam. And as Stan whooshed by us every seven minutes or so, it dawned on me that I was actually a lot like Stan. I might as well have been on that bike myself; I had the same restless discomfort. Constantly on edge, feeling anxious and overwhelmed, having difficulty relax-ing—it seemed obvious now why this boy was getting to me so much. And, with that realization, Stan and his wild cycling began to recede to the background. For a moment, I felt hopeful. Maybe I *could* adjust.

As Vern smoked, his breathing did improve. When he was able to breathe freely again, I reached out to hug him. "If you send him home, I'll serve you gourmet meals. I'll give you back rubs every night. Anything you want."

"I'm going to have to go in." Vern looked exhausted, I assumed from all the coughing.

"I mean it, Vern. I want some time with you, just the two of us, before the baby comes."

He reached for the open door. "I've had enough for one day, darling. Wake me at eight tomorrow morning. Water treatment if necessary."

Over the following days, Vern arranged for Rick and Carlos to scrape paint at The Point. Vern had complained that Herman was too slow and precise, and since he paid Herman by the hour, he thought hiring Rick and Carlos for the prep work might speed things up. I'm sure he also thought I needed some social interaction.

The boys showed up looking bedraggled—no shower, grubby T-shirts—but smiling and ready to do anything to avoid dealing with Mom and Dad, who had returned from another road trip and were in one of their moods. I went out to greet them on the side porch as Vern got dressed. I should've noticed the way they seemed to mirror Stan's angelic behavior after the fires, but I didn't.

Rick had a salesman's charisma. He was quick on his feet. Not a fast talker, but a down-to-earth nice guy who could tell a good story and was kind and softhearted unless it had to do with David, who—luckily for David—was singing and dancing at a show choir camp in Columbus. Rick said Mom and Dad were still upset about the piano and that David was little Mr. I-Had-Nothing-to-Do-with-the-Pig-Roast. David had been opening mail for Mom and Dad and depositing their checks in the bank while they were out of town and, according to Rick, had a chip on his shoulder because they kept making him help them at their gift shows and not paying him for it. "It's not *my* fault they picked David to help with the shows," Rick said, smiling. "He's good with the little old ladies. We aren't."

I didn't see why Rick and Carlos were so anxious to work for Vern. I quizzed them about why they were still in trouble with Mom and Dad.

"Oh, the septic system's all messed up," Rick said.

"From what?" My mind went to the hundreds of people at the pig roast.

"I don't know. When David flushed and it started overflowing, he screamed at the top of his lungs. Dad thought he was just using too much toilet paper. You know how Dad is. He comes in ranting and grabs the plunger, and then David starts gagging and Dad starts swinging." He chuckled. "I shouldn't have, but I started laughing. Dad didn't think it was funny. He noticed two condoms floating in the toilet."

"There were a lot of kids using that bathroom," Carlos said.

"Yeah, I think he flipped out when David started gagging." Rick hesitated, as if he realized he was schmoozing too much. "Does Vern have something for us?"

"Don't forget the underwear." Carlos snickered.

"Oh . . . yeah." Rick gave Carlos a boyish, good-humored smile. "You know how after the party we spruced up everything? The place was spotless—we even did the laundry—but Dad found a pair of BVDs in his dresser drawer."

"I don't get it."

"He wears Jockey. He was ranting to Mom, 'I've never worn a pair of BVDs in my whole goddamn life.' He wanted to know where they came from."

"Where *did* they come from?"

Rick waved his hand dismissively. "Hell if I know. They could've belonged to anyone."

The screen door slammed, and Vern appeared from around the corner. "How do? You ready for some scut work?" He led Rick down the driveway to the bridge, where he pointed to the peeling metal railing where it sloped down to the creek bed.

As Carlos took a side trip to the bathroom, I stepped in front of him at the front door, blocking him like a basketball player guarding the ball. I wanted to try again to see if he was willing to tell me who'd gotten hurt. I was mirroring my father, who wanted to know every detail about every party I attended as a child.

"You've got to tell me what happened," I said.

"No, Kim," he said. "Please—"

"Did you speak to Dad? Does *he* know?"

"Nobody knows," he said.

I raised my eyebrows. "*Nobody* knows?" I tried to imply I'd heard something. "Don't you want to get it off your chest? Maybe you'd feel better."

"The guys would kill me."

"What guys? Tell me. What guys are you talking about?"

"You can't say anything about this to anyone, Kim. Not even Vern. I swear to God." Carlos's hands were shaking. He lowered his voice to a whisper. He said he and Rick and six of their friends had gone to my parents' garage and grabbed whatever they could—bowie knives, sledgehammers, tire irons—to use as their "weapons of choice."

"Weapons for *what?*"

"We started driving," he said. "It was after midnight, and we drove around until we found a pig."

"Wait, what?" I was shaking my head, my palms upturned. This was not what I'd expected to hear.

"Kim!" He grabbed my forearm. "Listen." Carlos looked physically weak. Judging by the way he glanced to the driveway and then lowered his voice even further, I could tell he was scared. "We were so drunk, Kim. We found this sow in a field, maybe 130 kilos, and . . ." He shut his eyes for a moment. "We surrounded her. We beat the hell out of her. She squealed. And there was blood everywhere. She jerked in the air, like four feet, and then tumbled to the ground."

"Stop! Oh, God!" I clapped my ears shut. "How could you *do* that?"

Carlos's face was motionless. "She was half-dead, Kim."

"And so how did you get her to the house?"

"We had three guys in the front of the truck and about five guys in the back. We drove the truck right through the center of town, and she was still breathing and snorting."

"Past the police?"

He nodded. "One of the guys knew how to do the cleaning and salting."

"I'm surprised nobody got hurt."

"One of the guys did. Got his head cracked open—we were so drunk—and they took him to Highland District." Carlos looked stricken. "I don't want to talk about this anymore. I have to paint." He glanced out to the driveway, where we could still hear Vern's faint voice.

I drew a sharp breath and thought I might throw up. Just

listening, I felt as if I were an accomplice. I wanted to report this to someone.

Vern, I thought. There was no way I could keep this from Vern. I had to tell him.

I went straight to our room. As I lay on our bed, I focused on the outside sounds of water splashing, muffled voices, birds chirping, anything to blur the grisly images. I wish I could say I was worrying about Rick and Carlos and whatever it was that had allowed them and the other boys to do such a terrible thing that night, but I wasn't. Instead, I was thinking of the baby inside me. Was this genetic? Would our baby be capable of something like this? I lay in a fetal position, staring ahead, not blinking. I tried to recall the way I'd viewed Rick and Carlos—as lighthearted and fun-loving— before this moment. How would I ever get these images out of my head?

I wasn't allowed to tell Rick that I knew. But how could I not tell someone?

The boys plugged away for maybe a week longer. The deception was killing me. When they finished, I was glad to be rid of them. Vern thanked them for their work and sent them back to my parents, and as soon as they were out the door, I told Vern everything—every gory detail.

He eyed me a long time, his thick gray brows almost covering his eyes. He took several drags from his cigarette, staring down at the table. Then he said, "Do they know who owned the pig?"

"No."

"Well, it's done," he said. "You can't fix this, darling." As I nodded, he added, "I hope they learned something."

It took some time for me to realize the weight of their violence. The weight of their alcohol-induced, testosterone-fueled rage. Would Rick and Carlos and their buddies be forever altered by that grisly night out in the middle of the country? I know I was.

I couldn't stop thinking of that pig. The surprise, the terror, the blood, the pain. Wasn't it a crime? It had to be.

I thought back to the year I started seventh grade. I was twelve years old, and at school I learned that a young couple in my neighborhood—the Dumlers—had been tied up with lamp cord and shot, execution style, in their bedroom while their children slept. The newspaper reported that they had both been stabbed and shot, that it appeared to be personal and had undoubtedly been committed by someone who knew them. I kept asking myself, *How is this so different?* At more than three hundred pounds, that must've been an eight hundred–dollar pig. Would the police come knocking on my parents' door? The police had been at the party. Had they questioned where the pig had come from? And what about Carlos and his visa? Would they send him back to Brazil if they found out?

I didn't know if they'd learned anything, but *I* had learned something. I'd learned my brothers could be cruel. I'd learned I couldn't handle violence, that it could happen any time. And I'd learned that sometimes it's better not to know.

CHAPTER 11

"**L**et's go into town," Vern said the next morning. There was no washing machine at The Point, and since Vern had to go into Hillsboro for work anyway, we'd gotten into a rhythm of regularly driving the fifteen-mile journey for clean clothes and groceries. "The phone connection is better at the hardware store too. That is, if you still want to call Stan's mother."

"Yes, of course." It had been more than a month since Stan arrived. I shook my head.

We heaved Ben's bike into the back of the truck, the three of us squeezed into the front seat, and we rumbled out Cave Road to Route 50 west toward Hillsboro. With Chippie on the floor between my feet and Stan rhythmically tapping his knees together, I felt a touch of vertigo, so I rolled down the window for fresh air.

Even as we slowed through Rainsboro, past the dilapidated brick buildings of a once thriving town, I considered how picturesque it all was. I tried to focus on the positive, to fight off thoughts of all the worst things that could happen. We powered through the lush, rolling hills with their patches of fluorescent green farmland and the occasional clapboard farmhouse with its cast-iron bell, a remnant of the CS Bell Company that provided ship bells for the US Navy during World War II. I thought of the opera house, the foundry, the Bell Mansion—the legacy of just one family. This place had a deep taproot. To hear Vern talk, his family was a part of a lateral offshoot. His grandfather, Richard Barrett Fairley, had been a well-loved teacher in a one-room schoolhouse who'd worked his way up to school superintendent and later purchased the hardware business that his father had expanded into seven successful stores.

While my mind wandered, Vern quizzed Stan about the Wigwam. "What is it you enjoy? Do you play with other kids, or is it just you with a large machine?"

"You play against yourself," Stan said. "But I'm good at it." He bounced in his seat, his head bobbing on the half second.

Vern smiled the way he did when he drank with my father. As if he knew something he wasn't saying. I scanned the endless landscape, the scruffy brush and grass growing in the road's shoulder, and occasionally glanced over at him—at his tanned, wrinkled skin, his cigarette-singed hair. As I did, I thought of him as an extension of Hillsboro: struggling with his health, his business, and the way people perceived him. Like the old hardware building with its sagging floor and its south side leaning into the adjacent building, Vern wanted to be restored, or at least preserved. And so far, I was doing a damn poor job of aiding him in that effort.

On the way to Vern's office, we stopped briefly at our house to pick up the mail. When I handed the bundle to Vern, I couldn't help but notice another thick envelope from Stan's mother. Stan noticed it too.

Vern tucked the mail under the driver's seat and glanced at Stan, anchored between us. "This can wait," he said, and Stan bounced more slowly.

Please keep on bouncing, I thought as I watched. *Please, please. We don't need calm right now.* Calm meant flames on the dresser, flames on the bed. I could deal with bike riding, tree climbing, hooting and hollering. Not calm. Calm scared the hell out of me.

Stan would have been fiddling with the radio, had there been one. "Would you mind dropping me off at the video arcade?"

His innocent expression was hard to resist. Vern and I glanced at each other.

"Why, sure," Vern said.

I released a deep sigh and tried to hide a smile by looking straight ahead. If I hadn't been thinking of the thick packet under our seat, I might have patted Stan on the back or even said something affectionate, but I didn't want Vern to misinterpret.

I delivered my usual warnings: "Be careful of the cars. Don't talk to strangers. Don't get into anyone's vehicle. Try not to create a scene. Come home when you're hungry."

Stan nodded slowly as he stared off, his eyes fixed ahead.

We drove east on Main, across the broad lawn of the neoclassical high school with its central pediment and cupola, and the elegant 1844 Scott Mansion, now the home of Head Start and the WIC Program. We passed the Union Stockyards on the left and Great Scot, the grocery store, on the right. Vern swerved over to the curb, and I climbed out to let Stan out.

I patted him on the shoulder as he exited, then lifted Ben's bike from the back of the truck and placed it on the sidewalk. "Okay, get out of here."

"Can I stay for an hour?" He waited for an answer.

"Sure," I said. "Don't forget to come home for lunch."

As soon as Stan disappeared into the arcade, Vern pressed the gas pedal to the floor and screeched his tires on the hot pavement, leaving a patch of rubber behind us. "For now, we're rid of the little pain-in-the-sphincter," he joked. He laughed as he hacked, and our squealing tires drew attention from folks on the sidewalk. He lifted his chin—the Hillsboro version of a wave—as we drove past two of his customers on the corner by the historic cut-stone jail, then passed the glorious early-nineteenth-century courthouse with its front-facing pediment and ionic columns. We stopped at the light in the center of town where, in January of 1874, seventy Presbyterian wives and mothers, in dark silk hoop skirts and long coats, burned whiskey barrels to protest the sale of intoxicating liquors in Hillsboro.

"You joke that he's a pain, but you don't do anything about it." Stan was isolated in so many ways. If we wanted to help him— and there was a side of me that did—we needed to find him some friends, get him involved with other people, and help him socially so he wasn't setting fires for attention.

Vern stared ahead, one hand on the wheel. With his other hand, he shook his inhaler and took two deep puffs, followed by gut-wrenching coughs. I tightened my seatbelt. He turned the truck onto South High Street, his hands shaking on the wheel. We shared an uncomfortable moment of silence as he pulled into his parking space against the warehouse behind the store and coughed continuously for nearly five minutes.

"Why don't you open the letter?"

I grabbed it from under Vern's seat and tore open the envelope, hoping he knew there would be a surprise waiting. An organic farming brochure fell into my lap. Another one, detailing the virtues of breastfeeding, suggested as many as five years of nursing for health reasons and discussed the common problem of lactose intolerance. Stan's mother had circled in bright red magic marker the areas in the newsletters meant for our attention. I set the stack aside and read aloud her handwritten letter with its large flowing loops on lined white paper. She wanted us to know the man suing her had offered four hundred thousand dollars for the entire farm.

"Does this make sense to you?" I read something about the auction being advertised in *The New York Times* and the *Wall Street Journal*. She said dozens of important people were supposed to come. But then there was something about a bridge to the family homestead having been destroyed by a flood. Nobody but the developer was able to attend the auction. Stan's mother said she was ready to file a new motion with the court, but I couldn't understand her reasoning. I was beginning to get a strong mentally ill vibe. The legal details were technical and rambling. When I reached the part asking for our help another month, I slammed the letter on the dirty seat. "I can't read any more of this."

"I will need to see a doctor soon," Vern said, his voice barely audible. "I'm feeling more lethargic."

I waited for him to catch his breath. "You need me to go with you?"

Vern didn't blink. "You stay home and deal with Stan. I'll be all right."

Even though his health condition *was* serious, something about his manner made me think he was using it to change the subject. I reminded him that the situation with Stan was a priority, that he would need to respond.

"I know what you're saying," he said as we got out of the truck. "I will try to convince her to take him back. I'll call from the office. If she insists he stay, we will keep him one more month, and that's it. We will stick to it."

I waited while he quietly shut the car door, then said, "Vern, she *will* insist. Of course she'll insist. She has insisted every time, on what to feed him, what to do with him. On everything. She isn't the person to dictate to us, but she insists, all right. How are you going to stick to a deadline, Vern? Huh? You haven't been strong with her yet. How is this any different?"

Vern paced three steps ahead of me through the parking lot, past the alley, and into the building at its northwest corner. I could feel my heart racing; I tried to relax, but I wasn't finished. I followed Vern past the antique workbench, with its heavy metal vises and open drawers, past a haphazard array of green plastic boxes of merchandise, around an old shop vac, and up a set of stairs. As he unlocked the pale green door beside the sliding glass window, he said, "I will call her."

I entered Vern's office and nodded, straight-faced, at his two secretaries, Emma Mae and Anne, who sat in the outer room. I wanted them to know we were struggling, maybe unconsciously hoping to gather support.

Vern secured the door behind him and pointed. "Have a seat, honey."

Below a bulletin board of brown cartoons, colorful quotes, and a twist of tobacco leaves, I sat in one of three cracking leather chairs, repaired with duct tape. It was the same chair I'd sat in the first day I'd met Vern for what I thought was an interview. Delirious with adrenaline, carrying a résumé and slides of my artwork tucked under my arm, and pulling my skirt over nylon stockings sticking in waves on my legs, I'd been struck by the coolness of Vern's office, his smile, his effervescent personality, the energy and aliveness of the moment.

Now he sat slumped, his elbows on the desk, lighting a cigarette and squinting at the sepia photos under shining glass in front of him. He lifted a few files on the side of his desk and let them drop. Trying to lighten the tension, he said, "What's the old saw about the hurrier I go, the behinder I get?" He drew the curtains across his office's fish tank window, then picked up the heavy black office phone and dialed. "Hello, it's Vernon. How do?"

It irritated me that he smiled. He was way too cheerful to be firm.

As he chatted with Ruthann, I was reminded of the first moment I'd had the tingling sense I might be pregnant. It was before my twenty-fifth birthday, and I'd been juggling a number of projects. Vern had been telling me, "You're an artist. Take time to create art. If you need help, tell me. I'll hire someone for all the activities you don't want to do." He had trusted me to make many of the aesthetic decisions for the hardware store, the house in town, and the old furniture Herman was restoring in our basement. I'd felt he valued my talent.

Now, as I listened to his voice, it dawned on me that maybe he'd viewed me as if I were one of his workers. Yes, he valued my eye for design, and I liked his message about wanting me to express my creativity. But with Stan, he had signed me up for an activity I myself would never have chosen in a million years. When it came to this boy, had he thought of me at all?

Vern was mostly listening. At one point, he held up an open palm and shot me a look as if to say, *See? I'm trying. I'm doing this for you.* But as I sat there, eavesdropping on a conversation between his two secretaries in the neighboring room, he held out the phone with a huge smile on his face. Stan's mother had launched, in her operatic voice, into song.

I had assumed Vern was dealing with a woman at the end of her emotional rope—that she could be reasoned with and would understand the limits of our generosity. But hearing her effusive singing, I realized maybe we wouldn't be able to remove Stan even if Vern *wanted* to. This woman was not only eccentric; she was fearless.

Today, I wonder if Vern knew from Stan's father that Lawrence and Memorial Hospital in New Haven, Connecticut, had tried to commit Ruthann when Stan was born because she fought so vehemently to follow her own rules. Had Sam told Vern she was uncontrollable or suffered a psychiatric disorder? Maybe Vern felt a sense of kinship to her related to his own mental health.

He placed the phone on the hook. With his head hung low and his elbows on the desk, and holding a small stub of a cigarette so close it was a miracle he didn't singe an eyebrow, he looked at me with caged eyes. "One more month and that's it." He sounded tired and disappointed. There was no energy in his voice.

He said Ruthann had spent a long time describing her bread and how it prevented her from having even a single gray hair. "She was agitated. She's been ricocheting from lower court to upper court and back to lower court again."

"Okay . . ."

"Each time there's a ruling, it's followed by an appeal, a new judge, and a new ruling."

"Okay . . . so?"

"She's erected a billboard in her yard, quoting from Exodus,

'Thou shalt not covet thy neighbor's house' . . . Something like that."

"Oh, God, Vern." I was thinking we were using the wrong approach. We should be quoting the Bible. "Next time, why don't you remind her of the prodigal son?"

Vern must've secretly believed that the solution to Stan's family problems was for Ruthann to give up the farm—that if he couldn't coax her into doing it, he would speak to her older son, Sam, and persuade him. Years later, I found a note Vern had written to himself. At the top, it read, "Young Sam." Then, below, he had written, "What happened to the Roman Legions. Think their farm preservation effort a similar thing. If want to continue organic natural farming, must utilize less expensive land. Find quote from *Wealth and Poverty* (by George Gilder, 1981)."

But his phone call to Ruthann never got that far.

I folded my arms and sat stone-faced. "Well . . . I called it. I knew what she would say. Sounds like you've made up your mind."

"I have, honey," he said, glumly. "She said one more month. One more month and she'll get this settled."

I shrugged as my eyes focused on the floor. *Fine. You've made up your mind? So have I.* But I was kidding myself. I hadn't made up my mind at all. I decided to wait for Vern to see his doctor and then try to convince him to return Stan immediately after that.

I returned to a dusty house, glad to have a change of scenery but reminded of the difficulty of having too much to manage. Somehow, the weight of Caroline and Ben was more palpable in town—and now I had another month to contend with. I opened a few windows to let in some fresh air.

When Vern's mother's clock struck three and there was still no sign of Stan, I picked up the phone and called the Wigwam. Ann answered.

"Is Stan there?" I asked. "I'm worried. His bike's not here. He's usually home by now."

Ann said Stan was loaded with video tokens and that he'd worked on one machine for so long she'd had to lure him away with a piece of pizza from the snack bar. "You should've seen him gobble that pepperoni," she said, laughing. I could hear the frantic swirl of video buzzers and bells clanging in the background.

"Do you mind if I speak to him?" I wanted to remind him to be home in time for dinner.

Ann was gone for several minutes, and when she returned, her enthusiasm had faded. "Kim, I don't know where he went. He was here a minute ago."

I didn't want to appear alarmist, but Stan had seen the envelope from his mother, and I was sure he knew we would be calling her. I'd learned from the fires that phone calls to Ruthann caused a reaction in him. Was he somewhere setting dry leaves on fire? Or had he been lured away by some weirdo at the Wigwam?

I hopped in the car and frantically circled the neighborhood. My hands shook, my heart fluttered. I didn't know why the few cars on the road were honking at me as I zoomed past, searching everywhere from Main Street to West South and every old-brick Queen Anne in between.

I felt a panic that seemed in stark contrast to the peacefulness of the streets. There was little movement or activity. An old man I recognized, hobbling with a cane, staring at me from the sidewalk. A cat scratching its head against an old sugar maple. Slow down, I told myself. This is not dangerous. This is a beautiful town, a safe town, where people don't lock their doors, where everyone knows everyone. Still, South Street was eerily quiet— like the moment before the cocktail hour, when you know that after only a few sips the volume in the house will surge like an oncoming train.

I scanned neighbors' yards, down their driveways, up and down the side streets and alleys, all the way to Webster School, perspiring as I gripped the wheel. *This was my doing. I should've called sooner. I should've set a time.* I should've, I should've, I should've.

I sped left on Elm, east on Main, and up the hill toward the Wigwam, where I jumped the curb and jerked the car into park. Before I could get out, I said a brief prayer and took a deep breath, stretching my lungs. Then, weirdly, out of the corner of my eye, I caught Stan casually strolling out the front door of the Wigwam as if he'd been there all along.

Ann, with her infectious laugh, was right behind him, looking sorry for me. Her eyes seemed to be asking, *What are* you *doing here?*

She escorted Stan to his bike. He threw his right leg over it and sped off toward the house.

Ann met me at the car with an outburst of affection. "Apparently he was hiding."

I shook my head and blew out a mouthful of air. The tension was a spark of static electricity. I spread out my shaking fingers so she'd see them.

"Take a few deep breaths," she said. "And don't worry. He's a good kid."

But I got stuck on her words: *Don't worry.* Was she kidding? I *had* to worry. There was menace in the air. There was Ben's death and the unsolved Robin Gossett murder. There was a three-hundred-pound dead pig, for Godsake, and this kid was setting fires.

How could I not worry?

CHAPTER 12

A few days later, we were back out at The Point, and Vern drove himself to Cincinnati for his appointment. He arrived home that evening, struggling to breathe but in good spirits. It was hard to stay angry at him long. Clean-shaven and in his Brooks Brothers button-down plaid shirt and khaki trousers, with his lace-up leather shoes, he could've passed for a civil rights attorney—somewhat scruffy but professional. He reeked of cigarettes.

"I'm going to live another day," he said, kissing me in the kitchen. "I will have to be on oxygen, however." He explained that a five-foot-high oxygen tank would be delivered to the house, and he would have to be attached to it at night and whenever he was home during the day. "I also will be increasing my Lasix."

Vern's ankles were like mercury—up one day, down the next—so increasing his diuretic sounded positive. I'd known since college that with PMS, retaining water caused irritability. Anything that made Vern less irritable sounded positive.

"And what about the alcohol?" I asked, ribbing him.

"Thanks for the reminder." Vern palmed my waist and reached into the cabinet for a nearly empty bottle of Old Granddad. "I'd offer you a drink, but there's only enough for one." He smiled slyly. "How was *your* day, darling?"

I was mixing green grapes with sour cream and sprinkling the mixture with brown sugar, which Vern had said was a favorite dessert growing up, when Stan bopped into the room like an actor on a stage, his shirt covered in streaks of mud and large wet rings under his arms. He looked as if he'd been digging for treasures down by the creek. Vern still hadn't mentioned the extra month to him. But I guess you could say we were waiting for it, much like a painful splinter, to work itself out.

"So it was good," Vern said again.

It wasn't a question, but I nodded.

He fumbled with an ice cube; it pinged into his empty glass. "How would you like to call your mother, Stan? Would you enjoy that?" I figured he was hoping to transfer the responsibility to Ruthann as the bearer of bad news.

Stan showed no emotion. "Sure."

Vern picked up the phone, dialed, and handed Stan the receiver. The phone had a twenty-foot cord that allowed Vern to talk from almost anywhere in the house, especially from the small powder room he called his "library." Stan wandered into the living room for privacy, and I waited with Vern in the kitchen, hoping to calculate Stan's mood from the tone of his voice.

When he finished, Stan had visibly shrunk. "My mother asked you, didn't she?"

"Your mother asked us, and we readily agreed," Vern said. "It stands to reason, what with her legal matters and such, that you would be much happier here. We've enjoyed having you. We want you to stay longer, but it's entirely up to you." He paused. "How would you feel about one more month?"

Stan didn't speak at first. I felt an itch at the edge of my memory. My parents saying good-bye before leaving for Sweden for three weeks. The five of us, ages seven to thirteen, with no babysitter or way to contact them. A month to an eleven-year-old was interminable. How would Stan handle the thought of staying with us another full month?

I patted him on the shoulder. "We'll have fun. Come on, let's eat." I stepped onto the porch with the plates and utensils.

All through dinner, Vern sat with his back straight and lifted his fork to his mouth with his eye on Stan, as if he were demonstrating the proper way to eat vegetables.

Stan pushed around the green beans on his plate. "Is it definite?"

"Is *what* definite? Your staying with us?" I sipped from a glass of iced tea.

Stan nodded.

"It's definite if that's what you *want*," Vern said.

"We're happy either way," I added.

Stan set his fork on his plate and abruptly looked away. "Fine."

"You're welcome to call your mother any time," Vern said. "You know she wants to hear from you, right?"

"Yes, sir." He hardly moved, but I could see a few loose strands of blond hair bobbing.

"Though I'm dismayed she waited so long to tell us, I will say *this* for your mother: she keeps us guessing."

Stan's eyes looked puffy. I had a brief urge to reach across the table to comfort him, but something stopped me. A part of me believed the gesture would be fake. *How can I show him love and want him gone at the same time? Those are mixed messages, aren't they?*

Stan's abandonment haunted me until my head thrummed. I could easily recall the sinking feeling I always felt when my parents finally showed up back at home after a long road trip, their eyes revealing the dread of having to deal with five kids again.

"Why don't you call her back?" I suggested.

Stan didn't seem to hear me. He returned to toying with his green beans, pushing the rest of his food around on his plate.

"Aren't you hungry?" Vern asked. "Perhaps you ate too much at the arcade."

"I didn't eat anything." He stopped moving, his hands clutching the edge of the wire-mesh bench. He stared down at his lap. There wasn't a single blond hair shifting on his head or a single eye blink. It was scary witnessing his stillness. I couldn't tell if he was holding back, ready to erupt, or quietly retreating into his own world.

I figured, *Vern got us into this; Vern can get us out.* I wanted him to squirm, to feel some degree of responsibility, but he seemed distant too. He made a few clicking noises with his mouth. Then, all at once, as though he were speaking from the pulpit, he looked at Stan and me and said, "Well . . . it sure has been a delightful evening. Let us look forward to a glorious summer month." He pushed away from the table and lifted the salt, pepper, and butter to take to the kitchen.

I sat for a moment, poised to leap in to provide comfort. But Stan looked angry, not depressed. And I had enough anger of my own too.

I had gathered the dirty plates and was about to take them to the sink when Vern said, "Kim needs some help clearing the table, Stan."

Stan took a deep breath, cleared his throat, and clanked his fork on the plate—and then he darted through the screen door and disappeared into the backyard.

I didn't run after him. I didn't say a word. Vern took a series of shallow breaths. Then, as though we were finishing a household project, he turned to me and said, "I believe we're finished."

I cleared the rest of the table and placed the grapes in the fridge for later. After leaving the dishes in the sink, I sat on the porch sofa, swinging forward and back. All I could hear was the sofa's metal frame squeaking to the background *kshhh* of the water spilling over the dam. I'd always been slow to react, but why hadn't I seen this coming? This expanding time with Stan? Was it my mental training as a competitive swimmer that had gotten me into this situation? That had made me so used to letting someone else be in charge? The regimented environment at the pool had required shutting up and doing what I was told. I trusted Vern the way I'd trusted my swimming coaches. Was I passively acquiescing now?

Not totally. I was drawing the line Vern couldn't cross—it was just that then the line kept moving. Maybe this is what you get when you put your kids through a program that requires so many hours of solitude and grueling practice and provides them with no opportunity to express their own opinions or practice pushing back.

Vern joined me on the porch, and I mentioned that his high school friend, Jody Dobert, had called to speak to him that afternoon.

"Oh, okay, thank you, my dove," he said, with no added explanation. Usually he'd share *some* anecdote—you know, we were invited to something, or there was a meeting somewhere, or someone had called and he'd missed the call at the hardware store. Not getting any information at all . . . this was odd.

Before we were married, Vern had written me in California that he had dropped by Jody's house and she had served him bologna sandwiches. He had described her as a "doll" and a "lovely woman" and someone he had known since high school. I thought she was a nurse or a teacher, though I couldn't remember for sure. I didn't know what the thing was with Jody, why I reacted the way I did. I was jealous, though. I hadn't met her, and already I didn't like her.

Vern left the room to call her back, and I had to calm myself. She was married. She was a friend. She happened to be a woman. *So what? Why am I feeling threatened?* This was ridiculous.

The conversation didn't last long. Ten minutes later, he was back on the porch, settling into one of the wooden chairs, and I was mentally compiling a checklist: *How do you know her? How often do you see her? What is your relationship?*

As soon as I asked the first one, Vern saw right through me. "She's a friend. That's all." He seemed tickled that I cared enough to ask such an inane question.

"Why was she calling?"

"I called *her*."

"You did? About what?"

Vern looked dead serious. This was not his usual lighthearted reaction. Still looking at me, he patted a fresh Pall Mall on his book, then placed it in his mouth. As he was about to light the cigarette, his hand shook.

"I hadn't spoken to her in a while," he said. "Her husband, Phil, is a physician. They live east of Hillsboro." Vern closed his eyes and took a deep breath. "Several years ago, Phil was in a hurry on his way to work. His two-year-old daughter rushed out to say good-bye, and he backed over her."

"Oh, my God. He killed her?"

In his soft, scratchy voice, he said, "Yes," his cigarette dangling from his lips.

He got up to leave, and I wanted to crawl into a hole. For being jealous of a woman who had been through that kind of pain. All I could think was *What is* with *this town?* But then I remembered Ben, about how I was detached from him, and now I was detached again with the Doberts. This was more of Vern's history, a history I loved and valued and was drawn to but wasn't a part of.

Would Jody understand what it was like to be me? To be pregnant for the first time and taking care of this other woman's child? We hadn't even met, and I wanted something from her. I wanted her to say, "Vern, you need to move on. You need to think of your health, your wife, and your baby on the way." If she was in one of the helping professions—and I was pretty sure she was—she would see both sides, as a woman *and* as Vern's friend, right? She would *know* things.

Vern and I didn't speak for maybe an hour. When I think back, I can imagine that in order to cope, he was reaching for support from another person in the horrible fraternity of parents with dead children. He had a much longer history than I did with our friends—with Ann, with Jim, with the members of the Friday Night Club. But he was fifty-seven and I was twenty-five. There was no way for me to make up that history.

~

Vern sat in the kitchen, the light on, waiting patiently for Stan. I snuggled into bed by myself. For the life of me, I couldn't figure out why he was so determined to help Stan's mother. Did he truly consider our agreement to take Stan a gift to the boy's father? What kind of relationship had they had, anyway? Stan's older brother was Ben's age. Maybe, before his death, Stan's father had comforted Vern about Ben. Or maybe, due to his diabetes, Sam had already experienced a health scare and had asked for Vern's help with Stan if anything were to happen to him—and Vern had never returned the call. I was inventing a story. I wanted answers and didn't want them at the same time.

Stan sneaked into the house sometime after dark. At first, Vern spoke to him like a Dutch uncle, stating in a harsh manner that we had rules about disappearing in the dark. But then he paused, and a tenderness entered his voice. He explained that he had made choices in his life that were for other people. He praised Stan for his free-spirit style, for his intelligence, and for his athletic ability. He asked him to be patient and said that what he—Stan—was doing was a gift to his mother, and she would be grateful.

When Vern crept into bed and lay on his back, I rolled toward him and hugged him around his emaciated waist. My fingertips followed the contour of his body, stopping on the three-inch-wide gnarled and indented scar on his left thigh. He had said he'd been hit by a car crossing an alley on North High Street as a child. That it'd frightened him, made him realize the shortness and fragility of life. I'd seen photos of Vern from that time—short and chubby, wearing a white T-shirt stretched out around the neck, a crew cut under a ball cap with the bill sticking straight up, all the weight on one leg, and very few muscles.

Now, when I think of the tenderness of that night, lying in bed, remembering Vern's conversing with Jody and then listening to Vern's talk with Stan, I'm reminded of my perception of Vern as bruised, his life's assaults and his own mistakes as permanent as initials carved in a tree. I remember his initial harshness with Stan—the way a father might speak to his son—and wonder if his admonishment was meant as a note to himself. A note to be patient and that, in the end, we should all be grateful.

And maybe that's the reason Vern was stuck on keeping Stan longer. Vern was working on something too. On getting something out of *his* system. Maybe Ben. But also maybe Caroline. Maybe his own fears of being fifty-seven and becoming a father again. Was he thinking he'd failed in his duty as a parent the first time around?

Stan was there to help Vern through *some*thing. And whatever it was, he still hadn't worked it out.

CHAPTER 13

An oxygen tank arrived in early afternoon. Propped in our living room, against the wall and out of our way, it resembled a Kelly-green mannequin and made me immediately quiver, thinking someone was standing there, watching. In a way, someone *was* standing there. It was the side of Vern I didn't like to pay attention to: the red-faced, choking, smoking Vern; the silent, observing, and immobile Vern whose health was as precarious as a five-foot stack of bowling balls. One bad bump and the whole thing would come crashing down, wounding anyone in its vicinity.

Vern called from the office to remind me the tank was coming, and I told him it was already there. Then, as a weird segue, he said, "Why, say . . . when you speak to Stan, please avoid mentioning his mother." *Why?* I wondered. *Does he think if I don't mention her, the pain of her abandonment will go away?* God! This was common sense.

I rarely mentioned Stan's mother except to Vern anyway, so the request seemed strange, though also fitting, coming from Vern. For him, not talking lessened pain. *He* thought so, anyway.

A few minutes later, three boys—all younger than Stan, in dirt-streaked jeans, all chattering over each other—appeared on our doorstep. The oldest boy, big-boned with a prominent jawline, spoke first. "We seen you had a boy. Can he play?"

Stan rushed in from the back porch and stopped abruptly, his hand on the wooden bar that divided the screen door. "Can I go? Can I, can I?" He rocked back and forth as the screen door hinges groaned.

It had been a few hours since breakfast. I was starving. "It's lunchtime. Aren't you hungry?" I waited for Stan's eyes to meet mine.

"No," he answered bluntly. "Can I go?"

I pushed open the door. "All right. Come back when you're hungry."

The youngest boy pumped his fist in the air. "Yes!"

Stan dashed down the driveway, and the group chased after him.

My immediate thought was *Woo-hoo! My lucky day*. I hadn't slept all night, and my throbbing eyes ached in their sockets. I grabbed a handful of crackers to soothe my stomach and curled up on the walnut Jenny Lind bed that served as a sofa in our living room. *Why haven't I been able to even catnap?* I wondered. *Is this normal for three months into a pregnancy?* As I glanced at the oxygen tank, I felt a heavy weight pressing down on me. I wasn't ready to let Vern be a photograph on the wall.

I rested my head on a hard pillow, my forehead and neck clammy. Even as I munched crackers, the eggs from breakfast were crawling up my throat, but I'd gotten my wish: potential friends for Stan had shown up out of nowhere, like manna from heaven.

Sometime over the next hour, the screen door banged a couple of times. When I opened my eyes, Chippie had nosed his way into the house and was crouched beside me, panting. The way he looked, I thought he must've run a long distance. I leaned over to pet him, and he licked my hand, something he'd never done before. He was panting so hard he dropped his head to the floor.

"Hey, Chippie; what's up, buddy?" I petted his back and felt something wet and greasy, like tomato paste or gravy. I looked at my hand and jerked upright. Blood. A lot of it. A large clump on Chippie's back looked thick, black, and gelatinous. A clot!

I sprang from the sofa, shrieking, "Stanislaus!"

No answer. Then suddenly, footsteps. Stan appeared on the

front porch, out of breath, beads of sweat gathered under his eyes and trickling down his flushed cheeks. I shoved the screen door open and stepped back.

I was angry—no, furious—and I strained to get the words out. "You see this dog? He's bleeding." I'd vaulted up so fast the living room was spinning and I felt light-headed. There was no question Stan knew *some*thing. Chippie hung close by me, and I noticed it wasn't only his back. His whole body looked wet. With his tongue hanging out, he panted frantically.

Stan's eyes widened. He looked disoriented. "I don't know anything."

"You don't know *anything*? He's bleeding badly. Were you playing with him?"

"No."

"What were you doing?"

"Nothing." He shrugged and glanced around the room as if he were hunting for Vern.

Panic lurched up inside me, my mind racing in every direction. I led Chippie to Stan by the collar, noting as I did that his wire-haired legs seemed weak. "Look, stay right here and hold him while I call Vern."

I want to say it was a test.

Stan leaned over and carefully held Chippie's collar, standing at arm's length, his fearful eyes glued on the dog.

By then, I was trembling. When Vern picked up the phone, I began to weep. He couldn't understand my stammering. "Something's happened to Chippie. He's bleeding. It's terrible."

"Slow down, slow down. What happened?"

"I don't know. It's his back."

"His back?" Vern sounded anxious. "Does Stanislaus know what happened?"

"No." I eyed Stan, still holding Chippie's collar, his arm stiff. "Oh, God, Vern . . . I think he's been stabbed."

Vern sounded breathless. "I'll arrange an emergency appointment at the animal hospital. Go, quickly. But drive carefully. Don't speed." In a soft voice, he said, "Before you get there, drop Stan off in the center of town."

With Chippie in the front seat of the hatchback and Stan in back, I said a prayer as I drove maniacally toward Hillsboro. As the wind rushed into the car and dust swirled about, I avoided looking back. The tension in my stomach had intensified, and I didn't want to see Stan's empty eyes. I knew he'd hurt Chippie. This time, I knew. I wasn't going to be talked out of it.

Rob, Chippie's veterinarian, would be able to tell me what happened. I tried to take in the tranquil view along the road—*Calm yourself, Kim, stay calm*—but I couldn't. In Rainsboro, I looked both ways and bolted through a blinking light.

Stan sat motionless, his eyes on the far distant tree line. Chippie panted beside me, his back a riot of matted hair and blood.

Stan was rolling the window up and down in the backseat as we approached the intersection of High and Main. "You see the hardware store over there?" I pointed. "You tell Vern exactly what happened when you see him. You hear me?"

"But I don't *know* what happened," he said, jerking his head back.

Hearing incrimination in my voice, I tried to soften. "Okay, well, maybe you can think of something that *might've* hurt Chippie. Try to remember where Chippie was when you were playing with the boys." As he sat there, I searched his face for emotion, any emotion. His detachment haunted me. He stepped out of the car and jogged across the street in the crosswalk. I sped off down West Main Street, one hand holding back Chippie's neck as if he were a child without a car seat.

The air was a wet washcloth, and by the time I arrived in the crowded waiting room of the Hillsboro Veterinary Hospital,

Chippie had weakened even more. He uncharacteristically allowed me to pick him up, and I carried his limp body into the air-conditioned animal hospital, which stank of dog, cat, and body odor so ghastly—because of my pregnancy, I assumed—I thought I might gag. I tried not to breathe through my nose. There were little kids climbing on the chairs, an old lady in a hairnet and long dress. Dogs were yelping from rooms behind the office.

I stood in a short line, and when I reached the front, Melissa, Dr. Sharp's assistant, immediately ushered me to a back exam room, where I set Chippie on the clean linoleum tile floor. The antiseptic air was a pleasant relief from the waiting room and so was seeing Rob, who was my friend and not likely to think of me as an animal abuser.

Tall and thin, with dark hair and mustache, Rob wore a long white lab coat over his worn jeans. He carefully lifted Chippie onto a waist-high metal examination table, and Chippie's paws, usually going a mile a minute, hardly scratched the metal. "Sometimes we see injuries in this area of the back when a dog wiggles under a fence," he said. "Obviously, something has stuck him. Do you have a wire fence out at The Point or some kind of sharp object?"

"None that I know of." I tried to think of any neighbors who might've had a fence, but none came to mind.

"I could give you my opinion based on what I'm seeing." He petted Chippie under the neck.

I nodded. Despite the unbearable heat, I felt chilled. As he pulled open the wound, I had to look away.

"This cut is so deep and so clean, it's my opinion it was caused by a knife. Who would have stabbed him? Your new house guest?" Half country vet, half raconteur, this was Rob's sense of humor. I had called to vent to his wife, Susie, and had forgotten.

I told Rob that's where my mind was going. I petted Chippie under his neck, and he dropped his head down on the table, still panting, as if he were heat stunned. "Are you *sure* a knife did this?"

Unwilling to say definitively, Rob shrugged. "Let me clean him up. It'll take a few minutes." He lifted Chippie off the table. "You're going to be all right, old buddy." He carried him to another room.

I slumped in the examination room, worn out, my mind wandering. Was Stan's behavior escalating? I wasn't one of those overly possessive animal lovers who considered their animals their babies. I didn't take Chippie for walks. Never thought to buy him a wool coat for the winter. I sometimes even forgot to feed him until he nudged the bowl at my ankles. But stab the poor dog? I couldn't fathom it. How could someone do that to a helpless animal?

I had known what Rob was going to say, though I'd hoped I was wrong. But he'd confirmed my suspicions, and I trusted him.

I returned to the muggy waiting room and the old dog smell. I shook out my shirt to fan myself and counted the number of pets that looked exactly like their owners. Vern and Chippie matched each other too. Both older, running on half a tank, still young enough to tease and run around, old enough to know their limits.

Rob shaved around Chippie's wound and stitched it up, and then he placed him in a box so he would be easy to carry. He was a sad sack as Rob lugged him out to our hatchback and set the box in the front passenger seat.

"He's going to be all right," he said, ushering me around the car. "But he's an old dog, remember. He'll need some gentle care."

Rob winked as he shut me into the front seat of our blue hatchback.

I hadn't been waiting at The Point more than ten anxious minutes when Vern and Stan pulled up in the blue truck and Vern rushed in to see Chippie. I'd placed the box in the middle of our braided rug, as if Chippie were a turtle I'd found by the roadside. When Vern rubbed his head, Chippie opened his eyes wide. He didn't bark. Not a sound. It was a painful quiet.

Vern examined the stitches and the shaved area of Chippie's

back and then turned to Stan, seemingly hoping for a reaction. But Stan showed no emotion.

Vern stood up and placed his hand lightly on Stan's shoulder as they peered into the box. "What happened?"

"I don't know, sir." He looked tired and hot, his blond hair sticking to his face near the temples, his angelic expression vaporized.

"Were you extra rough with the dog today, Stan?" Vern's eyes showed serious contemplation.

"No, sir."

"How about the other children? What did you do with them today?" Vern scratched a wooden match on the pearly paneled wainscoting by the front door, and a violet flame sparked. He lit the cigarette dangling from the side of his mouth. "The children," he said again. "What did you do with the children?" He shook out the match.

"Not much."

I stared at Stan for a moment; something about him suggested anger. The thought crossed my mind that maybe he didn't do it and was angry with us for *implying* he knew something.

Vern sounded to me like a physician gathering symptoms for an accurate diagnosis. "Did you play games? How about hide and seek, or kickball?"

"No."

"Well, Chippie must've been there. Were any of the kids extra rough with him?"

"No, sir," Stan said again. His voice, his carriage, everything about him made me think he was telling the truth. If I hadn't seen Stan's attitude and posture the first moment Chippie came to me, I would've bought the whole story, hook, line, and sinker. But as Vern bent over to rub Chippie's neck, what I saw stunned me. It still comes back as a picture in my brain. Stan, now kneeling next to Vern's knees, leaned into Vern and closed his eyes. It looked like a tender moment. Even today, I wonder what it meant. It was as if for an instant something had fallen away and Stan had made a connection, or he was feeling something powerful and was able to express it. But what was it? Unhappiness? Loneliness? Was he reminded of his father? Was he grateful Vern wasn't jumping to conclusions?

Vern didn't seem to notice.

Stan leapt to his feet and peered out at the black-painted iron fretwork on the porch. Before he arrived, I'd loved that fretwork. Now, I didn't know why it was there. It belonged on an 1870 Italianate house, not our little 1920s cobblestone-and-frame cottage. It didn't fit. The house was trying to be something it wasn't. Which was the same with us. As surrogate parents to Stan, we were utterly out of place. How were we to know how to help him fit in?

Back then, I'd never heard of the autism spectrum, or Asperger's, or anything related. *Does he have some mental disorder?* I wondered at the time. *Is he a sociopath? Or is he just angry that nobody seems to care?* In retrospect, I'm sure he had ADHD and possibly was on the autism spectrum, but we had no sense of his history, no sense of any friends, not even a true sense of the life he led back in Connecticut.

I knelt in silence, petting Chippie. I wanted to believe Stan, but there was no chain-link fence anywhere around the property and no sharp metal object we knew of that could have caused his injury.

Staring at the dog, Vern said, "Tell Stan what Dr. Sharp said about Chippie's condition, honey."

"Chippie was stabbed."

Vern winced as he looked into Chippie's box on the braided rug. He took a long, deep, calculated breath. "*May* have been stabbed. We don't know."

I cocked my head sideways as my lip stiffened. "Okay, *may* have been stabbed." I felt like a fifth grader turning in the teacher's pet. I was ready to believe Stan was guilty, but Vern was right. We had no proof. I wasn't comfortable accusing him either.

And, honestly, a tiny part of me was willing to blame the whole thing on Chippie to end the conflict. I was reminded of the time my mother lost her car keys. Dad was convinced one of us had hidden them. Which made no sense. Why would any of us hide her car keys? And yet Mom had not intervened in the spanking. She must've believed on some level that one of us *would* do such a thing—just as now, even though it made no sense at all, a small part of me believed in the possibility that Chippie had done this to himself. Maybe there *was* an old wire out there somewhere. It was easier to call it a freak accident than think of Stan as capable of knifing a dog.

"Do you know of any kids down the road who would've injured Chippie?" Vern asked Stan gently.

"No," he answered immediately. I would've believed him because of the way he'd leaned into Vern, and because the expression on his face at that moment was so angelic—truly—the look of a kid incapable of stabbing so much as a fly. Until he stood there, not moving a muscle, his characteristic oddity, and I knew immediately. I knew my denial was blocking what was right smack in front of me. The little bastard had knifed Chippie.

"Well, we want to be extra aware from now on," Vern said. "If you notice anything strange with some of the children in the neighborhood, anything that seems dangerous, I want you to report it to us immediately."

Stan wasn't paying attention. He was creeping closer to the door, his eyes on a small gray-winged nuthatch on the porch railing. The bird's dark eye stripe bled into its beak, pointed high in the air. As it clicked its characteristic *ha-ha-ha-ha*, Vern croaked out the words, "This is a criminal act." Then he started coughing. He pulled out another cigarette and tapped it on his wrist.

Stan's long, skinny arms dug into his front-facing pockets, his narrow shoulders up near his neck. His posture seemed to say, "I don't know anything."

Vern glanced at me and shrugged. "Okay, that's all."

Stan burst through the door. Within a short while, he was maniacally riding the loop, loudly hooting and shrieking as he passed.

Vern and I bent over to comfort Chippie while Vern's cigarette rested in an ashtray by the door.

"Please tell me you didn't believe what he said," I pleaded.

Vern lifted the ashtray and was about to enter the kitchen. "I'm afraid I can't answer that."

"But you saw his body language."

"Yes."

"Well?"

"You don't know if *he* did it or if he saw someone else."

Is he protecting Stan because that's how he parents, or is he protecting him because he didn't protect his kids and wishes he had given them the benefit of the doubt? I stroked Chippie around the shaved area of his back, aware I was being more affectionate toward him than I ever had been toward Stan, while Vern was doing the opposite. It occurred to me that in protecting Stan, Vern was sacrificing someone he loved—Chippie—in the same way that he had been sacrificing me and our baby. What was it about Stan? What was Vern really protecting?

"Regardless," I said, "we should do something about the gun in the drawer in town." I shivered, thinking of that black pistol case, in plain sight. Why did we have to have it in our kitchen? Out in plain view? Where was Vern's intuition? Had he registered the brief warmth coming from Stan? Warmth I'd only caught a glimpse of for an instant?

No . . . he would've mentioned it.

The idea that he could look at Stan and think he might be covering for some other kid was beyond preposterous. Vern wasn't his defense attorney. Why was he giving this kid so much support? Had people been critical when Ben died? Had they blamed Ben himself? Blamed his parents? At every opportunity, I was blaming Ruthann for Stan's behavior. Maybe there was a Ben tie-in I didn't know about.

"We'll have to be more vigilant, that's all," Vern said, and he smiled in a fatherly way as if to say, "You'll understand when you're older." I knew that was what he was thinking, but I also loved that he said "we." Viewing the incident as having happened to both of us made me think he was beginning to take responsibility.

From that day on, I was more focused on Chippie. I might not have known where Stan was at any given moment, but I knew where Chippie was. The minute he dropped out of view for any reason at all, I would frantically leap from my seat—"Where's the dog?"

At the same time, Stan transformed into Superboy. Instead of throwing his bike on the lawn, he leaned it against a tree. He helped with the dishes. He took out the garbage. He even got ready for bed, smiled, and said good night without our prodding. I suspected his guilty conscience was at play—and so did Vern—but we wanted a break from conflict, so we simply noted it and continued.

I felt sure that the truth, like a dead body hurled into the ocean, would eventually wash up on the beach.

CHAPTER 14

It was Ruth's day to clean the hardware store, and Vern had sent her to the house in town to keep me company. I told her what Rob Sharp had said about Chippie. She took a step back and covered her mouth. "You think Stan did it?"

I shrugged. "We don't know. But after the fires . . ."

"I wouldn't put it past him," she said. "That boy's wild." She lowered her head to adjust her glasses. "Where is he?"

It was Thursday, July 29, the fourth day of the Hillsboro Festival celebrating Hillsboro's 175 years as a city. Nina, Ann's daughter, and her friend Tommy were going, and someone—maybe Ann—had suggested they invite Stan.

Ruth went right to her usual kitchen cleaning, and when I asked about her husband, who had been delivering appliances for Vern, she said he wasn't working, that he was upset with Vern. Perhaps it had to do with Vern's asking Archie Whiting, an older white man, to drive the old Fairley Hardware Model T pickup truck in the parade. She said he'd promised Paul and then changed his mind. Ruth's comment was "Hillsboro doesn't change."

I was thinking, *Well, okay . . . but it's time Hillsboro* does *change*. In a discussion of racial attitudes in Hillsboro the previous winter, Susan Gibbs, the wife of Jim from the Friday Night Club, had told me that when she and Jim moved to Hillsboro in the '70s, they still had a drinking fountain that said "Colored" upstairs in the Colony Theater.

When I mentioned this to Ruth, she said, "It was worse back in the '50s. The Black folks had to go to Lincoln School." She said

149

when she was twenty-nine and working for another family in town, the Black school was set on fire. Nobody knew who did it at first, but it turned out to be a white guy—Mr. Partridge—who was the county engineer, trying to force integration.

"He went to jail for it," she said. "It was real bad."

"And then they integrated?"

"No, they wouldn't let 'em. Those mothers, they marched every day to get their kids in school." Her head dropped again, and she adjusted her thick glasses.

"So what happened?" I asked. "Did they finally back down?"

She laughed. "They went to court. They even burned a cross. But the mothers, they kept on marching."

"My God, sounds horrible," I said—but in my head I was calculating if Vern had been in Hillsboro then. Why had I never heard of this? Ruth and I talked for a long time about change—adjusting to change, believing in change, forcing change—and my mind drifted to Ben's room.

I lifted a stack of Vern's papers and patted their edges on the counter to straighten them. "Speaking of change, how about we tackle Ben's room?"

Ruth shook her head as she swept up some crumbs.

"What's the matter? What are you thinking?" I asked.

"Mr. Fairley . . . he's not going to change."

If I have anything to do with it, he will, I thought. *He'll change.* Because there was no damn way I was going to keep Stan indefinitely. I didn't care how rigid and unyielding Vern was; he was going to change on that subject.

I told Ruth we had a few hours to work on Ben's room, and she flinched. "We have to? Today?"

"I think we should try." Some part of me believed that Vern wasn't thinking at all about our baby, that with all he was juggling—including Stan—he had a mental block. I wanted to wake him up, to help him feel something, and I thought changing Ben's room would do that. I told Ruth she didn't have to come immediately, but I was ready.

Wearing my embroidered blue Mexican muumuu, I grappled for a moment with the vacuum and dragged it up the stairs. Ruth followed behind me. I made it to the room and started scanning from the doorway, but she stopped on the landing, hesitation etched in her face.

"What is it, Ruth?"

"Oh, nothing."

I stepped into the room and looked closely at Ben's cork bulletin board, covered in certificates: Cub Scouts, Boy Scouts, awards for academic achievement. My eyes landed on a large gold stork handcrafted from natural fibers. "Where do you suppose this came from?" Uncertainty loomed large behind Ruth's thick glasses. I lifted it from a shelf and shook the feathers, which were made of a cane-like material. I sneezed from the dust.

One shelf held an abalone shell filled with metal soldiers; another, a foot-long red-and-black metal truck with wooden wheels. I lifted a blue souvenir *True Value* truck and realized it was a bank containing pennies. Close to it, on top of a stack of report cards and photos, was a small business card with a nickel glued to it. The card read, "Who says we don't give free samples?" Beneath the nickel, it was stamped with "The Hillsboro Bank and Savings Co., Your Friendly Bank Under the Time and Temperature Sign." Many of Ben's things looked old and rusty enough to have been Vern's when he was a child.

My mother, the queen of garage sales, would wander into my room while I was away at college and find things she could sell for pocket change. I returned for a holiday once and couldn't find a special pair of Mizuno shoes I'd received on a swim team trip to Japan. She proudly announced she had made twelve dollars on those shoes.

Maybe we value the most the things that don't come easily. I'd put in a lot of effort for those shoes. To Mom, they were clutter. I began to think of Ben's saved objects as achievements. Achievements for Ben, achievements for Vern, maybe achievements for the family. Ben himself had been an achievement. I'd begun to think of him as a lot like Vern—sometimes devilish, with a great sense of humor and sharing Vern's love of history. Removing Ben's things would be removing a part of Vern. Yet it seemed necessary.

Though Vern had mentioned that Caroline and their two daughters had taken what they wanted of Ben's things, to me, the room appeared loaded. I opened Ben's closet. Several cardboard boxes were stacked, tops smashed by the weight of the one above. In the corner stood a hockey stick, a pair of roller skates, a ski pole, a deflated football. A hook held worn leather belts; another, a plaid bathrobe. Some of his clothes still hung on hangers.

"What are we going to do with all this stuff, Ruth?"

She was standing in the doorway. "I try not to touch anything in there. I get a funny feeling." She looked unnerved by my digging through Ben's closet and was perspiring profusely despite the coolness of the house.

"A funny feeling like what?" I knew what she meant, but I wanted to hear it from her.

"I don't want to say." She glanced away.

"Just say it."

"It's Ben," she said. "Like he's listening." With the back of her right hand, she propped her glasses up higher on her nose and held my stare.

Ben hadn't been shot in his room—the accident had taken place in the family room—but hearing Ruth's comment, I tried to show the weird feeling didn't bother me. I bent over, and as I lifted a box, something under the cardboard flap moved. I dropped the box and slammed into Ruth's shoulder. We both inhaled, then burst into nervous laughter. A rock or shell had settled in the bottom. I shoved the box back into the closet.

I didn't want to touch anything either. To my city-slicker eyes, it bordered on an arsenal. Sharp knives, shotgun casings, cap guns, ammunition in boxes . . . It wasn't that big a stretch for me to imagine Ben's bedroom serving up something terrible.

"I've changed my mind," I said.

Ruth's whole body seemed to relax. She swiped a nearby shelf with a cloth diaper rag—undoubtedly one of Ben's—as a reflex.

"Come on, Ruth. This is too much. Let me talk to Vern. I don't even know if I *want* the baby in here."

Back at The Point that evening, Vern suggested we take a walk to the opposite side of the creek. He wanted to inspect his parents' old house to see if it was ready for visitors. Stan was zipping around the driveway, killing time, and dinner was cooling on the counter.

Vern dropped a couple of ice cubes into his glass of bourbon and water. "To your health, my dove." He lifted the glass, and I tapped it with my fist. We sauntered hand in hand across the bridge and up the weed-filled, winding stone steps to a mud-covered pathway.

"We need to get Tonybaloney out here," Vern said, "or someone of his ilk who can wrestle with the weeds."

I'd gotten to know Tony at the neighborhood gatherings Vern had invited me to on his front porch before we married. Tony, with his melodious voice, had played the guitar and serenaded the group with 1970s folk tunes as we sipped our whiskey sours. He was our neighbor Margene's son, and Vern liked to call him Tonybaloney for no other reason than he thought the name had a ring to it.

Vern clasped the rusty metal railing, and I followed him, flattening the poison hemlock, knotweed, dandelions, and thistle hugging the stairs. A thick poison ivy vine embraced the corner of the house like two brackets on an Italianate cornice. Along the path to the screened-in porch at the back of the house, Vern kicked a clump of dock weed, shredding the large leaf but leaving the root. He reached down, grabbed the giant leaves, and tossed them to one side. "It looks like rhubarb," he said, "but you don't dare eat it."

The house itself was like an old lady who'd fallen on hard times, struggling to stay positive. The interior smelled of mildew; its corners were filled with cobwebs and flies. A mass of crumbs sat tucked behind a broom in the kitchen, but there were piles of dead bugs everywhere. It appeared someone had started to sweep and, overwhelmed, had given up. Vern was in no condition to handle the dust. We ended up on the open side porch overlooking the pool, and Vern pointed out a small ceramic head and a couple of other relics tucked into the cobblestone pillars that supported the porch. We faced each other on two rusty metal chairs.

"This house gives me a weird feeling," I said, thinking of my conversation with Ruth that morning. "Kind of like Ben's room." I reminded Vern that while Stan was with Nina and Tommy at the Hillsboro Festival, I had been working with Ruth at the house. "Did you know Ruth has been doing the bare minimum? She's afraid to go in there."

Vern lit a cigarette, blew out the match, and tossed it over the cliff. "There's no reason to keep everything as it was. It's time to clean it up."

"But how?"

"What do you mean, darling?" He sipped his drink. "Mmm, that's good." He set the bourbon on a loose twelve-inch concrete tile on the porch floor.

"I don't know what to do with all the stuff."

"Toss it."

"Are you sure?" I told him it was significant stuff—certificates, antique toys, and rocks. To me they were markers, symbols of Ben's life. At the very least, somebody else might want them.

"It's only stuff, darling," he said. "Toss the rocks in the creek, and the rest, take a few plastic hardware boxes and fill 'em up. Ruth can help you."

"Well . . ."

"What? What is it?"

"Ruth thinks she can feel Ben's presence, that his spirit is hanging out in that room."

Vern reached for his bourbon, and his eyes swayed behind the wavy glass. It seemed he didn't mind if Ruth and I cleaned out the room, but he didn't want to go up there himself. In the past, he'd been reluctant to even walk through it. "What do *you* think?" He held my gaze. "Are you worried about something?"

"Well, do you think it's possible Ben's spirit is in that room?"

"Of course." Vern combed his fingers through his cowlick. His hands shook as he closed his eyes.

"You do?"

"I don't know if I've felt it myself, but it's entirely possible."

"But with Ben's death and everything . . . I don't know. Don't you worry something could happen to our baby if we put him in there?"

"Heavens no," he said without hesitation. "Ben's death had nothing to do with that room. If his spirit is lingering there for some reason, that's not a bad thing. It's good."

I leaned over to kiss Vern, and he held my arm and pulled me closer. I hugged his waist as he held out his right arm, holding the cigarette.

"These jobs are long overdue," he said. "You'll feel better when they're finished."

Maybe all I wanted was approval. While we sat on that porch listening to the mourning doves cooing and the water spilling over the dam, I recalled that Ben didn't have a tombstone. *Why?* Everyone else who'd died in the family seemed to have one, which I knew from a ceremony in the cemetery honoring Vern's mother, Tula, for her work with the DAR. I thought I would want one. At least something to say I'd been here, that I'd mattered to another person.

Does it matter to leave a legacy? My mother, joking, always said she wanted her endless pile of laundry done before she died. My father wanted to be missed by my mother. Maybe all that mattered was the here and now. Nobody two hundred years in the future would care a whit about any of us. It was the reality of Vern's age and the recognition that he wouldn't live forever that was getting to me.

We watched Stan across the creek, sprinting around the property, and something inside me shifted. Ben's room had been a monument to him. I thought about how Vern valued things in general. I'd fallen in love with him the day I realized he valued his inexpensive tan raincoat so much he'd written "Reward" and his telephone number on the inside collar.

Vern had contradictory impulses, as we all do, about whether to hang on or let go, preserve or move forward. His pain was so deep he couldn't bring himself to sort through Ben's things, but he recognized the need to move on in his life and so was willing to have *me* gather them up and toss them all out.

He wasn't, however, willing to toss out Stan.

Stan wasn't a *reminder* of Ben at all. He was a symbol. Maybe as long as Stan was there, Vern could convince himself he'd been a good father. He could convince himself that Ben's death had nothing to do with him—that it had been, simply, an unfortunate, tragic accident. Maybe it had been. I'd written a story in my head that cast Vern as a victim, but really, *Ben* was the victim. So was the little boy who was with him. Ben had been only fourteen, not even old enough to buy alcohol or drive a car. *What was Vern doing, giving him access to a gun and ammunition?* Had he just been too trusting of himself, and therefore of his son?

I didn't know Ben except through the things he'd collected and the opinions of other people. It dawned on me that my child might not know his father except through the things Vern collected. Besides all the furniture and mementos in our house, Vern also was leaving little scraps of paper as his legacy. His torn-out newspaper articles, comic strips, and quotes were a part of who he was.

I decided that for Vern's sake, I would change the colors, the furniture, the appearance of Ben's room. If I did that, maybe, with luck, some of Vern's pain surrounding Ben's death would drift away too.

As we ended the conversation and returned to the other house, I imagined a pure and uncomplicated life with two happy parents, no health issues, and lots of free time. Unreasonable, I know, since our family situation was anything but uncomplicated, especially with Stan—but still I dreamed.

And Vern had given me his blessing. I would wait for the new wallpaper I'd ordered. Then I would remove the twin bed, toss the curtains, and drop the rug off at Goodwill. Everything else I would label and take to the basement.

And there was something else. I would also start a file. Not just any file; this one would be filled with Vern's scraps—the small pieces of inspiration he was beginning to leave around the house everywhere. Torn corners of the newspaper with his favorite music jotted in ballpoint pen (Brahms Haydn Variations, Bartok Violin Concerto #2, Liszt Hungarian Rhapsody), or articles about age, time, or running a business. I'd fill the file with Vern's jokes and comic strips, and on top I'd place his latest quote, which he said was his father's most used business expression: "Eternal vigilance is the price of success."

CHAPTER 15

On the last day of the Hillsboro Festival, Vern arrived home after work with Jim Gibbs and Ann as I was pulling together a chicken tetrazzini casserole and salad. Jim took a close look at my stomach, loosened his striped necktie, and then hugged me in front of the stove. He'd heard in town about the pregnancy. Though I didn't know Jim well, I could see in his eyes a genuine affection and perhaps recognition that a baby could help Vern. Or maybe I just wanted to believe that.

Over one of our doors, Vern had placed a jar of saltpeter from his friend Jim Hapner and Jim Gibbs noticed it. The old joke was that the US Army put saltpeter in its food to suppress soldiers' sexual desires.

"You were in the Army, Jim," Ann said. "You must know about saltpeter."

Jim waved Vern's smoke away from his face. "I knew I should've gone straight home," he said. "Sorry, I can't stay long."

"What's the old saw about an hour of play versus a year of conversation?" Vern said.

By then, Jim was rooting through our near empty fridge. I knew what was in there: a few eggs, American cheese, moldy sour cream, maraschino cherries. He opened a drawer to a few stalks of limp carrots and celery.

Jim and his wife, Susan, were foodies before the word "foodie" was added to the common lexicon. Their guests got smoked pheasant, quail, and foie gras. I pulled out the American cheese slices and some Ritz crackers.

"You been on vacation, Vern?" Jim joked. "This box is bare."

Vern elbowed Jim in the gut. "Get out of there. I offered you a drink, not a three-course meal."

He handed Jim a small glass of bourbon on ice, and Jim leaned back in a chair, his fingers laced behind his head. "How long will Stan be here?" Jim had two boys, ages six and four, and he suggested the boys get together.

"He's with us permanently." I rolled my eyes.

Chippie let out a whimper in his sleep, and Jim bent down to pet him. "Hey, what's going on with Chippie's back?" he asked. "Are those stitches?"

"Oh. Vern didn't tell you?" I lowered my voice. "Chippie got stabbed."

Ann nearly choked on her cigarette smoke. "Are you sure?"

"Damn. I didn't see that coming," Jim said.

"Pretty sure. We think we know who did it," I whispered.

Jim pointed toward the living room.

"We don't *know*," Vern said harshly to me, as if he were talking to a child. He handed a drink to Ann. "I'd love to know who did it, but we have no proof." He dropped down hard on the nearest Windsor chair and lit a Pall Mall.

"They say they have no proof with Robin Gossett either," Jim said. He mentioned they had a few suspects—a couple of brothers—but not enough proof yet to indict, and then he glanced at Ann, knowing her husband, David, a lawyer, had firsthand knowledge of the details. "What's the latest?"

Ann lit a cigarette. "Nothing yet."

"*Some*body did it," Jim said. "He was shot five times in the back."

"Can't they arrest anyone?" I'd seen plenty of detective shows where they picked up dozens of people for questioning.

"There's no statute of limitations on murder," Ann said. "Someday, it'll slip out." She pushed open the smoke-stained curtains and opened the nearest window for air.

Jim yanked off his tie, unbuttoned his cuffs, and rolled up the sleeves of his monogrammed white shirt. "There. That's better." He tossed his tie on the kitchen counter behind him. "It's a murder case. Whoever killed that kid probably did some other bad things. If you think you know, Vern, you've got to do something."

"I understand, Jim, but we *don't* know." Vern's voice sounded weak.

The four of us sat at the kitchen table, sipping drinks and exchanging news from around town. I kept my eyes mostly focused on Vern. I'd pushed too hard. I knew I shouldn't blame Stan for Chippie's stabbing when I wasn't 100 percent sure either. Sitting at our kitchen table, comparing Chippie's stabbing to Robin's murder, was only making Vern resist harder.

"Life has really turned gray. I miss those damn cigarettes." Jim lurched forward, grabbing for Ann's pack on the table. "Give me one of those. Susan doesn't know, but I've been cheating." He tussled with Ann for one of her cigarettes.

"I thought you'd quit," she said, giving up the fight.

He shrugged. "As long as Susan doesn't find out, I'll be safe."

Ann lit the cigarette with her Bic lighter; Jim took several long puffs, then smashed the cigarette in Vern's ashtray. He appeared to be about to say more to Vern, but instead, he rose stiffly. "I have to get back to Susan before she calls the police. Besides, you two are a bad influence." He faced both of them, thanked Vern for the drink, and reached for his tie.

"I should go too." Ann laughed. "If I don't get home, my family will be eating dinner at the Wigwam."

Chippie's injury had sucked the limited oxygen from the room. *Here we go again*, I thought, *talking but not talking*. Ann's husband and Jim were close friends and had been two of the first on the scene when Ben died. Ben had babysat for Ann's kids, Nina and Wes, and had been back and forth across the street so much he'd practically lived at the Pence house.

Vern escorted Jim to the back door and Ann to the front. As I pulled out the casserole and spooned it onto three plates, I realized something: Ann and Jim were wrapped in the same cushion of silence Vern existed within.

I'd grown up thinking love was talking things out, no matter how painful. I'd say, "Dad, you're an alcoholic. Stop drinking," and we'd get in an argument. Inevitably, it would go nowhere, but I still felt better afterward. No secrets; no shame. Everything out in the open. All the covering up Vern and his friends did felt dishonest. I told myself this was polite society, that loving someone was not shoving the truth in their face but letting them accept it when they were ready. *But how long will that take? And what about our child?* I was running out of time.

That night, I put my hand on my belly and spoke to our baby. I told him, *No matter how long we end up with Stan, I'm going to protect you. I'm going to tell people what I'm seeing and feeling. I'm not going to live indefinitely in this cushioned, no-talk world. It's not respectful. And it's not healing.*

We returned to The Point, and for a week or more, Stan behaved. In fact, ever since Chippie's so-called "accident," he had become a different kid. He continued to ride Ben's bicycle in endless loops on the property, but he was so polite that I didn't want to do anything to interrupt the ambiance.

Then, one day, as he headed out to ride, I asked, "Why don't you play with the boys in the neighborhood? Wouldn't they be more fun?"

"No." He stubbed his sneaker on the linoleum floor.

"Why not? You seemed to enjoy them. What happened?"

Stan shook his head, wordless as a rock; then, without warning, he rushed through the porch door and disappeared. I figured he was back on his bike.

I found some sanctuary on the porch with my postage stamps, organized in flat blue plastic boxes that had once each held a swimming medal. I placed them on the coffee table in front of me. Each stamp, with its unique design and color, was its own little art piece, telling a story. The Queen Elizabeths, the George Washingtons, the Abraham Lincolns, the Liberty Bells; the flags, the dogs, the butterflies, the birds, the antique modes of transportation. They were all little blocks of history with enormous stories that I was sewing together with the idea of creating an art piece for the baby's room. I knew I should prepare for the nursery even if Vern wasn't so inclined, and somehow the idea of a quilt-like wall hanging had come to me. I arranged each stamp methodically, back to back, careful not to tear the paper or snap the delicate thread that held it all together.

Outside, I heard the ping of metal and glanced through the porch screen to see Stan with a long stick in his hand, descending the driveway with Chippie. An idyllic sight. Stan looked like the All-American boy, with his blond wispy hair, a striped shirt and sneakers, the dog by his side, and the backdrop of the bridge connecting us to Vern's parents' old place. It sure was a glorious afternoon. Sewing on the porch with the house in good order and the husband at work, I felt a wave of contentment. This was the good life.

I set the stamp sampler down and watched Stan meander toward the bridge. Then, without warning, he cocked his head back and, with his left leg, delivered a swift kick to Chippie's small body—which, legs flailing, dropped six feet and landed with a loud splash in the shallow part of the creek near the top of the waterfall.

I bolted through the screen door, nearly stumbling on the stone steps, shouting, "What are you *doing*?"

My heart thumped through my chest, and I felt nauseous as I sped down the asphalt pavement to the narrow stepping stones near the water, careful to avoid the poison ivy hiding within the ferns.

Chippie slowly clambered out of the water, his little paws sinking into the muddy bank. He gave a whimper, shook his coat, and sat beside the water, panting on a dry rock. Staring up at Stan and petting Chippie, I shouted, "You just kicked this poor dog into the creek!" As a reflex, I held my hand on my heart and took a deep, exaggerated breath.

I examined Chippie's stitches, worried the dirty water would infect his wound, but he appeared unharmed. I looked back up at Stan. "What were you trying to do? Kill him?"

"No, ma'am." Stan craned his neck to look down, as if he were surprised to see Chippie near the water.

"How did he get here?"

His tone was flat, robotic. "He fell in."

"Stan, I saw you kick him. Dogs don't fall off bridges." With my shirt sleeve, I wiped perspiration from my upper lip. I didn't know what he was thinking—didn't know and didn't care. All I knew was, I was being played.

Stan shrugged. "If I did it, I didn't *mean* to."

"You'd better not have meant to." I surprised myself with my sternness. I left Chippie down by the water, climbed up to Stan, and got right in his face. It was all I could do to keep from smacking him. "Don't let me ever see you do that again. You hear me? I'm calling Vern."

He waved his stick, pounding it on the bridge's peeling metal pipe railing. It clanked like a heavy chain. With his eyes averted, he repeated that he hadn't done anything, but the moment's weight had turned the soothing creek into a torrent in the damp air. I had an eerie feeling—the kind when you notice the underside of leaves, the backdrop of a greenish sky, the air is charged, and you know a tornado is imminent.

Vern swerved into the driveway twenty minutes later while I rocked forward and back on the porch swing facing the creek. I didn't know where Stan was. I hustled out to the truck.

Vern was wearing a button-down collared shirt, completely

unbuttoned, exposing his worn T-shirt. I bent over, still jittery, my elbows on his open window, and kissed his lips. He reeked of tobacco. But I felt safe.

"I'm beginning to agree with Rob Sharp's knife theory," he said. He removed his seat belt and sat there gazing over the steering wheel.

"He swears he didn't do it, Vern."

"How's Chippie?"

"He seems okay."

"You're *positive* you saw him kick him?" Vern's lip was shaking.

"I'm positive."

"Well, he's over on the neighbors' gravel road." He opened the door, exhaling his built-up frustration.

"I lost my cool, Vern. I wasn't nice."

Vern rubbed his eyes under his glasses. "It's okay. I want the boy over here. We need to talk to him." His neck was blotchy and red. I worried that this was too much stress for him.

"You want him *right now*?" I found myself regretting that I'd called. I was thinking of my own father and the way he would swing and shout when he was upset. I told Vern I'd definitely seen him do it, but I wasn't sure if it was intentional. I told him it wasn't an obvious kick but more of a scoot.

I guess every family has a troublemaker. After hearing the hideous pig roast details, I'd wanted to blame Rick for the crime. He was supposedly always our family's troublemaker, and yet long before my parents hit on the brainy idea of forcing us kids into swimming to keep us out of trouble, they'd often sent us to play together in the basement. I'd locked up poor Ricky in a dirty closet as a two-year-old. He'd screamed and bawled and banged on the door while my sister and I sang a rewritten version of "Little Rabbit Foo Foo," changing the lyrics to "Little Fatso Ricky" to make him suffer.

It's possible these memories had entered my mind when I saw Stan kick Chippie. I thought of Ricky and told myself that this was what kids did. Their behavior could be hideous. They were capable of all kinds of cruelty when left to their own devices. I identified with Stan because I'd been capable of cruel things as a kid myself.

Vern and I talked briefly about Stan's manipulating us. I told him Stan had said if he *had* kicked him, he hadn't *meant* to.

Vern frowned. "Are you saying it was an *accident*?"

I shrugged.

Vern's lip quivered. He looked angrier than I'd ever seen him.

I kept thinking of the cut on Chippie's back. Vern was right— we didn't know for sure if Chippie had been stabbed—but this time I knew for sure he'd been kicked. I also understood the dynamics at play—Stan's loss, his neglect, and his response to both—and Vern's line of questioning had brought me back to my parents' basement. They were saying, "Did you lock Ricky in that closet, Kimmy? Did you?" And with a straight face, I was saying, "If I did, I didn't mean to."

I reminded Vern that when I asked Stan to hold the dog after I noticed the blood, Chippie didn't appear afraid at all. The word "accident" whirled around in my mind as a link to Ben, but I didn't want to make that connection.

It was weird. I'd finally gotten Vern aboard the Stan-is-a-whack-job train, and now I was backing off. The more we talked, the more I whitewashed the narrative. Stan didn't want to be there any more than I wanted him to be there. We both wanted the same thing. Vern was the one with a different notion. Vern wanted Stan to stay. And to me, Vern was more important. If he was ever going to get past his grief about losing Ben, I had to let him work through this thing with Stan.

He and I decided to be more alert, more empathetic, and more loving toward Stan. For me, this was a huge challenge, since I wasn't even sure I liked Stan very much. But together, we agreed to make a special effort to give him the kind of attention we'd given him when he first arrived in Hillsboro. Vern didn't have to be at work ten hours a day; he vowed to be home more. I promised to, at the very least, *pretend* I liked Stan.

In the days that followed, we stuck to the plan. At dinner, Vern called Stan "Stan the Man" and made references to organic foods and Stan's unique life on his family's farm in Connecticut. Stan set the table, took out the trash, and straightened his room without prompting. To any outsider, he would have seemed like an angel of light.

But Vern would leave early in the morning, before Stan awoke. On one occasion, I found his handwritten note on the kitchen counter:

> *Boss Lady,*
>
> *Had very pressing personal business to attend to today and had to rush out before taking care of the house-boy routine. If you'll forgive and want me back on the job, I'll try to finish dusting and the windows later.*
>
> *-Alberto*
>
> *Oh, that nut from Ohio left a message for you that he loved you but that you were cruel (One cigarette till when?).*

I'd lost my sense of humor. When Vern arrived home that night, minutes before I put dinner on the table, I was so anxious to see him, and so exhausted, I nearly collapsed. I'd been gritting my teeth and quivering all day with Stan's every utterance. *Breathe, breathe*, I'd tell myself as he whizzed by on Ben's bike, shrieking.

And, though Vern didn't seem to notice, he and I were behaving more and more like unhappy roommates, disagreeing about the most ridiculous things. We got into a huge argument one night about how many days was appropriate to wear the same shirt. When Vern said, "You don't wear out your clothes, you *wash* them out"—trying to be funny—I took off like a fugitive down Cave Road.

For some reason, Vern followed.

"I'm supersensitive about many things," he said when he caught up to me, "a quirk others have found trying. How about this: I will do my best to listen when you need help and not expect you to do everything for Stan."

I scowled. Though I knew Vern was trying, he wasn't getting it. I wanted him to acknowledge he hadn't been pulling his weight. To say, *You know what, darling? I've decided to give you a break. I've decided to take Stan off your hands for a full day. To take him to work. To tire him out. Whatever I can do to help you. I will give you a total eight-hour work day without Stan.* And also—was this asking too much?—I wanted a timeline for Stan's departure.

But instead, Vern said, "Remember, Stan's mother also needs us."

I whirled around to face him. "*Our baby* needs us," I snapped, and then stomped back to the house, not wanting to speak to him anymore.

That night on the kitchen table, I found a stanza, written in Vern's shaky hand, that he'd memorized from *The Garden of Proserpine* by Swinburne:

I am tired of tears and laughter,
And men that laugh and weep
Of what may come hereafter
For men that sow to reap:
I am weary of days and hours,
Blown buds of barren flowers,
Desires and dreams and powers
And everything but sleep.

Reading this didn't make me want to cry; it made me want to scream. *You take the time to handwrite this piece of a poem? You leave it here on the kitchen table for me to see it? Yet you can't take five bloody minutes to talk about this little snot-nosed brat who's abused our dog and is driving me to the brink of insanity? Are you kidding?*

Vern was being disingenuous, and only paying lip service to our agreement. But as I really thought about it, I realized I was too.

I hadn't even tried to pretend.

CHAPTER 16

Vern's skin looked gray and clammy, his hands shaky. He was asleep in the large room off the living room, hooked to the oxygen tank, with plastic tubing running into his nose and onto the floor in a disordered pile. The chaotic bricolage of his daily life seemed to be strewn everywhere: inhalers, cigarettes, ballpoint pens, empty glasses, paper clips, mini-cassette tapes, a haphazard array of newspaper clippings and folders. I felt worried just watching him, concerned that the oxygen wasn't working. I had to push on his shoulder to be sure he was still alive.

He nearly jumped out of his seat. "For Christsake, honey. I'm fine."

Still warm and breathing. Relieved, I left him alone.

When Ruth arrived that morning, I greeted her at the door. It wasn't her preference to drive to The Point to clean, but knowing our situation, she was a good sport—until I asked if she would scrub the stove, her least favorite job. Then, suddenly, she didn't want to talk.

I told her we still had no confirmation about the cause of Chippie's injury, but I had my eyes open. I added that I didn't know much about Stan's home life, only that his mother was dealing with the estate and his father was a lawyer who'd died of diabetes.

She stopped abruptly and removed her rubber gloves, then impulsively covered her mouth, revealing her chipped red nails. "Maybe that's it."

"What?"

"His problem. Maybe he has *sugar*." Ruth averted her canny brown eyes.

I squinted. "Diabetes?"

She nodded. "Stan has to go to the bathroom all the time. I know people with sugar."

"Hmmm . . ." I thought about how many times he'd left a wet toilet seat. Maybe he was holding it too long. Was Ruth right about the frequency?

She hid her childlike amusement. "You could teach him."

"I'll let Vern deal with his bathroom problem. This was *his* idea."

Ruth turned away from me as if she were hiding a snicker.

"What? What are you thinking, Ruth?"

She shook her head, her lips a straight line. In many ways Ruth knew Vern better than I did. Our troubles, not entirely visible to others, were obvious to her. "I don't know if Mr. Fairley can help." She might've been speaking about his health, but I thought she was pulling old files out of her filing cabinet again—files I wasn't sure I wanted to open.

In the middle of our conversation, Vern woke up. He passed us on his way to the porch, and Ruth busied herself, dusting.

I was in such a fog it took me a moment to notice the lit cigarette next to the oxygen running into his nose. I couldn't believe what I was seeing. "Vern, what are you doing? Is the oxygen on?"

"Yes, honey." He kept on walking.

"What in the hell! Vern, can't you blow up the house with that thing?"

He flicked a mass of clear tubing over his shoulder. "Honey, the oxygen is diluted." He continued to smoke, his eyes on a book the size of a Russian novel.

I settled on the Jenny Lind bed in the living room, far enough away to imagine that if the tank exploded, I'd have a chance of survival. With each stitch in my postage stamp quilt, I thought about Vern. Should I remove the newspaper out on the porch? Should I secretly turn off the oxygen? Then there was Stan and his bathroom problem. Should I ask Vern now or wait until later, once Ruth has gone home? I was sure Ruth had cracked the code. It had to be diabetes, or something similar.

Where was the boy, anyway?

I sat pondering the choices I had made . . . and was still making. I told myself, if only Vern were in better health . . . if only Stan were back in Connecticut . . . if only I had time and a settled stomach . . . If only, if only, if only.

At some point, I set the stamps aside and nodded off.

In the middle of my daytime dreaming, there was a quiet knock on the screen door. When I glanced up, a young boy—younger than Stan, maybe seven or eight—with curly hair and dimples had his nose to the screen. I guessed he was one of Stan's friends, but we hadn't seen the boys in a while. He wore a clean white T-shirt and baggy shorts with large pockets like you might wear on a fishing trip. I imagined he was selling popcorn for the Cub Scouts.

"What can I do for you, sweetie?" I asked.

"My mother said we have to t-t-tell you something," he stammered.

I heard footsteps on the asphalt. In the hard glare of the late-morning sun, I watched as two other boys—*his brothers?*—loped toward us on the driveway. One appeared to be carrying a metal stake.

The oldest boy—the one I remembered, with the prominent jawline—was direct. "It's about Stan." He placed his hand on his brother's shoulder.

"What *about* him?" I asked.

"Um, well . . ." The youngest boy shifted from one foot to the other.

"What is it, sweetie? Here, why don't you boys come in." I held open the screen door.

"Just tell her," the boy with the jaw urged.

The younger boys spoke over each other—"When we were playing with Stan, we didn't think he would do it, we tried to stop him, and he, um, well . . . he tried to *kill* your dog."

"He whaaaat?"

The older boy handed me a bloodstained knife, and I felt the temperature in my face shoot up. It was a wide, pointed carving knife with a fancy metal handle—a knife from our kitchen. Dark brown dried blood was on its blade. I turned the knife over and over in my hand and felt a sharp sting in the pit of my stomach.

"Vern!" I shouted.

Never one to be rushed, Vern responded to my voice as if I were asking him to come watch the wind blow. "What is it, honey?"

"*Vern!*"

"Is there a need to shout?"

"Vern, this is important."

He arrived in his plodding, languid style, ankles hanging over his untied shoes, his false teeth full of food. Ruth was madly dusting around us as if the boys weren't there.

"Who do we have here?" Vern asked.

"These are the boys from the neighborhood. They've been playing with Stan." I handed Vern the knife, careful to point the blade away from him. In the shocked adrenaline surge of the moment, I wanted to scream for Stan. Instead, I collected myself and looked at the youngest boy. "Tell him what you told me."

The boy's voice lowered to a whisper. "Stan tried to kill your dog."

Vern's eyes snapped open wide. "And you were there? Who saw him?"

The boys began to talk over each other, and the oldest boy shushed them. "We were all there."

Vern held the knife with two fingers, blade down. "Is this what he used?"

Ruth stopped dusting, and I could see fear in her face.

Vern examined the knife on both sides, touching the blade lightly with his fingertips. "Start from the beginning. How did this happen?"

The youngest boy pulled down on his shirt with both hands. "I didn't think he would do it . . . I told him not to, but he did it anyway."

"Is that why you haven't been playing with him lately?" I asked. "Because you saw him stab Chippie?"

The boys nodded.

At that point, my mind shifted into protection mode. Until then I'd thought I was walking a tightrope one foot from the ground, but now I'd suddenly realized I was traversing a deep, rocky gorge.

"Thank you very much," Vern said. He handed me the bloody knife, and the three boys trotted out to the main road, where an old station wagon idled.

Vern pulled a cigarette from a pack in his pocket, his hand shaking. The room was airless and heavy. "Where is the little monster, anyway?"

I shrugged, stunned.

We sat in the living room for a long while, not saying anything. Vern smoked, and I breathed in the smoke, imagining its toxins traveling through my bloodstream.

Finally, he said, "I expect we should call his mother."

"You have to, Vern."

"Okay, okay. I expect you're right," he said. "This is serious."

And as we sat there, considering our options, something inside of me grew hesitant. Perhaps I was modeling a beaten wife who wanted to believe her husband would never hit her again.

"Maybe the stabbing scared him," I said. "Do you think that's possible? Maybe you scared him when you told him it was a criminal act. Because since then, he's been so good. I kind of hate to call her."

"If he would stab an innocent dog, he would . . ."

"What?"

"Never mind," he said. "I'm calling his mother." He stubbed out his cigarette in a nearby ashtray and tucked his pack and lighter into his breast pocket.

We were on our way to the kitchen when Stan bounced through the front door, panting, wet grass stains on his knees. His sneakers, apparently soaked with creek water, squeaked on the floor.

"Whoa . . ." I held my arm out to keep him from rushing past us. "Vern's going to have to call your mother."

"Why?"

Vern reached for his albuterol inhaler on the kitchen table and shook it. "Your friends said you stabbed the dog. I am forced to call your mother." Vern, standing with perfect posture, puffed the inhaler and then coughed.

"Call her if you want," Stan said. "But I didn't do it."

Vern sat next to the phone, gathering his thoughts along with his breath, and then picked the receiver up off the wall and dialed. It didn't take long for Ruthann to answer. While Vern described the deep wound in Chippie's back, he glanced at Stan, who was listening intently.

Vern clutched the receiver, his hand shaking, as if he were hanging from a steep ledge.

"Well, he *did* do such a thing," he said, his gravelly voice quavering. "We have proof." He explained that the neighborhood kids had reported it. There were three of them. He added that I'd seen him kick the dog off the bridge. "And no. She doesn't make things up."

My heart began to race. *Thank you, Vern. Thank you so much.* I clasped my hands together near my chin as the room, dark and damp, echoed his forceful tone. I was nodding wildly—*yes, yes*—hoping the added support would knock her over, that she'd finally understand the time had come, that Stan was past due for a ticket home.

"You're right," Vern said. "It's their word against his, but I happen to believe them." He listened a long while with his back hunched, holding a lit cigarette, smoke spiraling into his heavy reef of eyebrow.

"What is she saying?" I whispered. I sent him a look of warning.

Stan stood near the door. With one ear pointing outside, he listened to the riotous blue jays squawking in the sycamores.

"Well," Vern said, "I imagine we'll have a discussion." He paused. "Hello?" He listened for a moment. "Hello?" He placed the phone back on the hook, chuckling, and pitched his hands in the air. "She hung up on me."

"Call her back," I said. "She wasn't listening."

Ruth poked her head in the kitchen. "Bye, Ruth," I said. I'd been so preoccupied I'd forgotten she was there. "Sure you don't want to stay and join the conversation?"

She laughed and hurried from the house as if she were outrunning a tornado.

Vern tapped a fresh cigarette on his left wrist and locked his eyes on Stan. "Your mother said you were arrested."

Stan shook his head. "Not arrested."

"Then what?"

"I got in trouble with the police."

Vern glared at him. "What did you do?"

I expected to hear he'd tortured the cat or shot a squirrel. Stan bounced with every high-pitched chirp from one of the paw-paws outside. He nervously kicked the floor with his squeaky sneakers. "I looked in the neighbors' windows."

"Whoa." My eyes widened. "What were you looking at?"

"Honey!" Vern raised his voice.

"What? It's important to know what he wanted to see."

Stan stared through the porch screen, focused on old George, the neighbors' black dog, barking in the distance.

"Do you really think this is necessary?" Vern asked.

"Yes. Let's hear it. What was it?" I asked. "What were you trying to see?"

"Video games," he said. "They were on the TV."

"You mean like Pac-Man?" Vern asked.

Stan nodded.

Vern nearly coughed up his guts. I knew he'd thought it would be the neighbors having sex or something. "Now I understand the fascination." He tapped his cigarette ash into a nearby cup and took another drag, then smiled, apparently relieved.

"Wait. I don't understand," I said. "The neighbors called the cops because they thought you were watching them?"

He nodded. "But I wasn't. I was watching their video game."

"Okay, that's enough," Vern said. He pushed back his chair, lifted a folded newspaper off the table, and tucked it under his arm. "I've had enough for one day."

"Vern!"

"I'm sorry, honey. That's all I can take. Would you mind getting me that oxygen?"

Stan bolted through the back porch and into the backyard.

I threw my hands in the air. "What are you doing? That's *it*? You're not going to say more about stabbing the dog?"

"There was no point in talking with her, honey. She's too absorbed in her legal battle."

"But what about Stan? You're not going to talk to *him*? You didn't even mention his flight home!"

"He's not *going* home this weekend," he said sadly. "The oxygen, please, honey?"

"What are you saying?" I went to the room off the living room—the one Vern used as an office—to find the oxygen tank. The place was overflowing with paper. Some of it had been there so long it was yellowed from the daily smoke. I spotted the tobacco-stained end of the plastic tubing slung over a chair. The rest, which was sitting in a large mass on the floor, I detangled so it could extend twenty feet or more.

"Look, Vern, are you telling me we're keeping him even longer? What are you saying?" I slipped the tubing over his head.

"We have to, honey. His mother needs our help. She has her hands full."

"Oh, really? Well, so do *I*." I sat on the nearest hard wooden chair, rubbing my thighs. Had I been spoiled? I had so much going for me. I had a husband who loved me and a nice home—no, *two* homes, one with a waterfall and a glorious natural swimming hole. I should be endlessly grateful, without a care in the world. I had a source of income and family not far away, and I was pregnant with the child of a man I loved. Why couldn't I be happy with one little eleven-year-old boy?

Well, I don't know . . . because the psycho tried to kill our dog?

The thought of my selfishness brought back an adolescent reaction: *Why don't you pay attention to me?* "We *have* to go on these trips to pay for all you kids," my parents would say. But in their focus on the business, they seemed unaware of our needs. Vern kept saying, "We *have* to do this. His mother *needs* this." Why was Vern so afraid to put his own needs—our needs—above those of Stan's mother? It seemed he wasn't doing a damned thing to rein her in.

Outside, Stan continued his incessant riding, his endless loops like Vern's conversations with Stan's mother. No matter what Vern said, no matter how dire the circumstances, Ruthann just repeated her plea for more time. She was so damned predictable. And from where I sat, her desire to be free from her son was now understandable.

Across the table from Vern, I eyed him with my back to the driveway. "Why are you doing this, Vern? I don't understand."

"She hung up on me."

"So? Are you thinking you were harsh? Because you weren't. You weren't at all." I raised my voice. "You hardly said a word." I could feel my heart thrumming against my ribs. "This started as a two-week agreement. Since then, we've had two more weeks, and two more weeks, and two more weeks again. I'm sick of it. We are now at the beginning of August. Are you saying one more month? Why don't you say one more year?"

"I know," he said. "You need to lower your voice."

"No, Vern, I'm not lowering it. If Stan doesn't leave by the end of this week, *I will*."

CHAPTER 17

The next day was Sunday. Vern said he thought it would be too much for Stan to sit through an hour-long church service, but I managed to talk him into it. We needed to do laundry in town, and I wanted to garner support; I was hoping somebody in the congregation would say, *Oh, my God, he stabbed the dog? Vern, you have to send him home.*

We loaded the blue truck with our dirty clothes and rode into Hillsboro. On most Sundays, paper, soda cans, and cigarette butts littered the streets from the previous night of cruising. The high school students had a long tradition of parking in the diagonal spaces and sitting in lawn chairs in their truck beds, smoking or secretly drinking. The kids who weren't parked drove circles around and around the four-block area, their windows open, music blaring, horns honking, creating a massive traffic jam.

We fit right in with the look of the town on Sunday mornings, with our dirty laundry in black plastic bags in the truck bed and the cab smelling like an unwashed pillowcase. With our windows down, no radio, and our scruffy little half-shaved dog crammed into the front seat with us, we must've looked like a ragtag bunch.

We dropped Chippie at the house and sprinted in to change clothes, then raced over to the church.

There were two St. Mary's churches in Hillsboro: St. Mary's South (Catholic, where my parents attended) and St. Mary's North (Episcopal, where Vern had been confirmed in 1964, the year after Ben was born). St. Mary's North was a lovely circa 1854 Gothic

Revival stone church with stained-glass ogive-arched windows and a red front door.

There weren't many Episcopalians in Hillsboro. That day, maybe fifteen people, not including us, were there, and when we entered the church, some looked back and waved, as if we were returning from a long vacation. Vern quoted Emerson in my ear—"I like the silent church before the service begins, better than any preaching."

Our minister, Reverend Carson—who'd married us and whom Vern had affectionately named *Parson Carson*—was a few months younger than Vern and a religious scholar. Slightly balding, he was a tall man with a friendly, outgoing personality who wore a comb-over and large, wire-rimmed glasses. I marveled at the way he read from the Gospels every Sunday as if the church were filled.

As we sat, waiting for the service to start, I was struck by the beauty of the sanctuary, its colorful glass set within buttressed stone walls, the glorious Ascension window behind the altar.

Reverend Carson delivered an academic talk about forgiveness, and my mind wandered to Vern. We hadn't been connecting lately. It seemed all attack and defense, attack and defense, dissecting and chewing on this bone we called Stanislaus. I rifled through the *Book of Common Prayer*, wondering who I would talk to after the service and wondering what I would say. But as I scanned the pews in the mostly empty church, I saw no obvious person to nuzzle up to.

At the end of the service, Vern bolted upright and followed the last worshiper to Lacy Hall, the large, open parish hall with dark brown wood flooring and wainscoting. Stan followed—sandwiched between us—to the long conference table in the middle, which was loaded with an array of homemade baked goods.

Vern hiked straight to Parson Carson. "John, today's service reminded me of a Quaker meeting."

John seemed to glow, the room's nineteenth-century stained glass flooding his face with light. "I'll take that as a compliment," he said. He was more relaxed now, wearing his black tab-collar clerical shirt and black trousers. I stood a few feet from the two of them, my eyes on Stan, who was stuffing cookies into his pockets.

"Stan!" Vern let out a chuckle of embarrassment. "Come over and meet Reverend Carson."

Stan rushed over, chomping an Oreo, the front of his teeth sticking with chocolate. He could hardly talk his cheeks were so stuffed; I could hear his loud crunch above the *whoosh-whoosh* of the coffeemaker.

Vern sent me an urgent note with his eyes and took two steps toward Stan. "'They also serve who only stand and wait.' Have you heard that quote, Stan?"

Stan glanced to either side, as if Vern were talking to someone else.

"Come closer," Vern said, "so we don't have to shout."

Reverend Carson flashed his warm smile. "He's okay."

"Can you say hello?" Vern asked him again.

"Hello." Stan's blank face was still focused on the table. Small groups of parishioners were staring with warm approval, as if Stan were adorable.

Reverend Carson handed Stan a card with Saint Mary, the mother of Jesus, on one side and information about the church on the other. "Happy to have you here, Stan." He waited, hoping to catch Stan's attention, but Stan seemed obsessed with the sound of the coffeemaker. He swayed from side to side, as if keeping time to some internal drumbeat; seesawing, he drifted again to the cookies.

Reverend Carson mentioned something about the possibility of Stan's serving as an acolyte. "How long will he be here?"

I could feel a restless pummeling going on inside me. *Stan here long enough to be an acolyte?* There was no damn way I would let that happen. I pasted on a smile for Vern's benefit. I wanted to say, *John, pray for us, will you? Please? We're having a baby, we need help, and Vern is in some other world.* But my pregnancy wasn't obvious to everyone yet. I shook my head warily as I eyed John. "Anything to do with Stan depends on Vern," I said.

Nervously, probably in response to my tone, Vern said, "I'm afraid the chickens may be swept off their roost before he returns to Connecticut, John." He produced a guttural cough as two cookies rolled off the table.

I reached for his arm. "Come on, Vern. We need to go before he's sick from the cookies."

Vern was happy with me for presenting the illusion of every-thing-is-all-right. I felt like a successful con artist. John Carson was one of the gentlest, most understanding men in the world, so why had I avoided sharing with him the obvious? I felt like we'd dug our-selves a hole and had fallen into it.

"You okay, darling?" Vern held open the door.

I shook my head no. I was careful to wait until Stan was out of earshot before saying, "I couldn't believe it, Vern. For a second, I thought you were going to offer Stan as an acolyte."

"No, honey. That's up to his mother."

"Right . . . so is everything else." I stormed into the kitchen. "Look, he needs a haircut. Have you even noticed?" I tossed my purse on the counter.

"How about our staying in town for the night?" Vern was a mas-ter at changing the subject. "It's too damn much to get the laundry finished and leave at a reasonable hour."

Stan, who'd been listening from the living room, rushed into the kitchen. "Can I go outside?"

I rolled my eyes. "Ask Vern."

Vern nodded, and Stan disappeared through the front door, presumably to visit Ann across the street. I followed Vern into the kitchen and eased into one of the Windsor chairs.

"Can I say something?" I waited until I had Vern's full attention.

"What is it?" He lit a cigarette, shook out the flame, and, aware

I was watching him, set the match carefully in a large green ashtray on the round cherry table. "Honey, I love you, but it'll be a while. Here." He handed me a section of the paper. "Read about Princess Diana's baby."

I shook my head. *Princess Diana's baby? Right.* He flicked open the front page of the *Press-Gazette* and began reading, because nothing says I love you like a wall of newspaper in your face.

On the table, atop a stack of papers, was a quote by Austin O'Malley, written out in Vern's scratchy script: "You can not weld cake dough to cast iron, nor a girl to an old man."

I glanced at a lilting shaft of sunlight, my eyes tracking the two light gray and brown mourning doves I'd come to recognize as our spiritual companions. Vern glanced out the window and noticed the doves too, and in that moment, I knew what he was thinking— that he'd known these birds a lot longer than I had. From a nearby branch, their dark eyes, lined in white, guarded us. The purplish one flitted at the window, his short dark beak pecking the glass. He let out a brief *roo-ooh* sound, and I thought he might be trying to get in, that he wanted our attention.

Now I think that he, like Vern, was fighting his own reflection.

Chippie stood up from his flop spot in the hallway and stretched. He fell back on his hind legs and scooted his rear end along the kitchen floor. He rubbed in one direction, then another, and I sat there, a sour orange taste burning the back of my throat.

"Do you see him, Vern?" I pointed to the dog. "He's not doing well. We need to take him to the vet." Chippie had on occasion been dragging one of his hind legs lately. "We need to do so many things to get ready for the baby. I'm exhausted. Aren't you?"

"Somewhat." He gazed at me with a playful smile. "What did Scarlet O'Hara say?" He waited for a moment. When I said nothing, he said, "I'll worry about that tomorrow." He sat in a yellow-gray cloud of smoke, reading, his fingertips stained with newsprint.

This was my moment to pick up the phone, reach across four

states, and choke Ruthann with my words. Instead, I dropped my elbows on the table and held my head in my hands. "What about the baby? Don't you worry about the baby?"

"No, honey."

"Well, you *should*. You absolutely *should*. You know, I've never been pregnant before. I don't have the slightest idea what I'm doing." I tried to sound rational. But I wanted sensitivity too, maybe even tenderness.

Vern lit a second cigarette, not noticing the other one still burning in the ashtray in front of him. "Women have been giving birth since the beginning of time, darling. What are you worried about?"

"Eve-ry-thing." I enunciated each syllable. "It's all new, and I don't know what to expect." I waited for Vern to speak.

He noticed the extra cigarette, its long pillar of ash. He smashed it, then hesitated. "What you *should* worry about is my smoking."

Maybe attending church had reminded him of the small ceremony following Ben's death. And maybe he had glimpsed my future with our child growing up without him. His memories were always there, a heavy weight as unforgiving as a rock jetty. I could pound into him as much as I wanted, but nothing changed except me. Why was I so fluid in my response to him when he was so rigid, unyielding, seemingly paralyzed by Stan's mother? Had he always been this way and Caroline had finally decided she'd had enough?

I took a few steps toward him and hugged him from behind. A curl of smoke gathered near my face, and I twisted my head away. His hand on my arm felt warm and comforting, but I could feel him shaking. I stood back and waited for him to finish coughing. I was beginning to judge the day based on the depth of Vern's coughs. "You sound better."

"I need to get my medication on a schedule."

I nodded. The moment felt intimate and reminded me that we were still newlyweds. I loved that we thought alike in so many ways. Stan just happened to be one of those areas where we disagreed. It struck me that in the midst of an emotionally fraught situation, I still loved Vern, down to the tiniest particle.

I glanced down at a note he'd written to himself, unsure of how old it was. The quote read, "It boils down to this one principle: by this your child will know you love him—that you spend time with him." Vern was in one of his melancholy moods. I hesitated for a moment and watched him as he read *The Wall Street Journal*. I didn't know if he was lamenting the lack of time he'd spent with Ben, if this was something new related to Stan, or if he was thinking of the future and our child—but whatever thought was shooting through his mind, it dug into me. I stroked his head, tucked his hair behind his ear.

And as I continued to hug him, he said, "Darling, don't you have something better to do? I'm reading."

I climbed the stairs, drunk with hope that Stan would be on his way home soon.

CHAPTER 18

Because I still thought of myself as an athlete, I'd believed I was in decent shape, that a pregnancy wouldn't slow me down, but at three and a half months, my continuing nausea surprised me. The slightest activity wore me out. Food tasted like cardboard. I felt bloated and had aching pelvic pain and pressure, and I wasn't even showing yet. *How will I handle nine months if I'm having this much trouble in the early part of the second trimester?* I wondered. I worried my discomfort foretold of a miscarriage. Or that my anxiety would damage the fetus.

I dialed Mom and Dad.

"Hey, Butch, how are you?" Dad was always the first to answer.

"Hi, Dad. Is Mom around?"

"Bee-eej," he shouted. "Pick up the phone. It's your daughter."

While we waited, Dad grilled me about how things were going with Stan. I told him not well.

"What are you worried about?" This was my father's retort to anything I said.

"I'm not *worried*. I . . ."

"What?"

I tried to explain, but Dad thought it was funny to joke that I was the last person in the family anyone would call if they needed a babysitter. I asked again to speak to Mom, thinking, *Babysitting is not an option when you're swimming eleven or twelve miles a day. When did I ever have time for babysitting? Or energy for babysitting?* My parents had teased that if you put me in front of a child, I would be utterly

186

flummoxed, yet they'd readily left me to care for my younger siblings by myself.

When it came to Stan, though, I *was* utterly flummoxed. Maybe because I had been so young—I had barely turned twelve—when my parents left my sister and me in charge, some part of me believed I *was* inept. Jacquie, more of a pragmatist, had been better at thinking on her feet. As long as she made sense, I was happy to go along.

Mom picked up the other extension, and before I could even take a breath, I announced, "I'm having a baby."

"That's wonderful," she said. I could hear the joy in her voice.

Dad snickered. "That poor kid is not going to know what hit him."

"What poor kid?" I thought he meant Stan once he found out I was pregnant.

"Your baby," he said. "He's going to pop into the world and wonder, what in the hell is *this*?"

"Oh, Dick." Mom knew she shouldn't laugh, but she couldn't hide her glee. "What are you saying? It's wonderful news."

I had wanted to talk to Mom, to ask her questions about dealing with the pregnancy, but instead, I was shaking my head, wanting to get off the phone fast. They fired more questions—*How is Vern taking it? When is the baby due? Have you told anyone else?*—but a dull, numbing haze had settled over me. I hung up and immediately thought of Stan and his idiosyncrasies. How would I be a good mother when I was having so much trouble with him? I slid under the covers and lay there a while. This was becoming a habit.

An hour later, Vern's cheeks were alarmingly colorless. He sat at the kitchen table, rigid, in his own world, and asked, "Have you read *The Great Gatsby*?"

"I don't remember." I was supposed to have read it in school, but maybe I'd read the CliffsNotes. I hadn't found it memorable, had undoubtedly been waterlogged at the time. I didn't appreciate being reminded of all those hours spent swimming when I could've been reading.

"Read the last line." He lifted a stack of newspapers and shoved the book toward me.

I dropped down beside him. "I told my parents. Dad was the big jokester. He made a comment about our baby entering the world and wondering what hit him."

"I like him."

"Mmmm. Yeah." *He's not bad . . . unless he's your father.*

Vern shuffled through the scatter of papers and handed me a cartoon of a man lying in bed and the wife bending over him with her hands on her hips. The husband's words were "Tell the rest of the world I chickened out."

I didn't know how to respond. *Tell the world I chickened out about what? About Stan? About life in general? About having more kids?*

What was going on with Vern?

He had been scanning the store's summer retail sales numbers, and the expenses were higher than the returns. "It's hotter than a burnt boot," he said. "Even with all the fans running, nobody wants to buy anything."

He had tried his hardest to keep pace with other businesses, but the most successful business models those days consisted of sprawling warehouses packed with merchandise not there long enough to get dusty. It didn't take much to notice that Fairley Hardware was hobbling along on one foot. The third floor of the hardware store had become almost too unsafe to enter, with its leaking roof and boxes of faded Christmas decorations. Everything looked old—torn plastic wrapping on some of the merchandise, too many faded signs, and employees who were almost all over fifty.

Mom and Dad were struggling too. They could no longer afford to pay people to lug their boxes in and out of the showroom they rented at the Columbus Gift Mart. Many of their customers were going out of business, and the showroom was attracting fewer and fewer buyers. As big corporations increasingly offered cheaper prices with imports from China, old mom-and-pop stores focusing on personal service and quality merchandise from the United States or Europe could no longer compete. Meanwhile, in the midst of their turmoil, Dad had found himself dozing off at the dinner table. The costs associated with his subsequent diagnosis of sleep apnea and diabetes had added to their battle to stay afloat financially.

Maybe Vern thought of Stan as something positive in the midst of the business downturn, the losing proposition of Ayres Drugstore—it was now closed up, locked, collecting dust—and his struggle to keep the bank locally owned. I considered that maybe he was trying to help Stan because he wanted to feel *some* success during a moment when he felt powerless, but I decided against playing armchair psychologist.

"You know, Vern, you shouldn't be so hard on yourself," I said. "You have your hands full. We both do."

He pushed up the bridge of his tortoiseshell readers with his knuckle and stared at me. "Yep."

"What's the latest with Stanislaus?"

"We're going to continue." He dropped his nose back in the list of sales numbers, signaling the end of the conversation.

"What do you mean, 'We're going to continue'?"

"I *mean*, we keep the boy . . . until we don't. As the French say, *tant pis*."

It struck me right then that Vern's inclination to go along, to sail downwind, had led, in part, to the failing of the hardware business and was now undermining our marriage. The store—with its antique pitchforks, logging peaveys, and corn shellers hanging from the ceiling—was a walk back in time. Gone were the days when farmers hung out by the carriage bolts, grousing about their soybean production. Many were selling off their farms or parts of their businesses and working other jobs to put food on the table.

I wondered, *What do other couples do? What do they do when one*

*partner wants to negotiate a solution and comes halfway, and the other part-
ner won't budge?* I felt weak and housewifey. I must not have trusted
myself to be strong. I was in this predicament because I didn't *know*
what else to do. Vern undoubtedly felt the same way. The things I
valued, like having time alone or having time to be creative or even
visiting friends, had been great when we were first married. Now
they were just abstract ideas, because I couldn't carry them out.

I opened *The Great Gatsby* and angrily flipped to the last page.
"So we beat on, boats against the current, borne back ceaselessly
into the past."

I didn't know what Vern was trying to tell me. Was this line
recognition that we weren't in control of our life? Was he giving me
a coded, hopeful message? Or was it an expression of pessimism—
was he saying his past was an anchor that was preventing him, and
me, from moving forward?

Ruthann Coxe, like Caroline, had cast a long shadow on our
relationship. I had come to view her as a ranting old woman on a
street corner who fascinates you at first but whom you ignore and
rush past before the anger is directed at *you.* Maybe if Vern had
known—as I found out later—that when Stan was a toddler, Ruthann had been arrested for breaking into a breast-milk bank in San
Francisco, he would've felt differently about his willingness to help.
Then again, maybe not.

Vern opened a new pack of cigarettes and crumbled the cello-
phane outer wrapper on his dresser. He inched a fresh cigarette out
from the bottom of the pack and clutched it with his teeth. "Public
school will begin in the fall. She won't allow it."

"She'll try."

"No, look, if I insist on enrolling him, she will give in. Then we
will put him on a plane."

I would learn later that in the fall of 1976, when Old Lyme
was about to vote on a plan to build a new, seven-million-dollar
high school, Ruthann had the boys—Sam, thirteen, and Stan,

five—picketing against the plan at the local shopping center and, later, the polling place. The boys did not attend school because, in Ruthann's opinion, the district did not offer quality education. Having attended Catholic school herself, she believed her father's claim that public schools corrupted kids. To prove her point, she would repeat a story she'd heard about one public school student putting another student's shoes in the toilet and defecating on them.

But at the time, we didn't know all this. We were rolling along, dealing with each new crisis as if she were a fearless and unpredictable aunt with sharp elbows that we'd promised to protect. I took in a deep, jerky breath. "You actually think she's so opposed to public education that she won't allow it?"

"Yes," he said.

"For Godsake, Vern, she'll allow it. He stabbed the dog." I was whispering urgently. "You want him to stab one of us?" It was far-fetched, okay, but the thought had occurred to me more than once by this point. "What did she tell you when she sent him out here? Had he been torturing squirrels? If he could stab Chippie, he could do the same to us, you know. You want to take that chance, Vern? Huh? You want to take that chance?"

Vern refused to even look in my direction.

I upped the ante. "That gun in the drawer, Vern. You've got to get rid of that gun."

Vern removed his reading glasses and flung them on the table. "Stop your chatter."

"Stop my *what*?" I felt a sting through my whole body, to the arches of my feet. I felt literally sick. Would the clenching nausea in my belly damage the baby? Vern had never been so rude to me before.

"We have to teach him to mind."

There was a long pause. Then I said, "It's too late."

"Look, you must agree the boy has been cooperative lately. He shows promise."

I shook my head wildly, my voice shaky. "What is *wrong* with you? He's cooperative because he thinks he's going *home*."

Vern sounded determined to carry on a rational conversation. "I'm afraid I must disagree. Stan can learn to mind. You will simply have to put your foot down."

"You don't know what's going on, Vern. You're at the store all day. You're unaware."

"Verbose," he said. "Do you know the meaning of *verbose*?"

"Stop it, Vern. Stop right now!"

I told him he might think I was tossing out idle threats, but I wasn't. I was finished. I didn't raise my voice. I hardly took a breath. I said again, "I mean it, Vern. You have four more days. If Stan doesn't leave by the end of this week, *I* will."

Vern stuffed his cigarettes into his heavy, wool-lined jean jacket. Hand on the doorknob, he turned and, in a severe, stricken tone, said, "Do what you have to do."

I watched Vern from the corner of the family room as he met Stan in the driveway and talked with him briefly. Moments later, the two of them climbed into the blue truck, backed out of the driveway, and headed toward Main Street. As they disappeared over the hill, I gathered my anger into a solid lump in my throat. Vern had made it clear to Ruthann that Stan had stabbed Chippie, but the outrage had ended there. No more discussion. No more questioning. In my mind, Chippie's stabbing had plunged our life into mayhem. Hadn't the Boston Strangler abused dogs and cats long before he'd sexually assaulted and strangled women? Vern seemed oblivious to the seriousness of Stan's violence. I couldn't back down from my threat.

For maybe twenty minutes, I felt sorry for myself. Then I thought of the moment after we were engaged when Vern and I were each driving on our way into Hillsboro—he was following me in the same little blue truck, and I was eyeing him in my rearview mirror, and I was so full of excitement and love for him that I pulled over to the berm, hopped out, and rushed back to his truck. A few weeks later, he wrote me a note—"I think never again will I be impatient at a traffic light or stop sign. I'll always remember that joyous nymph popping out of the car and running back to implant the surprise kiss that I shall always cherish."

What had happened to Vern and me since that moment? I wanted to repair the damage but wasn't sure I even knew how. I considered that he might divorce me over this; if he did, I thought, it would be my own fault. I'd backed myself into a corner.

CHAPTER 19

It was the world's longest cigarette run. When Vern still hadn't returned after an hour, I stumbled across the street and knocked on Ann's door. She appeared wearing a stylish knee-length dress with a wide belt and V-neck front. I caught a whiff of expensive perfume.

"Hi, neighbor." She could tell I was upset.

"You have time to talk?" I asked.

Her broad smile flattened. "Of course. Come in. You hungry?" Her kitchen was filled with the mouthwatering smell of sautéed onion and beef barley soup. She patted the corner of her lips with a towel.

"I don't even know if I can eat."

"Just a moment." She smashed her lipstick-ringed cigarette in an ashtray cupped in her hand, then stirred the barley soup with a ladle. "Here. Have some soup." She scooped some of the steaming liquid into a bowl and handed it to me.

I sank into her chair. I'd been so absorbed in dealing with Stan I'd forgotten to eat lunch and was starving. I took a giant gulp of soup.

When I hesitated to speak, she shoved a stack of paperwork with her forearm to make room on her table.

Ann told me her round table had long been a magnet for friends and family needing solace. "If only this table could talk," she said, laughing, and for some reason that relaxed me. Though she complained she didn't know how to arrange furniture, she was a genius at making her eclectic collection of antique and upholstered furniture cozy and attractive but unpretentious. "They never write on your tombstone that you were a good housekeeper," she'd often reminded me.

I told Ann about my ultimatum—that Vern had to send Stan home or I was leaving on Friday. I added that it was my Hail Mary pass.

"Good," she said. She asked if Vern was drinking, and I told her yes, but not more than usual. Then she said something I'll never forget. "Some people say you have to let the alcoholic hit rock bottom before you can help them. But I'm learning you can bring the bottom up to them. It's about time, Kim . . . as long as you can do it."

Ann's smile was a salve at first, but it's funny, the more she supported me, the more I felt myself stiffen. This wasn't some annoying neighbor down the street; this was my *husband* she was talking about. Was she trying to say this was not a stubbornness problem but a drinking problem? I hated that. Vern *was* thinking of Stan, and of Stan's mother, which was pretty damned admirable. I wanted to remind her, "You know, I *am* a preservationist. It's how we got started in this whole mess." But my gut reaction felt childish.

I ended up letting out a few shaky breaths and saying, "I don't know what I'm going to do."

Ann handed me one of her attractive embroidered hand towels to blot my eyes.

"You're going to leave. You have to."

"Leave for where?"

"How long does Vern want to keep him?"

"Indefinitely, I think." I told her I didn't know what was going on with Vern. That he seemed bound and determined to keep Stan no matter what.

Ann bit her lower lip, accentuating her high cheek bones. "Does Stan have a return ticket?"

"No. Vern's already talking about school in the fall." I launched into a laundry list of complaints: he was hyperactive; he didn't listen; he took off in the middle of the night; he set the dresser on fire, and then the bed. "And we know now for sure that he stabbed Chippie." I told her about the boys and the knife.

"Oh, my God, Kim. I was hoping that wasn't true."

"We can't control him. *I* can't control him." I told her that every day, his energy accelerated. And every crisis ended the same way. "Vern tells me to be patient, that Stan will be leaving soon. Then he calls Stan's mother, and we're keeping him another two weeks. Or a month. Or whatever." I told her I felt desperate.

"Did Vern know Stan was trouble before he came here?"

"I don't know . . . I really don't know," I said. But I wondered.

She shook her head slowly from side to side. "Vern, Vern, Vern." In her chuckling, she seemed to understand more than she could say.

"Where am I supposed to go?" My mother was the obvious first choice, but she would have to tell my father, who would want to talk. With or without conversation, he'd broadcast all the gory details to the rest of the family, to his customers, the neighbors, anyone he happened to encounter on a street corner.

"You could hide over here," Ann kidded. "But leaving town would make the strongest statement. He's daring you to leave, you know. If you don't follow through, your word won't mean anything." She opened the kitchen door and switched seats with me so she could light up a cigarette and wave the smoke outside. "What about your parents?"

"No," I answered emphatically. "I can't talk to them about it. My father's a big drinker. They wouldn't be helpful."

"Who else then? Grandparents?"

My mother's family, considered the "good" side, might've understood, but I hadn't gotten over the hurt of my grandfather's ridicule when he'd received the invitation to our wedding. I had gone to a small printing company—the only one in Hillsboro—and chosen a template with a traditional engraved font style, which instead of saying "RSVP" had read, "Please respond." According to

Papa, my grandfather—we called him Papa—I had broadcast my lower-class status to everyone who knew the difference between classy and trashy. I didn't know why Papa was so class conscious—maybe similar to my father, he felt he didn't measure up in the eyes of his parents. Regardless, the criticism still stung.

"What about your father's parents?"

"Well, maybe." They lived with my father's sister in Sandwich, Massachusetts, on Cape Cod, and they and my aunt were the three biggest hermits I knew. There was no danger of their mentioning my visit to anyone, especially my parents.

"Are they good people? Would they understand?"

"I think so." I told her my grandfather, a surgeon, had delivered me and my two younger sisters. Mom had never gotten over my grandmother calling her a cow, but they were all right to me.

In some way, they were *my* people. They weren't *my parents'* people or *Vern's* people. They weren't even my sisters' or brothers' people. These were the grandparents and aunt who'd given me more presents than my siblings before I was mature enough to recognize the unfairness. They had proudly tracked me down and called me in California when they saw me on a silly television show about women beach lifeguards in LA County. Somehow, they "got" me. I began to think of them as my way out of the trap I was in—my personal lifeguards.

"The only problem is my aunt, Peggy," I said. "She hates my father." I told Ann that Peggy used to accuse us of stealing towels or breaking things on purpose to cause trouble when we were kids.

"They live far enough away, though," Ann said. "It might shake him up." It seemed to amuse her to imagine Vern's panic at finding out I was leaving.

The more we talked, the more I felt the anxiety dissipate. As Ann encouraged me, I cartwheeled in and out of memories of the house in Sandwich—their wide glassed-in summer porch, the steep slope down to the boathouse, their dock, their pontoon boat, and

Aunt Peggy allowing us to dive into the pond behind their house and watching us race across to a peninsula we thought was an island when we were kids. Maybe she hoped we'd break our necks or swallow water and drown. But a tiny part of me believed she might be kind and empathetic without my father around to drive her up a wall.

"You need to convey to Vern that you mean what you say. That two months is enough. It's been two months, hasn't it?"

"*Three* months." I could feel myself mentally rationalizing that it was *almost* three months, and three months wasn't exactly endless. I wanted her to come up with some middle ground where I wouldn't have to leave. "Can I ask you something?"

"Sure."

"Don't you think having Stan here is related to Ben?"

Ann took a long drag from her cigarette. "You mean Vern sees him as a replacement?"

"Yeah, maybe."

"Stan is nothing at all like Ben. Ben was never violent."

I asked her what she remembered of the night he died, and her eyes grew moist. She told me that while Vern and Caroline sped off to Highland District Hospital that night, the party guests—to comfort each other and wait for news—split off between Jerry's home on South 62 and her house. She said she fell asleep staring through her second-story window, clutching a few threads of hope that not seeing the Fairley's car meant Ben was still all right. But shortly after two in the morning, she'd awakened with a start. In her dream, she'd seen him on a white horse and heard him say, "Good-bye, Mrs. Pence." When the call came the next morning, she'd already known . . . Ben was gone.

Ann placed the empty bowls in the sink and ran some water over them. After a deep breath, she said, "It's time to think about Baby Fairley. I'll bet you haven't done anything for the nursery yet, have you? What does Baby Fairley want?" She raised her eyebrows as she waited.

I was immobile for a moment. "Well . . . Baby Fairley could use a warm bath and a fancy dinner in Cincinnati, maybe at the Maisonette."

"Yes . . . Baby Pence could use that too." She rubbed her stomach as she chuckled. It was a nice thought that tasted tender—but then, suddenly, trepidation set in.

"But Baby Fairley also wants this kid gone." I felt older than I ever had before. At the same time, more selfish. I swallowed hard. "Do you think that's bad?"

"Not at all, Kim. But I feel sorry for Stan." She lifted a few loose papers on the table until she found a fresh pack of cigarettes underneath.

That was the problem. I felt sorry for Stan too. Wetting the toilet seat, gobbling his food, dashing off in the middle of the night and hiding outside somewhere . . . It seemed he'd been a caged animal with his mother. A part of me shuddered at the idea of sending him back to her.

"It's time for Vern to explain to Stan's mother that Stan needs her," Ann said. "Enough is enough." She lit another cigarette.

I told her I'd picked out some wallpaper but Vern hadn't seen it yet, that we were both so tired.

Ann tossed her lighter on the table. "Where is Vern now?"

"Boone's?" It was a guess. Boone's was the drive-through liquor store on North High Street.

Ann sucked her cigarette and blew the smoke to her side and out the door. "I wish I could give you a simple answer, Kim. But I know Vern is wild about you. It may scare him if you leave, but he's not going to divorce you."

I dropped my head in my hands. "Why is this happening?" I looked up, my gaze frozen. Was this what Uncle Orrie and Jim Gibbs meant when they said, "Watch out for that guy?"

Ann smashed her cigarette in a small ashtray. "It's a test, Kim. Whatever you do, don't give in. If you give in, he'll never trust you to follow through on your word."

I nodded reluctantly as Ann stood. She handed me a book about children of alcoholics by Claudia Black called *It Will Never Happen to Me.* "It might help with your parents." She gave me a broad, congratulatory smile. Then she stood and wrapped her suntanned arms around me. "Call me if there's anything I can do to help."

Back at the empty house, I trudged up the stairs to our bedroom. The air was a smoky gray. I lifted the receiver—it was cold against my ear—and dialed.

"Are you all right, Kimmy?" My grandfather sounded surprised and happy to hear from me.

I wasn't sure how to answer. We rarely talked, and it was the first time I'd ever called him out of the blue like this. "I'm looking for some advice, is all," I said.

There was a long pause—then, "Is Vern hurting you?"

"Oh, no, nothing like that. I'd like to come and visit. Would that be okay? I'll tell you more when I get there."

After we hung up, I flopped on my bed, tracing the cracks in the ceiling. Was I doing the right thing? I'd put the plan in motion, and it felt terrible. I turned on my side. Hugged my pillow. After a few deep breaths, I sat up, picked up the phone, and dialed a new number.

"I'd like to purchase a one-way ticket from Cincinnati to Boston."

CHAPTER 20

Vern must've slept on the couch that night. He left for work the following morning in a cloud of stress and strain, his brow singed, a clump of hair yellow from too many Pall Malls the night before. I didn't kiss him, and he didn't make any effort to kiss me.

"Bye, honey," he said. "World enough and time."

I knew I couldn't go on like this.

Ten minutes later, I was cleaning the kitchen on automatic, my mind blank. As I put away the last dish, I noticed Stan's anxious blue eyes on Chippie.

"What do you think about giving him a bath?" I asked.

"Who?"

"Chippie. You want to see if we can clean him so he'll smell better?" I didn't know if he had rolled in something or what, but I could smell him from ten feet away.

Stan shivered when he heard a lawnmower and rushed to the window to see where the sound was coming from.

I explained to Stan that it would be a two-person operation, that one of us had to hold him and it wouldn't be easy, that Chippie might not enjoy the procedure. Together, we decided that I would lift the dog and put him in the tub, and once he was in there, Stan would hold him.

"Okay, Chippie, old buddy." I tucked my arms around his stomach and lifted him into the empty tub as he kicked his legs. "You have him?" I turned on the faucet and immediately started dry-heaving from the smell.

We managed to cover him with warm water. I rubbed a special hypoallergenic shampoo into his coat, and Chippie shook his body in a wave that flowed from his shoulders to his tail and back to his shoulders.

"Hold on," I said. I held his dirty collar, and Stan gripped his slippery body, soap splattering our shirts and faces. Stan, with his head turned away, managed to hold on. I released my grip. Stan rocked forward and back, his chin jutting as if the dog's energy was entering straight into his arms like a drug.

"He's getting away," he shouted, and in that moment I managed to cover Chippie with enough warm water that dark brown liquid streamed toward the drain. The dog shot out of the tub and scampered down the stairs, splashing dirty dog water, fanlike, into the stairwell. Stan, dripping wet, tumbled after him.

Chippie rolled over and over on the living room rug as if he were a wind-up toy, first wiping his nose on both sides, then grinding his soaking back into the carpet with his feet in the air. He darted from one spot to another, Stan racing after him. Stan thought he had him cornered and got ready to pounce, but Chippie jumped back just as he lunged.

"I can't get him," Stan said, smiling.

"Let him go. He's fine." I tried tossing a towel on Chippie. Each time I missed, Stan giggled. This was the same dog Stan had recently stabbed. I wondered, did he now find some affinity with Chippie, or was he likely to injure him at any moment?

"He can't stop. He's out of control." Stan was cracking up.

This was the first time I'd seen him so utterly amused, and I started laughing myself. *Damn*, I thought. *If only I'd known cleaning Chippie would make Stan this happy, I would've done it every day.*

I felt a wave of satisfaction—even pride—as I collapsed onto the couch. I'd done it. Despite my low energy and the tension and stress of having him there, I'd managed to find something other than bike riding to make Stan smile.

As I think of that moment now, maybe it was the relief of my upcoming trip to Massachusetts that made it happen. I allowed myself to get worn out washing the dog, knowing that in a couple of days I would be out the door and Stan-free for as long as I needed.

I was exhausted. At three and a half months pregnant, my pants were tight, and all I wanted to do was shop for baby clothes, pick up a good book on pregnancy, and pamper myself for the last months before becoming a parent. I knew I had to stand firm in my decision to leave.

Stan opened and shut the drawers of an antique octagonal screw cabinet in the living room.

"Why don't you go see Mrs. Pence?" I suggested. "Maybe she'll take you to the Wigwam." In that moment, I realized how far I'd come, encouraging him as if the Wigwam were a wonderfully wholesome playground for kids.

Stan barreled out the door. I tossed in a load of laundry. In our bedroom, I grabbed a small suitcase and flung my clothes for the trip on the bed. Then for twenty minutes, I folded with precision, tucking every article of clothing in its place.

Vern arrived home from work early and didn't seem to notice the damp, doggy smell of the house. He looked tired, his posture was hunched, and he grimaced as he hurled a stack of papers onto the kitchen table. I think he was hoping for a kitchen table summit. On top of what appeared to be business files was another flyer from Stan's mom—an article about Sill House Essene, the homemade organic flaxseed bread that Ruthann was making at home and selling to local stores. I pretended not to notice.

"I made a decision, honey," Vern said. He blew out a long breath and sucked in on his inhaler. I braced myself as he coughed. "I asked Ruth Captain to work an extra day."

"What for?"

"To help you, of course." He looked pleased. Had Ann called him at work? "It will give you more time to yourself."

"Four extra hours one day a week? You're kidding, right?" I crossed my arms. I would still be responsible, with or without Ruth. "You can hire her an extra day if you want, but I told you, Stan needs to go by Friday." I appreciated that he was trying, but his efforts were like bailing water to fix a clogged drain.

Vern grumbled something indiscernible. He sat on the closest Windsor chair and untied his shoes, leaving the shoelaces dangling.

"I don't know what to do about those sons of bitches."

"What sons of bitches?"

"How do you deliver a refrigerator to the wrong house?"

"Who are you talking about?"

Vern's dazed eyes looked watery, and I wondered if his medication was out of whack. "We hired a new delivery guy." He snorted. "He delivered the damn thing to the wrong house. We did some damage."

"To the fridge?"

"No, to the woman's woodwork." He pressed his finger into his ankle, leaving an imprint like one might on a ripe peach.

"Oh, God, Vern. You're swollen again."

By then we had oxygen tanks at both houses and long, tangled plastic tubing running everywhere. Vern twisted the nozzle of the tall green tank and attached the tubing to his nose. Once the oxygen flowed freely, he lit a cigarette as if he were on another kamikaze mission.

"What are you doing, Vern?" I shook the plastic tubing as he sat back down.

"Let *me* worry about it, will you?" He took a long drag on his cigarette with his elbow resting on the table and the cigarette near his eye. The tip glowed, sending up a flare that singed his eyebrow and burned a few loose hairs on his head. "Goddammit," he shouted. He wiped his head and dropped the burned hair into an ashtray. The acrid sulfur filled the room. Vern opened the cabinet for his pills. He poured himself a glass of water, then grimaced. "If you want to help, remind me to take my damned pills."

I stared at him, wondering if he was sick enough to be in the hospital—here I was, leaving in four days—but he smiled in a way that told me he was grasping for a solution to the conflict between us.

"When was the last time you spoke to your parents?"

"What do my parents have to do with anything?" I huffed.

"Maybe they'd make you feel better."

"No, Vern." I knew I was being a bitch, but my parents? Was he kidding? They were going to fix our problem? "Did you call them? Is that what this is about?" My voice sounded harsher than I intended.

"No, honey."

I pivoted on one foot and climbed the stairs to our room.

CHAPTER 21

A couple of days later, I woke to the sweet, fatty smell of bacon. When I stepped into the kitchen, dirty dishes filled the sink. Two pieces of cold bacon lay on a paper towel on the white Formica countertop.

Vern had gone to bed after I'd fallen asleep and woken before me. His ankles were back to normal—presumably due to medication—and his sour mood had lifted.

On the heels of mentioning how much work he had at the hardware store, he reminded me that it was Thursday, the day the church ladies volunteered at the Union Stockyards, serving the best homemade food in town. "Care to join us?" He made it sound as if he were taking Stan on a field trip and inviting me on a date. But his ashen eyes were wistful. He seemed to be trying to prop himself up. Before we were married, in the flush of our romance, we'd been to the Union Stockyards together. Vern had written me a letter of invitation saying that I would make the stockyards diner an exciting place for him.

But why now? Why, in the midst of our struggles, was he wanting to go there? At the stockyards, I would have to pretend everything was copacetic, when I was about to shock Vern and fly off to Cape Cod the following day.

Vern had been complaining so much that it confused me to hear he wanted to spend any time at all with me. "Didn't you say you were swamped at the store?" I asked. The kitchen air was dead but for a few hissing flies; for a moment, I swatted them.

"You'd be a lovely distraction," he said.

I resisted the urge to kiss him when he shot me his warm smile. Even in that lukewarm moment, I felt a strong attraction to Vern.

He steered the conversation to all the fun we were going to have with Stan. When I didn't respond, he said, "How is my beauteous blue-eyed cupcake?"

"Green-eyed, you mean." I looked away coldly. Once again, it seemed he wasn't listening. Maybe he sensed I was no longer willing to play along.

We drove down to the Union Stockyards, a one-story frame, open-barn structure near the old railroad tracks on the north side of West Main Street. One of the only remaining stockyards in a downtown commercial district west of the Alleghenies, it was across the street from the grocery and down the hill from the historic Scott Mansion. Trucks hauling livestock pulled up to the back. With all the trailers and cars parked in random lines in front of the building, Vern had a hard time finding a parking space.

Stan held his shirt over his nose as we drove into the gravel lot.

"Aren't you accustomed to the smell?" Vern asked him. "You live on a farm."

"It doesn't smell *this* bad." He dropped his shirt and pinched his nose with his fingers.

"What do you use for fertilizer?"

"Seaweed," he said.

Vern nodded his approval. "Well, the smell is the hogs. Not the heifers. For a lot of these farmers, that smell is money." Vern parked the truck and held the door open for Stan. "You'll get used to it."

We found three seats in the back of several rows of buyers in cowboy hats and ball caps who were wearing plaid shirts and holding pens and small notepads. Below, in front, four cows ready for slaughter with white numbers painted on their hind ends pushed and shoved through one gate and out the other with swarms of flies on their backs.

Watching a group of Holstein steers, I couldn't stop thinking of the pig roast. Those boys had hurled that sow on the back of the truck half-dead. *Was she unconscious? Or was she in pain, shrieking?* I tried to block out the thoughts, but these animals looked frightened, cornered, overheated. Panicked. The idea tormented me like one of those little biting flies at my neck. Why at this time—this exact moment, when I was about to leave—was Vern taking me to see these animals on their way to the slaughter? Was this some kind of private message? With every squeal, I wanted to take those poor animals home.

"Hundred dollar bill now one, two. Hubida dubida three, four, five, six here, now seven. Bid eight. Give nine. Ten, eleven, twelve. Hubida dubida thirteen." The auctioneer nodded to bidders, his index finger pointing. Stan rocked in place as if to music.

Animal cries blended with the auctioneer's pace, and the stench, humidity, and lack of ventilation grew more suffocating. Stan rocked. Vern smiled. Time slowed as my mind drifted. I thought of Vern and how he must feel, alone in his opinion of what to do about Stan, and of the way he escaped into his books. I thought of Stan riding those damned endless loops. He was the most alone of all of us. Deserted by his father, deserted by his mother, and now deserted by us—or, I should say, me—wanting him to move along, return to Connecticut. I realized he was an eleven-year-old orphan.

"How about some lunch?" Vern asked after a few minutes. He rubbed his grizzled eyebrows.

I shrugged. "I'll try."

We stepped past the bidders in our row and down a couple of steps into a separate, air-conditioned room where women wearing street clothes and using loud voices served a dozen or so people at a time, seated on fixed vinyl stools in front of a long Formica counter.

With his tortoiseshell reading glasses, now hanging from a cord around his neck, Vern scanned a laminated menu. These were the best burgers in Hillsboro, even with the stench of cow manure creeping in under the door and through a dirty window air conditioner. "Three burgers?"

I doubted my ability to hold down much of anything, but I nodded.

Stan seemed anxious. When the woman behind the counter handed him his plate, he removed his two pickle slices with this thumb and index finger and devoured the burger. "Great," he said when he was done, wiping his mouth with the back of his hand. Vern pulled out a napkin from a small dispenser and set it in Stan's lap. He chatted with a woman behind the counter, introduced Stan, and allowed him to pick from three varieties of homemade pie. I thought again of our little family—of Vern, Stan, and little Baby Fairley. We *were* a family, whether I was willing to admit that or not. Vern looked so happy with Stan at the stockyards that I felt guilty that I was about to ruin everything. I once again began to doubt my decision to leave.

Our trip to the stockyards *was* fun for Stan, and I could tell Vern was enjoying his enthusiasm. It was also clear to me that Ann *had* called Vern. I had a brief flash of the thought that maybe Vern would surprise me by changing his mind and sending Stan home.

But when we left the stockyards, Vern skidded out of the lot and up the hill to the west, then swerved onto Oak as I gripped the dash above the glove compartment, trying not to heave up my burger. As he pulled into our driveway on the corner of West South Street, I knew by his silence my positive thought was wishful thinking.

I fell into a defeated slouch, and I couldn't hold back my resentment. I climbed out of the truck. "*That* was fun," I said as Stan dashed past me and into the house. "A nice way to end my babysitting gig." I was testing Vern to see if he believed I was leaving, but there was no smile of recognition as I slammed the door.

Vern screeched the truck into the street, the exhaust fumes spewing behind him, and drove off.

⌒

In the morning, I called Ruth. "Please, if you can, keep an eye on Stan *and* Vern. I don't want anything bad to happen to either of them." I read aloud my grandparents' phone number, and she wished me luck.

I slipped down to the kitchen late. I had blown my hair dry and donned a small amount of makeup and a long navy jumper, loose-fitting, for comfort on the plane. As soon as Vern saw me lugging the suitcase, I could see his alarm.

He must've thought I was performing an act, that he could use his well-honed powers of persuasion. "Have a seat," he said. "Let's talk." Stan sat beside him, smacking his lips as he chomped Rice Krispies in orange juice. The spoon scraping the bowl reminded me of a loose utensil in the dishwasher.

"There's nothing to talk about, Vern. I told you I would be leaving." I dropped an English muffin into two sides of the toaster and waited.

Vern smashed his cigarette on a large, filthy ashtray he'd brought in from the living room. "Have you spoken to your parents?"

"My parents have nothing to do with this." It bugged me that his first thought to make me happy was always to reach out to my parents. Was that a normal reaction or related only to our age difference?

"Maybe you should call them." He tore open a brand-new carton of cigarettes and pulled out a pack. "Maybe they could talk to you."

"I told you, Vern. My parents have nothing to do with this." The more he pressed, the more I wanted to storm out.

"I believe you," he croaked. "I do not condone what you're doing, however."

The muffins popped in the toaster. I buttered the two sides, sprinkling them with cinnamon sugar. With the small plate in my hand, I sat at the table and nibbled.

"Do you have any idea where you're going?" Vern pulled together the newspaper and a stack of yellow legal pages.

"Yes."

"Where?"

"My grandparents' in Sandwich, Massachusetts."

"You have a ticket?"

I nodded. I had a plane ticket to Boston and a bus reservation to Cape Cod. It seemed like he was juicing up the courage to ask me how long I'd been planning this, but he didn't say anything for a moment. I was afraid he was going to stop talking altogether.

Finally, he pushed up the bridge of his glasses. "Ann talked you into this, didn't she?"

"No."

"I know she did. Jesus Katy Christ. Ever since she's started this counseling gig, she's been finding alcoholics under every bush."

"What are you talking about, Vern?" I hadn't said a thing about alcoholism. He was putting the pieces together in his head and missing a few.

I placed my empty plate in the dishwasher and glanced at my Timex watch. The bright light of the day had cast an ominous shadow across the kitchen. I spotted Chippie; he was panting, and I couldn't help but remember Stan's swift kick and his fall off the bridge. Vern noticed me watching him, which was unsettling. I leaned over and let Chippie nuzzle my hand.

"Love me, love my dog," Vern said.

"Well, you may have to tell Ruth to keep a special eye on him." I didn't want to be too direct with Stan sitting there.

"We'll keep an eye on Chip."

I tapped Stan on the back. "Good-bye, Stan."

There was an emptiness in the room, as if the news of my leaving had caused a gust of cold air to blow in. The chairs were askew, the table cleared, showing countless cigarette burns. Caroline's smoke-stained eyelet curtains were untied, revealing yellow streaks. It was as if my departure was brushing away the clutter, exposing Vern's unexpressed sorrow.

But the charade was over, thank God. I lifted my purse strap over my shoulder and picked up my suitcase. Vern followed me to the car. I hugged him somewhat coldly. Even then, I wanted him to beg me to stay and promise to send Stan home. I strapped myself into the car, still hoping. Again, wishful thinking.

"Good-bye, honey," he said, closing my door. He looked worried and tired, his head dropped low, his shoulders hunched. I wanted to change my mind, but I knew I couldn't. I rolled down the window. "Do you know how long you'll be gone?"

I imagined maybe a week, maybe a month. With luck, only a few days. But all I said was "As long as it takes."

Vern leaned through the driver's seat window and kissed me. "Please be careful. I love you very much."

"I love you too," I said, and I was on my way.

CHAPTER 22

I pinned my hopes on a belief that my absence alone would scare Vern. I told myself he would reevaluate our situation and, out of his love for me, would send Stan back to his mother. I was testing the old absence-makes-the-heart-grow-fonder notion. I'd heard for so many years about my grandparents' lack of understanding when it came to my father that I didn't actually have much faith in their ability to help me. What I wanted most was a brief vacation that might shake Vern up.

I arrived in Hyannis on a shuttle from Logan Airport and took a taxi to my grandparents' home on Triangle Pond. Theirs was a lovely red frame house with two gable ends facing front, a porte-cochere on one side, and a bay window in the middle. As my driver pulled into their circular drive, I noticed a cluster of rhododendrons so voluminous that from the front of the house, they hid the trunks of the towering pitch pines along the street.

Mom-Mom and Pop-Pop and Aunt Peggy all came out to the breakfast nook near their side entrance. Peggy opened the door, and her black lab, Lucky, the size of a horse, reared back and shoved his front paws on my chest, slobbering. My suitcase fell to the floor with a thud.

"Down, Lucky," they all shouted.

Lucky sniffed and pawed at me for a moment, then trotted off.

I'd forgotten how much I loved my grandfather's welcoming laughter. "Come in. Tell us the news." He wrapped his strong German arms around me and guided me to their built-in breakfast nook.

Pop-Pop had lost weight since he'd gotten a pacemaker, a diagnosis of diverticulitis, and two surgeries, one on each hand. With his skinny legs and the tight belt he wore around his middle, however, he still reminded me of Humpty Dumpty, as he had when I was a child. Standing somewhere around six feet tall, he towered over my birdlike grandmother in her tight, perfectly tailored purple dress. Together with Peggy, whose height was somewhere in between my grandparents', they made me think of size A, size B, and size C. They were all three so different. Perhaps if one of them didn't have a solution to Stanislaus, another size might fit.

The house had that deep earthy smell of wet topsoil mixed with cedar. I couldn't tell if the cedar smell was the house or the breakfast nook bench, which looked like it might've held blankets.

Mom-Mom and Peggy hugged me, and the words poured out— "I'm pregnant."

The three of them warbled a succession of congratulatory remarks. *That was quick. How lovely. How wonderful. You must be exhausted.*

"Here, have a seat." Mom-Mom pointed to the breakfast nook. "You need to rest the baby."

I slid in around the table—their cozy spot, with its worn leather seat cushions tufted with buttons and its philodendrons in the bay window, their arrow-shaped leaves pointing toward the light.

Covering the table were packs of old letters—dozens—tied in off-white cord, that I recognized immediately as having belonged to my great-aunt Selena, who had died within the previous year. Selena had organized her letters like a quilt. I thought of how Mom-Mom collected and organized her glass paperweights and how she'd wallpapered their front hall with Peggy's paintings in matching black frames, placed in a tight grid. I was reminded of the stamp quilt I was making to decorate the baby's wall. Like my grandparents and aunt, I gravitated toward order. In a sense, we were all trying to hold ourselves together.

Mom-Mom whisked Selena's letters to a side counter and out

of our way. Then she wiped the table clean with a damp cloth.

"So let's hear it," my grandfather said. "What's going on?"

"Well . . . we have this eleven-year-old boy." I rushed through the details—how he appeared one day for a two-week visit and then moved in as if he were a member of the family. How his mother was fighting a lawsuit to save the family farm. As I listened to my own voice, I recognized my defeated tone, and my eyes grew watery. "It was supposed to be two weeks. It's been three months."

"Whoa," my aunt blurted. "Sounds like you have a son." Peggy's silky auburn hair cascaded down the sides of her face in loose waves. You'd think as an artist with that beautiful hair and a degree from Wellesley she would've been married by then, but at forty-two she was still at home, taking care of her parents and, according to my mother and father, deeply resenting it. Mom said her boyfriends had never measured up to her parents' expectations.

"I don't think Vern plans to send him home," I said.

"What about his mother? Where's she?" Peggy asked.

"Connecticut," I grumbled. "She's too busy dealing with the lawsuit to deal with him."

My grandmother tapped her gnarled fingertips together whenever she couldn't hear the conversation. She was hard of hearing and didn't seem to be wearing her hearing aids.

Peggy sneered at me. "I think he's yours."

"He's what?" Mom-Mom asked.

"He's her new son, Ma," Peggy shouted. "She has a *son*." This was Peggy's code for *I know what it's like to take care of people*.

Mom-Mom scowled. "That mother needs to have her head examined."

Pop-Pop had no problem with long pauses in the conversation, and this reassured me that he was listening carefully. I was reminded of my father's comment that Pop-Pop was known for his talent as a diagnostician.

The more details I provided, the more they nodded and listened.

They didn't exactly support me, but they didn't say anything in Stan's defense either, which was a welcome change. I let out pieces of the story as if they were sections of anchor chain, the metal slowly digging in and gripping their empathy. When I ended the story with Chippie's stabbing, the anchor latched onto a rock.

Pop-Pop looked deeply concerned. "Are you sure the boy stabbed the dog?"

"I'm sure," I said. "The neighbor kids told their mother. She made them tell us."

"This should be reported," Peggy said. "Have you gone to the police?"

"No." I nervously twirled a few tendrils of my shoulder-length hair.

"Well, you should. How long ago was this, anyway? Stabbing a dog is criminal. Was he trying to *kill* the dog?"

For a moment, I felt a headache coming on and rubbed my temples. Was I embellishing the story? Blowing things out of proportion again? Maybe Stan was showing off. Why was Peggy getting so worked up? I worried she would call the police herself. I mentioned there had been three boys with him. Younger boys.

Mom-Mom, who was tapping her fingertips together, reached out to rub my hand on the table. The phone rang, and she rushed over to grab it. I could hardly hear her voice, but Peggy knew instantly when Mom-Mom turned away, cupping the receiver. "It's your father," Peggy groaned, her tone caustic.

I frowned when I realized Dad was tracking me down.

The way my grandmother kept tapping the receiver, it was obvious she heard nothing. Pop-Pop and Peggy shouted loudly to have him call back later, but Mom-Mom couldn't hear them either.

"Just a minute, Dick." She handed me the phone.

"How are you doing, Butch?" My father sounded composed, his words measured, but it didn't matter. I didn't want to talk to him.

"I'm fine," I said.

"You're fine?"

"Yeah." Other than getting tracked down within minutes of my arrival, I was fine.

"Well, if you're so fine, what in the hell are you doing in Massachusetts?"

Instantly, the guilt swept through me. I scrunched my eyes and glanced at my grandfather, hoping he would rescue me. "I'm visiting. Why?"

"We need you home, Butch. Vern's having a conniption. So is your mother."

"Like I told you, I'm fine," I said. "Could you stay out of this for once, Dad? This has nothing to do with you."

Pop-Pop stood two feet away, leaning against a tall barstool. "I'll talk to him," he said.

I handed my grandfather the phone.

"Dick, she just walked in the door. She's here for now. Why don't you tell Vern she's safe and not to worry?" He said good-bye, hung up, and looked at me. "You have to give it to him. He sure is persistent."

My grandfather was a wise man who, from what I could tell, had a long history of feeling let down by my father. He'd wanted him to be a doctor, and Dad had no such inclination. Sometimes, I felt sorry for Dad that he'd always been viewed as such a disappointment.

While visiting my grandparents in New Jersey as a child, I'd been drawn to a small doghouse plaque that hung near the kitchen. The plaque had four wooden dogs on hooks, each representing a member of the family. For some reason, whenever we visited, the dog named *Dickie*—their name for my father—always hung in the doghouse. When nobody was looking, I would take the Dickie dog out and place it on a hook beside the Mom, Pop, and Peggy dogs. But by the time I passed by it again, the Dickie dog was always back in the doghouse.

"Did you notice whenever we visit, Dad's name is always in the doghouse?" I finally asked my mother.

"Your father has dealt with this his whole life," she said. "Always in the doghouse."

I'd believed the doghouse plaque was one of my grandparents' sneaky ways of expressing disappointment. It had bothered me as a kid, but as an adult, I felt the same sense of letdown when it came to my father. He would stand too close, touch me without permission, and violate my sense of privacy, so much so that I had to put up walls to keep him away. Why couldn't he stay out of my conflict with Vern?

I fell back on one of the breakfast nook cushions and blew out a mouthful of air. "He can be so frustrating."

"Tell me about it," Peggy said. "No, on second thought, *don't* tell me about it."

Peggy could be a bitch, but I didn't mind her sense of humor when it suited me. At the same time, I felt disloyal to my father.

"You need something to eat," my grandmother said, and before I could respond, she said, "I'm going to fix you two meals: one for you and one for the baby."

"Thanks, Mom-Mom, but do you mind if I lie down first?" I tried to speak loudly, but she peered into the refrigerator.

"She wants to lie down, Ma," Peggy growled.

"Oh, okay." Mom-Mom waved me toward a back guest bedroom with walls covered in 1940s-style blue floral wallpaper and a bed with a white crocheted and fringed coverlet. The house was cool despite the summer heat. I set my watch on a small antique nightstand, removed my headband and black flats, and curled up, my hand cradling the baby inside me.

That night in their cavernous living room, between two baby grand pianos, on a couple of enormous oriental rugs, with seventeen antique clocks ticking around us, we sat with the evening news blaring and a fan pointed in our direction. Mom-Mom and Pop-Pop were in matching La-Z-Boys with their feet up. Peggy and I sat on rock-hard chairs near them.

"You can't let him dictate your life," Peggy said.

"Who do you mean?" Was she talking about Vern?

"The boy. Who else? You're walking on eggshells around him."

Pop-Pop listened but didn't chime in. He pulled up on his thin black belt in the same way my father always did.

"What do you think, Pop-Pop?" He was the most logical, reasonable person in the room, and unlike my father, who would be dominating the conversation, he wasn't saying much.

"You're an adult now," he said. "We should wait."

"We should *what*?" My grandmother had one ear pointed toward Pop-Pop.

He frowned as he raised his voice. *"Wait*, Ma. We should *wait*. She needs to think about this for a few days."

"Can't we turn off the television?" Mom-Mom said politely.

A testy exchange followed, ending with Peggy reluctantly turning down the volume.

"Where were we?" Pop-Pop asked.

I said something about how I didn't sign up for this when I married Vern. Pop-pop said he thought it was a game we were playing.

Peggy raised her eyebrows and squirmed in her chair. "She needs to work this out with her husband," she said, trying to get Pop-Pop's attention. "She can't stay here indefinitely." Peggy was seemingly trying her hardest to hold in what she thought about not wanting me to stay too long, but it was oozing out through her pores. I undoubtedly was reminding her of my father.

Mom-Mom pushed back the leg rest on her La-Z-Boy. "How about some ice cream?"

"I'll have some. A tiny bit." I remembered the huge scoops of butter pecan and coffee ice cream my grandparents would dish up when I was a child.

My grandmother smoothed her tight purple dress over her small belly and patted my arm. "What's the matter? Aren't you going to feed the baby?"

She exited the room, and Pop-Pop winked at me.

Mom-Mom was back in seconds, handing me a bowl mounded high with chocolate mint ice cream.

"We will come up with a plan, Kimmy," my grandfather said. He glanced at me over his narrow black readers. "Try not to think about all this tonight. Get some sleep and we'll talk tomorrow."

CHAPTER 23

All night I imagined my grandfather's plan of attack, afraid it might sound something like confession—"Say two *Our Fathers* and three *Hail Marys*, and you're good to go." Instead, in the morning my grandmother invited me to their back porch in front of a wall of windows, where Peggy sat peering out to Triangle Pond and Pop-Pop quietly read the paper.

Until then, I hadn't realized how much their yard reminded me of my parents' place. Both had a steep slope down to the nearby water, though at my parents' house you needed a machete to forge a path to the lake, while my grandparents had built a series of winding wooden staircases interrupted by a small gazebo with an asphalt-hipped roof, crisscrossed and vertical hanging timbers, and two benches facing each other, as if to ensure that even in their old age they'd have access to this magical landscape through wild rhododendrons and pitch pines.

My grandmother, at seventy-nine, didn't look a day over sixty. Now, wearing her hearing aids, she looked more muscular. I noticed her thick upper body, the tautness at the nape of her neck, and her dowager's hump, all traits I'd inherited; they prevented a proud posture but, fortunately, had made me a strong swimmer.

My grandfather dropped the newspaper in his lap and sipped his coffee. "How was your sleep?"

"Glorious." There had been a cool breeze of fragrant pine wafting through the window, the periodic rustling of leaves, and my sheets and pillowcase, seeping cedar. But my grandfather's serious expression had me worried.

"I hope you don't mind that I called Vern."

I collapsed in the nearest chair. "Oh, well, how was he?" I had been reassured when Pop-Pop had insisted we wait a day to discuss a plan, since my father would've dropped everything to iron out the difficulties immediately without any reflection. I appreciated the differences in their approaches. But now I fretted that he was about to tell me he agreed with Vern, or that I needed to return to Hillsboro.

"So what did he say?" I tried to sound indifferent. I wasn't ready to be shocked. I wanted consolation.

"He was very nice. I like him." Pop-Pop looked embarrassed. His expression told me he'd tried and failed to improve my situation. "Vern told me the boy will be there for another full month."

I snorted. "No comment." I could feel my entire body tensing. *Here we go again*, I thought. *Now I'm about to hear advice from grandparents who live eight hundred miles away and don't have a friggin' clue about my life.* What was I even doing here?

When Pop-Pop hesitated, Mom-Mom jumped in to fill the void in the conversation. "You need to go back there and deal with this, Kimmy." She and Peggy eyed each other.

"I can't go back there."

"You have to." My grandmother tried to be cheerful. "You can stay married or quit."

I was reminded of my mother, the way she let my father back into the house after he'd run off with the woman from the cosmetic counter at Mabley's department store when I was eight. I'd wanted her to put up a fight, to make Dad suffer. Now, I wanted payback for all the hurt and betrayal. But my grandparents were telling me, *Go back, let Vern off the hook.* How could I? His little love affair with Stan would continue, and I'd be an unwilling participant.

"I wish you could see this kid." I laid out again my litany of complaints about Stan's high level of energy, his constant motion, the time and effort required to deal with him.

"Who have you told about your situation?" Pop-Pop asked.

"My neighbors and one other friend." I told him Ann kept an eye on Stan when he showed up at her house or the video arcade.

"That's all?"

"Pretty much." I bit my bottom lip.

Pop-Pop rubbed his chin. "Does Vern know how much you're suffering?"

"Well, yes. He knows about everything."

"How about the toilet seat?" Pop-Pop sounded clinical, as if he were speaking to one of his patients.

"Yep, I've told him." I added that Vern had an aversion to bodily fluids and that he didn't appreciate my complaining.

"Well, that explains it," Mom-Mom said. She believed she had solved a mystery, that there was no more to discuss. "You may think he knows, but Vern has no idea what you're going through."

Peggy looked tickled. "Sounds like you need to let *Vern* sit on a wet toilet seat. Let *Vern* scrape off the chewing gum and candle wax."

"You need to let everything fall apart," Mom-Mom said.

They were talking over each other.

My grandfather crossed his arms over his broad belly. "You said the boy had tried to leave in the middle of the night, right? Next time, let him go. Let Vern answer the call from the police." Pop-Pop creased the newspaper with his fingernails. "You've been making it too easy for him." He said I was letting Vern continue to enjoy his daily life while I picked up all the slack. "I'm with Ma and Peggy," Pop-Pop said. "This doesn't seem serious to Vern because Vern doesn't see what you're talking about. Show him. Don't tell him."

The morning sun rose above the porch roof, and a warm gust of air blew through the screens. A large spider dangled from a web near the ceiling. "Did you say Vern spends the day at the hardware store?" my grandmother asked. "You spend most of the day with the boy, right?"

"Yeah."

"Let Vern take him to the hardware store from now on," she said. "Plan your own activities. He'll see for himself." Mom-Mom snickered. "He'll get in trouble up there. I guarantee it. He can only go so long."

"What am I supposed to say when they call to tell me Stan has gotten into trouble?"

Peggy seemed unable to hide her devilish glee. "You say, 'Wow.'"

"That's all?" I kind of liked the idea. No argument, no judgment, only a comment.

"That's all. You say 'wow,' and then you wait."

My grandmother reached out and rested her hand on my forearm. "*You* stay home and look pretty."

"He's going to drive Vern bananas," Peggy said. "Be prepared for Vern to go into a full-blown breakdown over this."

Hearing that, I felt empathy for Stan. "If Vern has to take care of him full time," I said, "Stan is the one who will suffer."

"He won't suffer. How will *he* suffer?" Peggy asked.

It was easy for me to think back to my childhood, when my absence created problems for my siblings. If I didn't show up to help clean up the house, the work was divided four ways instead of five. Somebody had to do it. Not participating in this project—our Stan project—would force Vern to take over.

I hated to admit it, but I wasn't sure Vern would keep Stan safe.

"What if he hurts himself?" I asked. It confused me that the three of them weren't concerned with the danger, but as I thought back, we were frequently injured as kids with nobody there to help. David got his hand nearly chopped off. Rick cracked his head open. There'd been occasions when one or more of my siblings went missing and we kids went on all-out hunts; several times, this ended with our discovering Rick conked out in the bathtub. I easily recalled the terror of being alone at night in the middle of a thunderstorm. The fear of being kidnapped. *What if we get lost? What if we run out of food? What if something really terrible happens?* I knew I had been feeling all the anxiety and responsibility from my childhood in dealing with Stan, but dammit, those dangers had been real, not imagined.

There was a long pause, and then my grandfather said, in a fatherly tone, "I have a question for you, and I want you to think about it before you answer." He paused a moment. "Are you loving generously? And what I mean by that is, are you loving without sacrifice?"

"I think so."

Pop-Pop's tone was bright and compassionate. "You love Vern, and some side of you is saying you need to be selfless and take care of the boy. But you're not showing you *trust* Vern."

I returned a lopsided smile. I could see examples of my own judgment and lack of trust. In my head, I was building a checklist of all the areas where Vern was falling short—the drinking, the smoking, the parenting, the hardware store—and in building the list, I was stepping in at every turn, choosing to deal with Stan directly rather than trusting Vern to handle him. I told myself I was protecting myself and the baby. *What am I supposed to do? Let him burn the house down?*

But I didn't really know what my grandfather meant by "Are you loving without sacrifice?" The minute Vern dropped Stan into my lap, I'd become my twelve-year-old self again—head of the household, without the slightest clue what I was doing. Stan was a stand-in for my siblings. As a grown-up, I had no idea how to deal with him.

"I worry about Vern's health," I said.

"I understand," Pop-Pop said, "but you're worrying about his health more than he is. Let *Vern* take care of himself. He can be the fire warden and the lifeguard—even the police."

Mom-Mom and Peggy each extended a heartfelt nod.

The gravity of Vern's age and poor health tugged at me, and

I felt myself slump. In that moment, I realized another reason I had resisted Stan's presence so fiercely: time was a commodity in my relationship with Vern. He complained about old age and the passage of time, and yet he was giving our precious time away willy-nilly to Stan.

Pop-Pop was right. As in the Don Marquis essay that Vern loved and often shared, he—Vern—*was* doing what he wanted. Viewing himself as Marquis, an old man in the last ten years of his life, *Vern* had strapped a forty-five-caliber revolver to one arm of his chair and was shooting out the lights when he wanted to go to sleep. He was throwing a silver candlestick through the front window. I, meanwhile, was sweeping up the pieces.

What Mom-Mom, Pop-Pop, and Peggy were telling me was to recognize that Vern and I were partners. To protect our partnership by letting everything fall apart. To notice the broken glass and let it sit there. To give Vern back his dignity by doing nothing.

Loving without sacrifice? This was a totally new concept to me. Loving *was* sacrifice, wasn't it? My mother had been a chemistry major at Cornell. She'd sacrificed her career to help my father. We kids had sacrificed a part of our childhood to help our parents with their gift business. We'd learned this in Sunday school—that Jesus Christ had loved us so much he'd sacrificed his life for all of us— that loving was sacrifice. For staunch Catholics, my grandparents sure sounded like heathens. It seemed they and my aunt were telling me to prevent destruction by allowing Stan to be destructive, that in my way I was enabling Vern, and that I could do more for him by doing less.

I gave Peggy a half-hearted smile as Lucky put his chin in my lap and nudged me with his cold, wet nose. "You hungry, ole buddy?" I asked him.

Mom-Mom's eyes brightened. "That's right . . . It's almost noon. You need some breakfast. You're eating for two." She leapt from her chair as Peggy got up and disappeared into the house.

"We don't have to implement this plan right this minute," Pop-Pop said.

Mom-Mom lingered at the door. "Why don't you stay for a few days and give Vern some time to feel desperate?"

What I heard was not some altruistic idea to show my deep love for Vern. What I heard was a new way forward. For my own sanity. Twice, I'd been the first to rush into the smoky bedroom. I'd been the first to notice the toilet mess and the gum on the furniture. The first to discover Chippie's injury. I'd believed I was allowing Vern to make up for the missing time with Ben by continuing to feel he was helping Stan, but it had come at a price—and *I* was paying it.

There was no reason why I couldn't let Vern react first.

Now that I had a plan, my impulse was to purchase a ticket on the first available plane home, but I needed to stall for time. To let Vern sweat. It was the ages-old *hard-to-get* scenario. You have to back off sometimes to make them realize they want what *you* want. Somewhere in the back of my mind, I believed Vern would come around. I imagined walking into the house, his hearing my voice and rushing out to greet me, our bodies snapping together, two magnets in the middle of our family room.

Pop-Pop suggested we go the next day to an organ recital in North Truro, on Cape Cod. As a member of the Hyannis Retired Men's Club chorus, he had met two men who, through their connections, had salvaged a 1929 Wurlitzer pipe organ from a Connecticut silent movie theater.

"You might enjoy the music," Pop-Pop said. "They play a smattering of everything."

My grandfather's enthusiasm for an organ recital at the home of two gay men struck me as strange when I considered my father. It fascinated me that Pop-Pop was so open and tolerant when the only thing liberal about my father was in telling me his personal secrets that I wished I didn't know. *Going to the home of two men who were musicians and had installed a pipe organ off their living room?* I couldn't see my father *ever* doing something like that without a painful, cringeworthy conversation.

"It's hard to find happiness in this world. So when you find it, you stick with it." Pop-Pop flashed me his wise grandfather smile, and I let the warm, chocolatey softness in his voice envelop me. He wanted to make sure I didn't give up on Vern. What he didn't realize was that I would never give up on Vern. The biggest risk was my giving up on myself.

Pop-Pop arranged the return ticket to Cincinnati and promised not to call Vern to warn him I was coming. I thanked Aunt Peggy. She returned my half-bent-over hug as she held Lucky back by the collar. Pop-Pop loaded my suitcase into the trunk of their car, and he and Mom-Mom drove me to Hyannis for the bus to Logan Airport.

The drive to Hyannis became a moment of quiet gratitude. The warm air, the tree-lined drive past Mystic Lake, the large, open fields with lush green grass and white rail fencing. My mind went straight to the Wurlitzer organ, the gold wings of an angel and stylized winged lions on the top of it. Of all the things that could've bolstered my mood and helped celebrate the good in my life, the organ recital had been far better than anything I could imagine. The audience had been a small, appreciative group of friends and neighbors. And the music—well, there was nothing more soothing. Too much time had passed since I'd been to any kind of performance or show. Music was a part of me that I'd silenced.

I don't know if my grandparents realized the gift they'd given me with that organ recital, but it was better than an appointment with a psychologist. Better than church. Better than an ocean swim from Manhattan Beach to Hermosa. The organ had opened up something in me, with its moving parts, its wind-breathing system, its reverence. I'd breathed in that organ's warm tones, and it had felt sacred. It was that feeling you get when the hair stands up on your arms and the chill travels through every nerve in your body. You don't know what hit you. But you feel connected to the person sitting next to you and the person sitting next to him, and then you realize you're connecting to a whole universe of people before you. And you're letting go of something, too. Something heavy and unnecessary.

Mom-Mom suggested I take a few trips to Cincinnati when I got back, to buy myself some maternity clothes. She warned that Vern might be difficult. "He will be happy to see you, but it may take him a while to get over your leaving. But don't give up." She twisted in her seat and handed me two sandwiches over her shoulder.

"Oh, thank you. One is fine."

"What? Don't you want to feed the baby?"

I felt my grandmother's warmth fill me. I wondered if they were making up for the lack of support they'd given my father or if the story of Dad's maltreatment was a warped narrative my parents told to make sense of their own struggles. My grandparents and aunt had been gentle, maddeningly wise, and caring. There was so much more to them than the image I'd always seen through my parents' harsh lens.

And I couldn't wait to get back to Vern. To his sparkling eyes, his reassuring smile, his warm, deep voice, the feeling I got whenever I hugged him that I'd known him all my life.

I held out my purse. "Thanks."

Mom-Mom dropped the two sandwiches into it. As I thanked them again and climbed onto the bus, she said, "Remember us to your father and mother."

CHAPTER 24

It was raining when I arrived in Cincinnati. I drove the hour to our house hunched over the wheel in what became a blistering downpour with our torn wipers flapping against the windshield. Deafening thunder and lightning struck close enough to hit the car. When I pulled into the driveway beside Vern's blue pickup and parked on a diagonal, I could see the TV light flashing in the window.

The rear screen door, ajar, banged in the wind. The rain blew sideways, pattering onto the gravel. I dashed toward the house, hauling my luggage, and as I was about to push open the door with my hip, I noticed that my two pots of impatiens, hanging from the porch's main beam, were both dead.

In the kitchen, Vern was slumped at the table in a smoke haze, half-awake. He dangled a cigarette two inches from his nose and oxygen cannula, poised to send himself and *The Wall Street Journal* up in flames.

"I'm home," I announced in a high-pitched singing voice.

Vern jerked awake, set down the cigarette, and flashed the winning smile I'd fallen in love with. I couldn't wait to hug him, but I also knew that, for my sake, I needed to stay guarded. I placed my hand on his shoulder for a moment and eased myself into a chair across the table from him.

"You came back," he said.

We exchanged silly smiles.

"It's so good to see you, my dove."

I wanted to say it was good to be home, but I held back. "Where's Stan?" By then, my harshest criticisms of Stan had blurred and faded.

Vern smiled as if I were trying too hard. "I believe he's watching television." He lifted his cigarette and rolled the extra ash off the tip.

I peeked my head in the living room, and there he was, glued to the screen. "What are you watching?"

Stan burst into hysterical giggles as he listened to a silly jingle, "Brush your breath with Dentyne." It seemed nothing and everything had changed.

In the kitchen, smoke burned my nostrils. The rain had stopped, and outside the sky turned green—the air, still—as passing cars swished past on wet asphalt. I jerked open two windows, hoping for a cross-breeze.

"What did your grandparents have to say?" Vern asked.

"They suggested I let you take care of Stan. They thought I was protecting you too much."

"Me? Oh hell, you're not protecting me. Protecting me from what?"

"From Stanislaus," I whispered as I smiled. It seemed the answer to a riddle.

Vern had a peculiar look on his face. "We had a glorious time . . . cutting down weeds and honeysuckle along Distillery Creek. Chippie and Stan are getting along beautifully."

"No problems?" I glanced at Chippie. He was curled up and panting on a mat by the door, a welcome change from his typical deafening greeting. I was so happy to be home, to see Vern, and to know they had survived.

Vern had a sheepish look on his face. "Well, we did have one problem the day you left." He said his accountant, Tom had to stay late that day, so rather than leave Stan alone at the house, Vern had given Tom the keys to the office. A few hours later, the police had arrived, shouting through a bullhorn, "Come out with your hands up. The place is surrounded." He said someone had seen the light on in the building, and a couple of them had called the police. This was the blessing and curse of a small town. Everyone was in everyone else's business.

I didn't want to laugh, but it struck me as funny. Stan wasn't making trouble at all, but Vern's having to watch him had caused a near catastrophe at the hardware store. A catastrophe I normally would have prevented.

"Whatever," Vern said. "We need you *here*, darling."

For a moment I felt a twinge of manipulation, but I viewed it as taste testing—as Vern dipping a spoon in a saucepan and measuring for temperature and sweetness. It tickled me to see the ashtray in front of him overflowing with bent cigarette butts and small wads of chewing gum. The kitchen counter, clean when I left, was a cluttered, dirty mess. The house felt voluminous, a large empty space. I could hear the back door tapping against the casing.

Vern started to rise. "Let me help you with the suitcase."

"No, no, I'm fine," I said. "Call if you need me."

"I need you and I'm glad you're home."

I trudged up the stairs with my suitcase, and before I could put away my clothes, a door slammed.

Vern shouted, "Jesus Katy Christ, Stanislaus. Can't you see the mud on your feet? You need to take off your shoes."

I let out a faint laugh. *How did he get outside so fast?* I pointed my ear to the door, hoping to hear more, but that was the end of it. I flipped off my shoes and lay in bed, then hugged my pillow. It was so great to be home, to be a family again. And to have a solid plan.

That night, Vern sent Stan over to the Pences' so we could talk. I was clearing the dirty dishes and storing the leftovers when he pointed to the nearest chair. I sat down slowly, positioning my stomach so it wouldn't bump the table's edge. The directive felt like a return to childhood. The days when my father lined us up, all five of us, to interrogate about who had gouged the table or eaten the icing off the Kroger frozen cake in the freezer.

Vern edged one cigarette from its tight red pack and tapped it on the table. "We don't have to talk about your leaving," he said. "But I want to talk about Stan."

In that moment, I had a sneaking suspicion that what he *most* wanted to talk about was my leaving, but I went with it.

"I'm going to tell his mother we will put him in public school," he said. "If she allows it, which I don't believe will happen, we will send him to school here."

I immediately thought of my grandmother's warning that Vern might be difficult. I smirked. It was obvious Vern was still chapped by my departure. He hadn't appreciated my turning into a stage manager of what he considered a short mockumentary, co-opting Ruth and Ann to embarrass him.

I swallowed my last swig of iced tea from dinner. "Yes, we discussed school."

"I want to call her on Friday, the day for hiring and firing." He said this as if he were going to break the news to Stan's mother gently, so as not to upset her too much.

Something inside me cringed, but I tried not to show it. I knew the subtext. Vern wanted to wrestle with me. He was setting a familiar trap that had defined me as a child. A trap of argue, guilt, and Kim to the rescue. Defending myself or arguing would be walking into the trap that I knew would end with Vern's digging in his heels and Stan's staying longer.

"Sounds good." I tried to sound nonchalant. "Whatever you decide is fine with me." I emptied my ice in the sink. "Is that all?"

"That's all, my dove," he said.

CHAPTER 25

I woke one morning to Vern's gravelly voice chatting with our neighbor Margene, who was pruning her vine-clenched chain-link fence. The happy tone in Margene's voice told me he was inviting her to The Point.

Suddenly, I was wide awake. I leapt out of bed, threw on some baggy clothes, and scrambled down the stairs. There was no way the other house at The Point could be ready in one week. With a couple of broken windows, damaged screens, and mold on many of the walls, the project would take several people, and Vern's handymen, Herman and Margene's son, Tony, were busy with other jobs. Not only that, but the natural pool wasn't even filled, and the gate was still broken. Had he really invited her? I loved Margene, but cleaning up that house was one more thing to add to our list when we were already overextended.

At the bottom of the stairs, I stopped, adjusted my belt, and took a deep breath. I told myself that our baby was *my* new project. *I* didn't need to paint the house at The Point. *I* didn't need to get the place ready for visitors. There were scores of people looking for jobs in Hillsboro. Even my brother Rick and honorary brother Carlos could help whip the other house at The Point into shape. So I would fix myself some breakfast and then make it clear to Margene that Vern was underestimating the time required to get the house ready. If she wanted to come anyway, that would be her decision.

I couldn't wait to see Ruth. On my way to the family room to say hello, I peeked my head in the powder room and felt an instant panic in my gut. The seat was soaked with urine.

But then I took a deep breath and said, "Zippidy-doo-da."

I banged the door shut, giddy with excitement. It felt strange to be home, to see Ruth dusting a painted wooden bird as if this were any other day when it seemed my whole life had changed.

"Hi, Ruth."

Her mind was somewhere else; she recoiled when she saw me. "I'm so glad you're here," she said. "He missed you. He can't handle this." Her voice was contemplative but neutral. It took me a while to understand exactly what she was saying.

"You mean he can't handle Stan?"

Her lips pressed together. I think she was expecting life to return to our previous version of normal now that I was home. She glanced through the sliding glass doors; Margene was back to pruning her vines, and Vern was striding toward us.

I took a step closer so she could hear me. "I have a new plan, Ruth. We're going to let Stan do what he wants, and we're not going to clean up after him. You should see the toilet seat right now, but don't touch it. That goes for gum on the furniture and muddy footprints on the floor, anything else like that. I want to leave it all for Vern."

Ruth glared over her oversize glasses. "He's not gonna like it."

"That's what we want. We want him to not like it." My emotional conversion felt colder than a dive into a freezing cold pool.

Vern stepped onto the back porch.

"Morning, Ruth." Vern dashed past us on his way to the powder room. He flipped on the fan and poked his head out. "Don't you ladies have chickens to pick?"

He didn't wait for an answer. He locked himself inside the powder room, and Ruth swatted at his books with her cloth.

His voice rang out like an alarm. "Goddammit!"

"Oh Lord have mercy." Ruth ran her rag over the shelves as sparkling dust particles floated in lines of light.

She and I locked eyes for a moment, and I covered my laughter with my hand. I made my way toward the kitchen. As I passed the powder room, feeling powerful, I rubbed it in; through the crack in the door, I asked, "You okay, Vern?"

He answered the way he often did when I banged on the bathroom door. "I told ya I loved ya, now get out." Years later I learned these were the lyrics to a popular song sung ten years before I was born by a singer named Anita O'Day whom I'd never heard of. What the lyrics meant to me was that Vern was back to being Vern.

Ruth wandered into the kitchen. Sometimes when I talked to her, she had a way of pretending she wasn't paying attention, going about her dusting or scrubbing as I jabbered away. But I knew she took in everything.

"Maybe he can't help it," she said about Stan, her back to me as she stacked dishes.

"He *can* help it." I explained that even disabled kids can learn to use the toilet without making a mess.

Ruth lowered her voice. "Did I ever tell you I ate dirt?" Her voice was conversational.

"What?"

"Yeah." She nodded. "When I was pregnant, I would take a spoon and go outside, and find a good spot, and swallow a spoonful. My mother got mad. She would holler and I would hide. But I couldn't help it."

She dropped her ample breasts over the kitchen sink and sank her hands in the warm, sudsy water. Steam rose and clung to her like winter moisture on a window.

"It's not the same, Ruth."

She removed her glasses and wiped them with the hem of her knit top. There was a luminosity in her brown skin, a gentleness in her voice. "Girl, you're brave."

I shook my head. "This is a survival technique, that's all." I dug my hand into one of the lower drawers of the refrigerator, pulled out some blueberries, and sprinkled them on my oatmeal.

I believed that Ruth was clairvoyant. She knew everything. The way she laughed, I intuited that she approved of my plan.

I had just set my bowl on the table when I noticed her eyes fixed on the yard. Stan darted across the grass toward the driveway, chasing a squirrel.

"Does he know Mr. Fairley's looking for him?" She wiped her wet hands with a clean towel. Now that I'd backed off, Ruth had become more focused on what Stan was doing—which, I realized, wasn't all that bad.

"Nothing to worry about," I said in a low voice. "Think of this as a show."

"Think of *what* as a show?" Vern hurried into the kitchen. He kissed me with my mouth full of food, and I detected a faint smell of laundry starch under his shroud of smoke and perspiration. I felt my skin prickle. He wore a short-sleeved Brooks Brothers shirt, frayed at the collar, and a pair of khakis. As he gathered several papers from the counter and table, he said, "The world is too much with us, darling."

Vern's recitation of early-nineteenth-century poetry seemed an attempt at reconciliation. I read it as his code for *We are still together and I still love you, despite the conflict.*

"Where's the little rascal, anyway?"

I swallowed one last bite and handed Ruth my bowl. This was my cue to get up and leave. While I hunted behind a box on the counter for my purse, Vern said Margene and her family would be coming to The Point in a few weeks, and I nodded.

Vern was about to sneak away. He gathered a stack of papers into a file. "I'm off," he said, and then realized I was on my way out too. "Where are you going, honey?"

"Cincinnati," I said. "Why?"

"What about Stan?"

"What *about* him?" I shook my head, feigning confusion.

"You know I found Ben's damn bike on the street side of our lilac bushes? He's lucky it's rusty and not tempting to thieves." He reached in the cabinet for a glass and filled it with tap water. "Well, I have to get to the bank. I have a meeting."

I positioned the strap of my purse on my shoulder. "Okay. Well . . . have a good one. Bye, Ruth." I weaved past her and into the hallway.

"Wait. What about Stan?" Vern asked again. "Where is he?"

I shrugged and headed for the back door.

Vern tossed a pen in the air, and it snapped on the Formica counter. He followed me into the family room, where he cocked his head to one side and frowned. "Come on, honey. You know I can't take him with me."

"Wow," I said, thinking of Peggy's suggestion. All I wanted was to throw my arms around Vern, to kiss his freshly shaved skin, to squeeze him. But I put on my look of serious contemplation. "I'm sure one of the ladies up at the hardware store would watch him. You'll figure it out." My tone was gentle but unapologetic.

Had I not gone to Cincinnati, things might have turned out differently. But I did. I tore off down Route 138 with the side window open, my left elbow resting on the door and my right hand on the wheel, my hair billowing every which way. The seatbelt was tight and my feet swollen, but I knew I would be treated well at the maternity shop, and I wiggled my toes in anticipation.

I loved the drive from Hillsboro to Cincinnati. I loved the curves and roller coaster drops, the small farms with their grazing cattle, the gray, unpainted barns buttressed by silos and stacks of tractor tires, the clumps of dandelions, and the heat rising from the asphalt. I inhaled the scent of hay and grain, then roses and sweet alyssum, like a dab of perfume behind each ear. I felt pride in Hillsboro—its stately older homes, a unique collection for such a small town. The Point, with its lovely setting, its incredible dam. I was one lucky woman. With parents, grandparents, siblings, friends. Lots of people who loved me. A nice house. A dog. A baby on the way. I had it all. Even a husband who was still hanging in there with me, despite my distancing act. If only I could get Vern to come back as an equal partner, I thought, my life would be perfect.

When I arrived in Cincinnati, I saw women with babies in strollers, women with older children, young women, old women, women of all shapes and sizes, and reminded myself of how strong I was. Most women wouldn't take on another woman's eleven-year-old boy; I knew they wouldn't. They would've been screaming and shouting a lot earlier. I was damn strong. I was generous. I was also resilient. Now, thanks to my grandparents and aunt, I was balancing my own needs with my desire to help Vern. I was optimistic—but it was a fragile optimism, reminding me of the way I used to hold my breath under a train on an overpass.

I was the only customer in the store that day. Racks filled with maternity clothes of every pattern and color imaginable filled the small space. The sales clerk—in her forties and stylish, with dark hair and eyeliner—brought me armloads of maternity clothes and commented on each outfit: *Not your type. Too young. Too serious. Too something or other.* She was an easy laugher, and her compliments sounded genuine. She saw more in me than a young pregnant woman with a worried look and an old man for a husband.

I twisted and twirled, throwing my shoulders back, in front of the three-way mirror. I tucked my brown hair behind my ears and rubbed out the deep vertical crease between my eyebrows. When my legs ached, I put my feet up on a stool in the dressing room and allowed myself to feel nurtured, as I had with my grandparents.

I hardly thought at all about Stan and Vern and what they might be doing. Until I was about to pay for the clothes and glanced down at an open page of the *Cincinnati Enquirer* near the register. Tucked into page two was a small article reminding parents of measles vaccinations required before their children could attend school. The article focused on preschool, but I couldn't help but wonder about Stan.

"Thank you so much," I said before leaving the store.

She accompanied me to the door like I was a houseguest.

I drove home in a party mood. Upon entering the back door, I felt as if the house were charged with electricity, like flicking a switch would blow a circuit. Would there be a confrontation? A crisis of some sort?

The TV was blaring. Stan knelt in the living room, five feet from a Western rerun. In the kitchen, with the oxygen tank turned off, its plastic tube wrapped around the tank like a noose, Vern was sleeping with his head down.

"I learned something interesting today on my trip," I said, startling him.

"Well, how do?" He sat up straight and pitched his shoulders back. "How was Cincinnati?" His laugh turned into a soggy cough that he covered with his fist.

I unwrapped the tubing, unscrewed the nozzle, and handed him the nasal cannula. Then I leaned down and kissed him on the neck. "Did you know Stan will have to get vaccinated before he can attend school?"

"Hadn't thought of it," he said, "but I expect he shall."

I clicked open the refrigerator and started slicing into some cheese. Stan hurried in from the living room.

"Have you been vaccinated?" Vern asked him.

He shook his head. "I don't know."

Vern sighed. "We'll have to find out, I reckon."

"*We* won't have to find out. *You* will have to find out." I gave him a sly smile.

Vern returned to his book but looked up again after a few moments. At first he said, "The game is over, darling"—but when

I didn't respond, he continued to make his point. "I've told you before, but I'll risk repeating. You can go back to the dear, sweet girl I married. If Stan attends school, everything will change. I'm sure you're aware that you'll have more time." He was gentle and unhurried, but authoritative. After a long pause, he added, "I'm missing the euphoria, darling."

"So am I, Vern," I said. "So am I."

Vern waited to see if I would call the school to inquire about Stan. When I didn't, he took his time and then called. He had a list of items he intended to discuss with Stan's mother and wanted to make sure he had all the facts. "If Stan has never received the proper vaccinations, that's a lot all at once," he said.

"Yup," I said. I wanted to acknowledge his efforts without adding my emotion. It wasn't that I was holding back—I still felt anxious—but I told myself this was a dance. Each time Vern stepped toward me, I stepped back.

Vern dialed Ruthann's number, and I busied myself in the kitchen, tiptoeing as I put away the dishes and wiped off the counter. I'd been following my grandparents' advice and letting everything go to hell. It's hard to say if it was serendipity, his getting his medication balanced, or the reduction in tension between us, but Vern's ankles were no longer swollen, his skin no longer gray. I expected him to surprise me this time.

He sat up straight at the table, nervously scribbling on a yellow notepad, a radiant smile on his face for most of the call. At first there were lots of yeses and howevers. But I found myself paying less attention than usual. "Thank you," Vern said at one point, which I considered a good sign. He then explained to Ruthann that Stan would have to attend school as long as he stayed with us.

But something wasn't right. Vern set his cigarette on a small plate and closed his eyes as he listened. When he opened his eyes, he said, "Yes . . . yes . . . okay . . . we'll make do."

As he placed the receiver on its hook, I felt my stomach drop. His complexion had reddened; his body had stiffened. He dug into the back of the cabinet for a glass tumbler and set it on the counter with a thud. He grabbed two ice cubes with his bare hand and poured himself a scotch.

"What happened? What did she say?"

He shook his head slowly, holding up his index finger.

"What?"

The call had harvested Vern's limited wind. He hunted for his inhaler and shot a puff of albuterol into his lungs. He coughed and gasped, then downed his scotch in a single swig, as if it were medicine. He sat down and sighed. "On August twentieth she had to pay for her half of the property, plus everything else: legal expenses, court costs, back tax. She couldn't do it. She asked for an extension."

"And?"

"Well . . . she started crying." Vern looked tenderly at me. "Her tears got to me."

"Okay." *And what about my tears?* They apparently hadn't done a damn thing for him. Was it our age difference? Was he treating me the way he treated his kids? Or was he missing his relationship with Caroline and therefore connecting to this woman, Ruthann, who had lost her partner too?

I couldn't go there. It was too hard to entertain these thoughts, though I still wonder about them today. He must've felt as isolated as I did.

I listened without letting the emotion swallow me. Vern's hands were shaking.

"She quoted from the Bible. Something like 'You shall not afflict any widow or fatherless child.' She repeated herself over and over."

I rubbed my stomach as I listened. Something had changed since my trip to Massachusetts. I was no longer making a mental checklist of all the problems since Stan's arrival. The heavy weight of the previous months was now on Vern's shoulders. "It's not your fault, Vern."

"I don't know what else to do, darling." He seemed to be implying that Ruthann was doing everything she could to resolve her legal troubles, and we had to do our part too. "She said she's gotten thin and frail, that it's affecting her health."

"It's affecting ours too," I said, but I didn't shout. I tried to breathe and slow my thoughts. I told myself, *No defense. No argument. This is Vern's decision. Vern's deal. I will let it blow through me.* "What about school?" I finally asked. "And vaccinations?"

"You heard the conversation."

"No. I heard *you*, but you didn't say much."

Vern snapped his lighter a couple of times, unable to get a spark. "She said it was more than a farm, that she was fighting over principles." Vern's eyelids drooped; he took in a deep breath, clearly expecting me to say something, but I didn't. "Goddammit," he said. "I need a new lighter."

I could tell Vern sympathized with Ruthann's frustration. I did too, in part. Working the organic farm sounded like a messy business. Vern said her neighbors had complained the house was an eyesore, was lowering the value of their property. She had sent us an article that had run in the *Hartford Courant* a year earlier that described her house: "The roof sags, the siding is mildewed, tall grass overwhelms a broken picket fence, an abandoned car sits in the yard and chickens meander about the entrance." One of the neighbors, who'd asked that his name not be used, had said, "We'd like to get her out of the house, the neighborhood and the town before the house goes to wrack and ruin." These were the kinds of comments people in Hillsboro used to rationalize tearing down historic buildings.

Through my work in historic preservation, I knew the benefits of saving old structures, especially the long-term financial benefits. But I also couldn't count the number of times I'd heard someone say, "You can't fight progress." It seemed Ruthann was leading the preservationist charge, and we were her troops in the field, managing her son.

"She's filing another appeal," Vern said, as if Ruthann was close to winning her case. He seemed to be trying to convince himself as he thumbed through a stack of her letters on the kitchen table.

"What about Stan?"

Vern's mind was in Connecticut, on the organic farm, or perhaps in San Francisco, where he'd met Stan's father.

"Stan, Vern. Did you hear me? What about Stan?"

"Well, I think she was resigned." Vern stared down at the table, glassy-eyed. "Her exact words were 'I don't like it, but I guess you'll have to put him in school.'"

CHAPTER 26

Vern was afraid to tell Stan about school. He sat in the living room, smoking and making comments while Stan watched TV—"Hillsboro has a good school system. Maybe you'd enjoy it. Have you talked to Nina about her class?"

Like me, Vern worried Stan would feel rejected by his mother the moment he heard the news. I tried to go there in my mind, to feel what Stan must be feeling as Vern dropped hints. It was easy. All I had to do was imagine my parents at the front door, kissing us good-bye—"You kids be good. Call if you need us"—before carrying their boxes of samples and food for their next two weeks out to the motorhome.

I stood with one foot in the hallway, raging inside at the thought of Stan's living with us longer. *This will blow over*, I told myself. It had to. I needed to let Vern deal with the logistics of his attending school. But the situation was beginning to feel permanent. As if Ruthann were giving us her son. I thought I should throw glasses and plates and show Vern just how unhinged I could get, but I couldn't muscle up the emotion. Instead, I repeated my grandparents' advice in my head—*Let everything go, let everything go, let everything go.*

"Maybe Nina would like to play with you," I told Stan.

I'd heard from my father that Stan had been difficult at the Festival of Bells. He had stopped by my parents' booth—they were selling discontinued gift samples for ten cents on the dollar in front of Ayres Drugstore—with two other kids, presumably Nina and Tommy. My parents had encouraged him to help. "He was a pain in the ass," my father said. "Touching everything, not listening. I wanted to beat the living daylights out of him." But with all the activities we were juggling, I had failed to mention this to Vern.

"You had fun at the Festival of Bells, didn't you?" Vern asked Stan.

Stan rocked in place more slowly. "Yes, but I don't want to play with Nina."

"Why not?" Vern held his eyes on me, which seemed like encouragement.

"I've noticed you haven't been to the Wigwam lately either. What's going on?" I asked.

"I don't want to." As he bounced, his rhythm slowed to almost a dead stop, and I could feel my neck tensing. I should've said, "Wow," and let Vern handle this one, but I couldn't help myself. Despite the little voice inside telling me I should go upstairs and hide in my room, I wandered over to the Pences' to see if they knew anything.

Ann was uncharacteristically tight-lipped, which was weird.

"Did something happen with Stan?" I asked her. "He hasn't been over in a while."

"I should let Nina tell you." She shouted for Nina, who scrambled down the stairs and into the hallway. She seemed to know why I was there. "Tell Kim what you told me about Stan."

"What did Stan do?"

Nina, at almost thirteen, was easily ten years ahead of Stan in maturity. She tucked her long, wavy hair behind her ears and then pulled at her knit shirt, hemming and hawing, seemingly unsure if she should tell me. "I don't want to hang out with him anymore," she finally said.

"Why not? Did he hurt you? Was he rude?" I wasn't sure how to respond.

"I don't think he would do it, but . . ."

"What?"

"He scared us."

I gulped, trying to suppress my own fears about Stan. "Scared you how? You don't think he would do what?" I was thinking he must've threatened her in some way. *Did he try to kiss her or grab her or something?*

Nina's broad, capable shoulders seemed to collapse around her crossed arms.

"It's okay. You can tell her," Ann said. She smoothed the back of Nina's head.

"He said he's going to build a bomb."

"A what? A *bomb*?" My head jolted back. "That's ridiculous. He can't build a bomb."

But Ann and Nina looked serious. *Would an eleven-year-old know how to build a bomb with fertilizer?* I wondered. Was it possible he'd learned, working on the farm?

When Nina disappeared upstairs, I stood in Ann's hallway, shaking my head and looking down at the floor, trying to make light of the situation. "You know, Father Gude, a Catholic priest, lives out at The Point. He said he would pray for us, but so far it hasn't helped." I chuckled.

Ann was devastatingly direct. "Stan probably needs counseling, Kim."

I pushed open her squeaky screen door and stepped onto her concrete stoop.

"I'm sure he's harmless," she added, "but, you know, I have to think of Nina. I told her she didn't have to be friends with him anymore."

"Right." I nodded. I spoke through the screen door. "I'm trying to let Vern handle all this, but . . ."

Ann sighed. "How can I help?"

"You want an eleven-year-old boy?"

"No thank you." Ann laughed, but I detected a thread of sadness. She *was* happy to help but also happy to have her own problems and not mine. It seemed I'd taken a step backward. Once again, I was allowing myself to get disoriented in the problem-solving. Why couldn't I be more Buddhist—nonreactive? A patient observer of life and joy in the present? Was I intervening because I didn't trust Vern? Was I trying to prove I was right about Stan?

"You know what I'm thinking?" I said to Ann. "Maybe I should report this news to Vern and then stay out of it." He was only eleven. Surely he was boasting. How would he know how to build a bomb?

"Good call," she said.

I took a long, slow walk across our narrow, tree-lined street, telling myself I had done my research. I didn't need to kill the mood at home or come up with a backup plan. Stan was still Vern's baby.

Vern sat at the kitchen table without his teeth, nursing a bourbon. His eyes looked bloodshot; his maroon cardigan was riddled with cigarette burns.

"Nina doesn't want to play with Stan anymore," I said.

Vern pretended he didn't hear. "School is a sticky wicket."

I knew the old Kim would have responded with an obvious suggestion, but instead, I shrugged. I felt sneaky and dishonest and manipulative at the same time. Something about his uncertainty made me want to hug him. But I didn't. I sensed he detected my coolness.

"Tell me, darling. Why *doesn't* Nina want to play with Stan?"

I could feel the discomfort gathering in my chest. "You should ask *him*," I said. But I was tempted to get into it again. Did I have no restraint at all?

Vern gave me a crooked smile. "What is it, darling?" He set his bourbon on the table.

"You want *me* to tell you?" I wanted him to drag it out of me.

He reached for his JTS Brown in a lower cabinet as he locked eyes on me.

"Nina told me he wanted to build a bomb."

"Oh, for Christsake." Vern's shoulders dropped, and he dramatically swung the bottle onto the kitchen counter.

"It's confusing, isn't it?" I nervously straightened papers on the counter. "Do you believe it?"

"That he would say that? Yes."

"No. That he would build a bomb."

"Of course not. How's he going to build a *bomb*?" Vern looked disgusted with me for the suggestion. "He's showing off, that's all. Things are going well for him, finally."

I rolled my eyes. Things were far from going well. We had an eleven-year-old animal abuser, arsonist orphan who'd never been to school, and we were signing him up to live with us beyond early February, when the baby was due. I knew there was no end ahead for our problems.

I reminded myself that I'd handed Stan back to Vern. If there was any hope of sending him home, Vern was the one to do it.

CHAPTER 27

Word traveled fast in Hillsboro. Or maybe Mom and Dad just drove by and noticed my car. I was upstairs, folding tired clothing into brown paper bags, preparing to load my winter clothes in the closet, when the doorbell rang.

I figured it was a delivery of some kind. But Mom and Dad were in the driveway, huddled near the back door. Mom wore a polyester pantsuit, unbuttoned in front; Dad, a pair of khaki pants with a blue button-down oxford shirt. They had come from a sales appointment.

"What in the hell were you thinking?" Dad said.

I chuckled. "Hey, great to see you too." I knew they would've wanted me to call when I first got home, but something had stopped me. Maybe it was fear of their joining forces with Vern, or fear they'd want to get more involved in our conflict. Whatever the case, I tried to hide the tiny part of me that wasn't overjoyed to see them.

"Can we come in?" Dad stood behind Mom, uncharacteristically hesitant, and he and I fell into a clumsy embrace.

I led them into the living room where we sat, awkwardly, feeling cold. Or maybe it was just that *I* was. Completely out of character, I offered them each a drink of JTS Brown and 7 Up. These were the first alcoholic drinks I'd ever made for my parents as an adult, and I expected them to be shocked, since I'd made an announcement as a teenager that I would never serve them an alcoholic drink again. Instead, they just sat there, straight-faced.

Dad drained half of his drink before finally saying, "Did you have to fly off to Massachusetts?" He wore his hurt in his shoulders, which were shoved up into his neck like he was about to punch someone.

"If I'd known you could help, I would've called. You said you were busy all summer." I leaned back on the sofa, my feet up on the coffee table, as they sipped their drinks in Caroline's wingback chairs. "How is it going with the boys?" I asked. I assumed I would hear Dad's version of the BVD underwear or the condoms in the toilet, because it wasn't like him to miss an opportunity to tell that kind of a story. Instead, he launched into a new tale about how he and Mom arrived home from a business trip to find a giant hole in the wall of their bedroom. It was a silhouette of a head, a neck, and a torso.

"We were sure it was Rick," Mom said, "but David did it."

"What do you mean?" Rick was twice the size of David, and twice as strong. It didn't make sense.

Mom started to giggle. She said the boys got into a fight and David had finally had enough of being pushed around.

"And so what are you saying?"

Dad's smile withered. "We're saying David slammed Rick through the wall."

"Your father has been leaving the hole in the drywall so he can show it off to everyone," Mom said. "He invited Mike—you know, Mike the UPS man—to come in and see it." Mike had been Mom and Dad's friend ever since their dog, Mustard, had shredded the seat of Mike's pants during a delivery.

"We've been busy," Mom said. "Rick and David and their problems have been the least of our worries." She went on to mention all the places they'd traveled and to describe their business as "coming out from under a cloud, finally."

"But no matter how busy we are, you should call us," Dad said. "That was embarrassing, hearing you were in Massachusetts with my parents."

Dad usually enjoyed a good conflict, but my visit to his parents had clearly stirred up something in him. He started to grin, though, as the alcohol began to work its way through his veins. "Are they, um, doing okay? My parents? Were they nice? Were they helpful? What are they doing these days? How was Peggy?" He had a slew of questions.

I'd grown up hearing plenty of negative stories about my grandparents—they'd been "cruel, selfish, too demanding and controlling." But when I praised Mom-Mom and Pop-Pop now, mentioning how welcoming and helpful they'd been, my father loosened up; his shoulders relaxed, and he even seemed pleased. "I'm glad. It's good you felt you could go to them."

I'd never heard Dad sound so generous about his parents. His words buzzed in my ears like an apology. He guzzled the rest of his drink as he stared at me. "Sonuvabitch. I'm sorry. We should've been there for you. Are you doing okay with the pregnancy?"

I nodded. I didn't bring up Stan. I hadn't enjoyed their past efforts to problem-solve for me and wasn't about to start now.

Dad made some joke about Vern, about how he spoke in riddles and it wasn't always easy to understand him. He said, "I'm still sorry for pushing so hard with Vern about Ben." He flicked back the hair from his cowlick.

"That was ages ago," I said. "Not a problem."

"Sometimes you talk too much, Dick," Mom said. "And on that note . . ." She stood and waved him toward the hallway. "Come on. We need to get home so I can get dinner started."

Escorting Dad from the living room, we passed the totem pole, its tall black, red, and blue figures looming over us, and a weird chill passed through me. Vern and I still had only talked around the details of the tragedy. He'd never told me about that night Ben died. But it was comforting to see Mom and Dad. Their openness, their willingness to discuss anything, had been one of the reasons I'd felt sure they'd accept my marriage to Vern long before he'd driven out to meet them.

I patted Dad on one shoulder. "Vern is sensitive about Ben. It has nothing to do with you, Dad. But I'll tell him what you said."

Dad was three paces behind Mom. When we got to the door, he looked back as if he'd forgotten something.

"What is it?" I asked.

"I'm curious about something, Butch. You know Charlie Jordan?"

Charlie was a well-known realtor in town, and Mom and Dad's secretary's husband. I nodded.

"Do you know if he was in Vern's class in school?"

"No, Dad." I smiled as I patted him again. "I would give up on guessing Vern's age if I were you."

As the September's weather grew colder and darker, I felt more restless. Decisions related to Stan and school were now Vern's bailiwick and I should've been less stressed, but I wasn't. Stan would be entering the fifth or sixth grade. Had Vern registered him? It seemed to be all or nothing with Stan. I now had no idea what was going on.

When Vern quietly stepped into the kitchen, the crinkle of his keys in his pocket made me so anxious I'd tremble for several minutes. At night, I would toss and turn with restless leg syndrome. In the morning, jaw sore, I bit my nails to the nub, my brain concocting irrational fears of what might be going on in my body. Was the stress finally getting to me now that I was letting Vern handle everything? Were my bodily aches and pains related to the pregnancy or something more sinister? Something in the water or food we were eating? With less stress, I should be feeling better. It didn't make sense.

One night, Vern said he wanted to talk about Stan. We sat on the front stoop, and as I listened, I scraped lines in the brick steps with the points of overhanging holly leaves.

"I don't believe there's a need to further discuss the bomb," he said smoothly, deftly.

"Wow." I waited.

"They may have to test him." Vern drummed a fresh cigarette on the brick step beneath us as we glanced across the street.

"You talking about the school starting soon? They have to test his aptitude?"

"Well, yes. I'm having doubts. Maybe it was a mistake to keep Stan so long. We should've asked him what *he* wanted to do." Vern looked thinner and more frail than I'd seen him.

I wasn't sure what to say. In my determination to make room for Vern to be more proactive, it was as if I were letting the current sweep me downstream and was no longer prepared for the rocks. "There's nothing you can do," I said, and there really *wasn't* anything Vern could do, short of sending Stan home. I felt sorry for Stan but also for Vern. My distancing act was working; I needed to keep letting things fall apart. But it hurt. Vern was battling at the hardware store, battling at the bank, battling his health, battling the aftermath of his first marriage, and now battling me. Worst of all, he hadn't yet digested the idea of a new child.

There's a sense of peace that comes with finally waving the white flag, with giving up the fight. It doesn't happen instantly, but after more than a week at home, waving the white flag was beginning to feel good. Vern had been a faraway train stuck on the tracks. As we stared at each other, somewhere in my mind, I detected a faint *whoop-whoop* of a whistle, felt the vibration of the rails and the *trup-trup-trup* of the tired train about to start moving.

"There *is* something I can do," he said. "I can call the old rip and tell her I've changed my mind. It's too damned much." Vern winked as he put his hand on the black metal railing. He looked determined and, finally, sure of what he wanted to do.

I was thinking, *Wait, what? Did I hear you correctly?* There was no last straw. "Vern, are you *sure* about this?" Inside, I was tingling.

He didn't wait for my reaction. With his foot he crushed his cigarette on the brick, pushed up from the step, and returned to the kitchen to phone the Pences.

A moment later, Stan was in our kitchen.

Stan seemed to anticipate what Vern was about to say. He bounced off the walls, scuffing his shoes, his gaze riveted on our two mourning doves, who were bobbing their heads in unison outside our bay window.

"Stan?" I tried to get his attention.

He swiveled on one foot, glancing back and forth at us. "Yes, ma'am."

Vern pointed. "Have a seat." He grabbed a tissue to wipe his nose, then donned the oxygen cannula.

I nervously wiped loose ash off the table with a damp sponge. Stan's chair sounded a rhythmic clap as he rocked back and forth on an uneven patch of flooring.

Elbows on the table, I covered my eyes with my hands. All I could think was how Stan's mother was putting us through a test, maybe unwittingly. I felt a tug of guilt, then remorse, and when I opened my eyes, I was carving ashy lines in Vern's ashtray with my fork.

Vern poured water from the tap and topped it off with scotch. "We realize your mother has some trouble at home with all her legal battles," he said. "But school starts here soon, and you will need to return to Connecticut."

Stan nodded. He looked calmer and more confident. Relieved. He looked less like Dennis the Menace and more like I imagined my own child might react.

"So I will call your mother over the weekend and arrange for your return." Vern's voice seemed to tremble.

"So you mean I'm going home this weekend?" With his hands in his lap, Stan batted his long, skinny legs together. He quivered in his chair.

"Hopefully, Monday morning," Vern said. "I'll see what I can work out."

Stan leapt from his seat and was about to disappear into the living room when he turned to face us. "Is that all?" There was a buoyancy in his voice.

We both nodded. I had no words for Stan. I had no words for Vern, either. I sat for a moment, feeling weak, somewhat dizzy—in shock, I suppose. After all my obsessing about how much I wanted Stan gone, he was finally going to leave, and now I felt panicked. I was reminded of the endless moments as a teenager when the five of us would count the days until my parents would leave to go back on the road. Then, as they pulled away from the driveway, for some strange reason, I'd have an impulse to run out to the motorhome and shout, "Wait! Wait! You forgot something . . . me!" It was a weird sense of panic. I didn't want them and I did.

And just as in those days, as Stan wandered toward the television to catch a few shows before I prepared dinner, my first impulse was to reach into our wooden kitchen cabinet, pull out the Baker's chocolate, and bake a batch of brownies.

CHAPTER 28

As I descended the stairs the morning of Stan's departure, I could hear Chippie yapping. Upon poking my head in the family room, I found him dancing around Stan, nipping at his shoelaces, as if this were Stan's first day and not his last. Most of Chippie's shaved hair had grown back. Stan leaned over to pet him, the two now apparently the best of friends.

I was five months pregnant. Summer was winding down and school was about to start. In so many ways, our lives had changed and not changed. My brain was no longer addled but clear. I felt both sorrowful and relieved—sorrowful because I knew Stan was returning to mayhem and relieved because I no longer had to protect him from it.

I sat on one of the kitchen chairs, shaking out the pressure in my legs as if I were warming up for a swimming sprint. Vern held his hand on my knee to settle me and leaned in to kiss me on the cheek.

"Stan has been waiting a long time for this day. You may have been right all along about his wanting to go home," he said. "I don't suppose you'd want to drive him to the airport?"

I inhaled and sighed audibly. "Sure."

"I'm kidding. I want you to stay here, darling. I'll drive him. You do something for Kim. Plan the nursery, read a book, go for a walk. You have a lot to decide over the next few months."

I reached out to hug Vern. With my arms tucked under his, I felt the heat of his cleanly shaven neck, the drumming of his heart against me. Vern was back and I could feel it.

I fixed the two of them a huge breakfast of bacon, scrambled eggs, orange juice—no milk—and toast, then followed Stan and Vern to the back door, where I hugged Stan good-bye.

"Have a safe trip. Write to us," I said. "Keep in touch." I fluffed his hair, and his long, narrow face hardly moved. But this time, I sensed a difference. He looked happier; his eyes were more expressive.

Vern tipped his imaginary hat. He held open the door for Stan, who whizzed past us and into the Nissan like the Road Runner evading Wile E. Coyote. As Vern backed the car into the street, Stan hooted and hollered. Vern honked, Stan waved. Blood rushed into my head.

From the moment I'd met Stan, I'd wanted rest. To watch him, to hear him, to be near him, had exhausted me. Now he was gone, and I thought I'd feel lighter, more energetic—but I didn't. I had expected an instant recovery. But to be a mother was not an easy task, and to be a mother to another woman's child, it seemed, was exponentially more difficult. In the last few months, I had often hidden in our bedroom to contain my grousing or to recover from the drain of instant motherhood. Now that Stan was gone, I felt the same urge.

Instead of hiding out, I went straight to the phone to call Ann. On the kitchen counter was a torn yellow-lined page from a legal pad. On it, Vern had written, "This ticket entitles you to two lunches or dinners at the Maisonette or three lunches at Izzy Kadetz or four lunches or dinners at the Wooden Spoon. Theater, Symphony, or Opera optional with the Maisonette entrée. Offer expires 12/25/82."

In a reverent whisper, I prayed, "Thank you, God." Then I picked up the phone and dialed Ann.

When she picked up, the tone in her voice told me she'd seen them leave.

"He's gone," I said. "I can't believe it, but he's really gone. Thank you so much. I can hardly believe how much you've helped me."

Ann laughed, and I felt both lighter and restless. "It wasn't my help. It was you. It was your following through," she said. "Congratulations."

Vern returned a few hours later. I was sprawled on the maroon couch in the family room with my feet up, thinking about my grandparents and all the great advice they'd imparted. I felt more experienced, as if Stan were a hurdle of adulthood, preparing me for the arrival of my own child.

Vern had a grayish pallor. He reeked of cigarettes. He took one look at me and asked what was wrong. He said he hadn't returned Stan to Connecticut just to see me depressed.

"I'm not at all depressed," I said, kissing him.

For a moment, I wondered if he was regretting his decision. Regretting his standing firm, feeling he'd somehow let Stan down. But I think now it was the long view. It was Vern's understanding of the brevity of moments with others. The way you wake up one day and realize you don't have much time left—that even though you did your best, your contribution was, in the end, rather small.

"I'm fine. And tired," I said. "Did it go okay?"

"It went well. Stan was happy to go."

"Then what's wrong?"

"Nothing's wrong," he said. "I'm okay if you're okay."

But Vern wasn't okay. I was delighted Stan was gone but heartbroken Vern seemed to be focusing again on Ben. Or at least, that was my hunch. There was a cool breeze, and I glimpsed a spiraling of red and yellow leaves through the sliding glass door. Chippie wandered in, his long nails clicking the linoleum. He scratched the rug, making himself a bed. I removed the back cushions so we'd have more room, and Vern lay down close to me, across from the wall of hand-carved and painted birds. He glanced up at the towering totem pole.

We had been through something. It was impossible to know exactly what was going on for Vern. He looked weak and more fragile than before he left. I could feel his heart pounding. Sending Stan home was removing the bandage on an old wound.

The day the wallpaper arrived for the nursery, I called to arrange for its installation. Tony and Herman helped move Ben's furniture to the warehouse. I folded the curtains and rolled up the rug. I'd made a habit of rushing through Ben's room, hardly looking at any of his belongings, but this time, I sat with them on the bare wood floor, sorting objects into boxes. I went through everything, item by item, turning them over as I examined them closely. It wasn't all ammunition and weaponry, as I'd thought. There was a small lamp made from a ship's lantern, a toy car he'd made as a Scout, a wooden snake, a coin collection, a trophy and medals, and puppets. These were the kinds of objects I hoped my own child would collect. I'd never seen so many interesting rocks and shells. Ben had learned to ski and sail, play football and baseball.

The more I looked, the more I ruminated about whether or not I'd have a boy who would value this stuff the way he did. Or a girl. Maybe she'd be a tomboy who'd roam the woods, climb the tall oaks, or collect knives. Maybe she'd be interested in the martial arts, in how to protect herself. With Stan gone, my mind was clear to imagine an infinite number of possibilities. I carefully assembled each item in three large plastic hardware boxes and stacked the boxes in the bare closet.

With the room empty, I imagined soft blankets flung over Vern's grandfather's rocking chair, a colorful mobile overhanging the crib, a handful of toys, cushy stuffed animals, teething rings, and wooden blocks. Music playing "Rock-A-Bye Baby," the sweet perfume of laundered diapers, light streaming in through the window, and our future—wide open, expansive, and, most of all, hopeful.

CHAPTER 29

We continued to make occasional trips to The Point, but when the weather grew too cold for showers under the waterfall, we packed our things, locked up the house, and, with some reluctance, settled back into town. The warm weather had flown by too fast. The window to prepare for the baby was about to close—it was now November—and we never had gotten around to filling the pool. Still, there would be next year. There were upstairs rooms to be painted at the Highland House Museum, meetings of the Esoteric Club, and Lamaze class with Vern to prepare for the baby. Susan Henry from the Esoteric Club and Madeleine Crouse, Ann's sister-in-law, had even offered to host a baby shower.

To me, it seemed Vern and I were back. There was still time to plant bulbs, bake a pumpkin pie, and replace the wilting impatiens with colorful chrysanthemums.

Ben's room sat silent and sleepy—much larger than I expected, but cozy and perfect. It made good sense as the nursery since it was a part of a Jack and Jill configuration and connected to our room by a small bathroom.

Vern had encouraged me to do the planning. He had seen my wallpaper choice, and we'd discussed the use of glossy white for the woodwork. Still, I couldn't wait to show him the completed package.

So, one night, I invited him to take a look. I pulled him up the stairs, holding his hand like a child excited to show what Santa Claus had brought. I had purchased a soft rug that had that new-carpet-adhesive smell. The wallpaper, mostly white, was washable for little hands and set off by brilliant white and folding louvered shutters that let in plenty of light. Even the adjacent bathroom looked brighter. Most of all it looked authentic, respecting the house and its history.

We rested on the landing, and Vern seemed to brace himself. "Just a moment," he said as he caught his breath. My stomach was in a pucker, all jittery with enthusiasm. This was my gift to the baby but also to Vern.

When we reached the top of the stairs, he glanced into the room and stopped abruptly.

"What's the story?" I asked. "You seem disappointed."

"No, not at all." He took a moment to catch his breath, then dug in his trousers for his inhaler, shook it, and took a few puffs.

I stepped around him and into the room, holding up my arms. "Do you like it?"

"Lovely," he said. "You did a magnificent job."

"Come in and look," I said. "Did you see the cradle?" His mother had saved a late-eighteenth-century walnut cradle with four rounded finials and a carved-out heart at either end. Vern had said he'd slept in it as a baby. There was also a crib—painted bright white—that had been stored up at the hardware store and now sat in the corner between the two windows. *Had Caroline and Vern bought the crib for Ben?* I tried to block the thought. I wanted so badly to celebrate our new child that my mind erased what it could of those reminders. The closer we got to the birth of our baby, the more I wanted to pretend the Ben tragedy had never happened.

Maybe Vern picked up on this. Maybe my steering away from conversation about Ben caused Vern to hold on more tightly to what was left of him.

Fresh light danced on the new carpet, but Ben's secrets, questions, loves, and resentments were still tied up in that room. I could feel him. His twin bed, his dresser, his belongings were all gone, but he was still there, taking up space. I felt a wave of sadness for the child inside me, but I understood. Of course the moment would feel bittersweet for Vern. He'd said he wanted me to design the room the way I wanted, but we were still in those dark days of winter when you prune the garden and you know it's going to look barren and stark for a while. I had forged ahead, and Vern wasn't ready for the change.

He scanned the room for a long time. "It's lovely, darling. I'd love to ravish you, but I'm afraid I'm going to have to lie down." He turned on his heels and took the long route around the stairway to our bedroom, apparently not wanting to cut through the nursery.

Near the end of the week, we heard the Friday Nighters might be meeting. Jerry's office was covered in drywall dust—too much for Vern with his lung disease—but one of the members had promised to call if they decided at the last minute to meet somewhere else. Tony, our neighbor Margene's son, had come from next door, and we were sitting on our front stoop, listening to his velvety voice as he strummed familiar folk songs on his guitar. There were hardly any cars. Somebody was grilling hamburgers, and there was an occasional flurry of burnt-umber leaves and the thud of car doors as neighbors arrived home from work.

It was one of those nights when everything seemed right with the world. Vern sipped his bourbon. I drank something resembling a Shirley Temple. Feeling married again, I leaned my head against Vern's shoulder, wanting to squeeze back into the partner I'd been before Stan's arrival.

We were soaking in the lyrics of Tony's current song, "Blowing in the Wind," when the phone rang. Vern leapt to his feet and pushed open the door.

He was gone a while; eventually, I excused myself to Tony and went in to check on him. Vern was leaning against the counter on his elbows, his face ashen.

"I know. I know. I'm sorry," he said.

I figured someone must've died. I could hear faint feminine sobbing through the receiver.

As Vern mostly listened, I pulled out the nearest chair and, holding my stomach, wiggled into a comfortable position beside him.

"I'm sorry," he said again. He sounded understanding. But then he shook his head and said, "We paid our dues." It sounded like he was speaking to a political party fundraiser. Stan was so far from my mind I couldn't imagine who it was. "It's too much," he sputtered. "No, we can't. I'm sorry. You know, we're having a baby."

We had spoken plenty about the baby ourselves, but this was the first time I'd heard him speak about the pregnancy directly to anyone else. He didn't say *Kim* is having a baby but *we* are having a baby. I felt a kick, and it was as if the baby was saying, "Woohoo! He's talking about me!"

Vern grabbed a cigarette from his pocket, stuck it in the side of his mouth, and flicked his lighter. "No, I believe he needs a proper school setting."

That's when it jabbed me——*Oh God, it* has *to be Ruthann. Surely we don't have to deal with her again.*

Suddenly the sobbing turned to shouting, scorching Vern's every word with her rage. Vern held the phone away from his ear. Calmly, he said into the receiver, "You're not the only one who's been struggling."

In disbelief, I watched Vern's left hand curl into a tight knot. *Come on, Vern*, I silently urged. *You did a great job in sending Stan home. Now you need to be strong. You need to say no means no.* I scanned the kitchen, clean and uncluttered. No stacks of newspapers or bills, overflowing ashtrays, or dirty dishes. We were stronger, had more energy. Our lives had become enjoyable again.

At first I glared at him. Then, on impulse, I glided over to his chair and hugged him. When I heard Stan's mother still emoting, however, I sat back down in my chair.

It terrified me to think Vern might be moved by her histrionics and take Stan back. Waiting for his answer was nearly unbearable.

"Well, at any rate," he added, "I strongly believe he should attend school. Perhaps a private school." He took a deep drag from the cigarette and tapped the ash into the sink with his index finger. He leaned over, his elbows on the edge of the kitchen counter. "Yes, where he would receive more attention." Vern was unable to break through her tirade, but he remained calm. She came at him in waves, and each time, hoping to disengage, he tried a different rational argument. Nothing worked. Still, he avoided insulting her and managed to be supportive.

"Yes, he would thrive," he said. "I might add, one must intervene, or you are liable to suffer some grave consequences." Vern sat down, and a dark shadow seemed to pass over us, the light in the kitchen dimming. With the phone caught between his left cheek and shoulder, his right hand holding a pen, he hunched over a notepad.

Not convinced Vern could stand firm, I paced and prayed.

"Yes," he said, "I believe it *is* wrong." Then he hesitated a moment. "Hello . . . Hello?" He slammed the phone, and it rang as the receiver smacked the jack. "She hung up on me."

"Yippee!" I squeezed him tightly.

Maybe it was his smile or his reaction of surprise—but in that moment I could hardly contain my joy. "Whoa, whoa. You're going to knock me over." He shook his head in disbelief. "Stan was arrested."

I took a step back. "What? You don't mean *really* arrested . . . by the police?"

Vern looked confused. Something didn't add up. "She left Stan in the car while she dashed into a building to file papers for the lawsuit. She told him to wait for her. But he wandered into Burger King and ordered food. Apparently he gobbled the food without paying, so the manager called the police." Vern grinned.

"They can't arrest a *kid*." I felt an instant wave of outrage and empathy.

"No . . . I know. But that's what Ruthann said. She said she charged into Burger King, shouting that the food was horsemeat. The upshot is, Ruthann didn't call to complain—she got the conflict resolved with the police—but she does want to send Stan back to us."

"Well, you told her there was no way, right?"

"No, I . . . um . . ." Vern held his hand over his mouth, hiding a smile. "Would you care for a drink, darling?"

"Vern, so help me . . . if you left one ounce of wiggle room . . ." I leaned forward, my eyes boring into him. "If you said anything she might have heard as 'yes,' you are dead meat."

"Horsemeat," he said.

"Yes, horsemeat."

We returned to the front stoop, where Ann was chitchatting with Tony. Nina stood next to her mother, wearing a faint smile, as if she knew something but wasn't saying.

"You two look happy," Ann said as we opened the door.

Vern turned to me and delivered a smile that felt like a secret handshake. "Glorious night . . . an Indian summer." He set his drink to one side as he sat on the top step. Apart from the sound of stiff branches scraping our windows, there was a hush over the neighborhood.

Ann handed Vern a cigarette, her bright smile all-knowing. "Everything okay?"

Vern lifted his moist glass, its ice mostly melted. "To your health." He glanced around at all of us, then handed me his drink. I knew he was toasting the two of us.

"Cheers." Everyone clinked glasses.

"Please." He turned to Tony. "Don't let us interrupt."

Tony strummed a few notes, and as he bathed us in his soothing, liquid chords, I leaned against Vern's shoulder and hugged him around the waist.

World enough and time, I thought.

CHAPTER 30

A **year after Stan left,** Chippie's health deteriorated. Arthritis had developed in his hind legs, and no longer able to struggle up, he spent most of every day barely moving on the floor by his water bowl. Several times a day, one of us would lift him, carry him outside, and set him down to urinate.

On one such day, I was composing a grocery list when Vern entered the house gasping. Though he'd seemed to have fewer lines in his face and walked with a lighter step since the birth of our son, his face was grayer, his hands were colder, and, on this day, his optimism was also blunted.

He stood for a while, fishing for a pack of matches in his pocket. When he lit a cigarette, he stared at the burning tip.

"I expect we'll have to put him down."

I stopped writing. Chippie was on the floor, soaking wet, his damp leg tapping the linoleum, his long nails ticking like a stopwatch. His head was down, his lids barely open. He looked depressed.

I went to Vern, stood behind him, and, hugging his hunched frame, buried my face in his neck. Richard, our sweet little baby, named after Vern's grandfather, was now "George" because we both thought it was better to call him a name that historically meant "farmer" rather than "mighty king or ruler." We knew three Georges—George Gude; George Steele, a friendly realtor in town; and George the neighbor's dog—and we loved all of them, so George it was.

George was peacefully catnapping in a carrier on the kitchen table. With his smooth, hairless head and large jowls, he resembled Vern's baby pictures. His size, beefy like my father, also reminded me of my father's family. He was bright and blue-eyed. Perfect. And ever since his birth, our lives had felt more settled. When he fussed at night, I placed him in the bed between us, and listened to his soft breath as he slept. He was a satisfied baby, restful and snuggly. I, though I didn't know it yet, was already pregnant again. And although the congestion in Vern's lungs was always there, simmering like a toxic stew, he was consistent with his medication and using his oxygen. Our lives seemed to me, pretty darned perfect.

"We have to do something about Chippie," he said.

I told him Chippie was too much to think about right then. "You'll know when it's the right time."

At first, Vern didn't say anything. The furrow in his brow cut deep, and he didn't look up.

"What's wrong?" I asked.

"I want to take him today." He hesitated, then added, "As long as you're okay with it."

"Today? Are you sure that's a good idea?" I was struck that Vern had asked me. But I wasn't sure I was ready. We were drifting in a good place, adjusting to the new baby, our lives revolving around feeding times and diaper changes. George had just taken his first steps. I didn't want to add depression to our daily lives. "What about the girls? Wouldn't they want to say good-bye?" Vern's daughter Laura was still in the area.

"The girls have said their good-byes," he said. "I think it's time."

Outside, the sky was gray and still. It looked like it could rain. I had a low-grade headache and had learned not to make big decisions at times like these. I was afraid Vern would regret it. "Why don't you wait. Take some time to decide."

Vern didn't listen. He slowly pulled his tan raincoat over his pewter-blue sweater with braided leather buttons and donned his wool hat. He was stoic, his gray-green eyes resigned. He picked

Chippie up, his dark little tail tucked under in back, and, cradling him in his arms, he said, "Say good-bye, Chip." It was as if Vern was steering into the wind, the sail luffing.

"Good-bye, Chippie." I rubbed my fingers around the back of Chippie's neck the way Vern had taught Stan. "I love you." He dropped his head onto Vern's arm and didn't move. There was no resistance. Vern carried him to his truck and slowly veered off toward Main Street. I burst into tears.

In the afternoon, the puff of the muffler and the scratch of tires on gravel told me Vern was home. I met him at the edge of the hallway to the family room. In his arms, he carried a box the size of Chippie. He was out of breath; the box looked too heavy for him.

"Are you okay?" I asked.

Vern rubbed his hand along the top of the cardboard. He reeked of cigarettes. "I went to Doc Sanders. Doc wasn't there, so I told the girl I was ready to pick up my dog." Vern sort of chuckled. "She caught me in a blue mood, I guess. She said, 'Let me see if he's ready.' My retort was 'He's as ready as he'll ever be. He's dead.'"

Vern wore a smile, but I knew it was a cover-up. He placed the heavy box on the desk that had belonged to his grandfather and— standing tall, his shoulders back—set a cigarette at the edge of his mouth. "At any rate . . ."

"Are you okay, Vern?" I could see his lip quivering. I reached around him, and as we hugged, I felt him shaking. It was as if I could feel his heart splitting open.

"He was Ben's dog." His voice cracked. "We got him when Ben was born." He pulled a handkerchief from his pocket and blew his nose. "Chippie was like Ben. He could be a rascal."

"Wasn't he like you?"

"No, he was like Ben." Vern's eyes grew watery.

"I'm sorry, Vern. I'm so sorry."

We stood wedged between the sliding glass window and the

totem pole, not speaking for a good while. He breathed deeply, trembling, and then his face straightened. For a moment, he propped himself against the sliding glass door. I wondered if we were standing where Ben was shot.

And then as if he were reading my mind, he mentioned that horrible night for the first time.

"It was hard to lose him. When we got to Cincinnati, I wanted to at least donate his organs." His voice trembled. "They wouldn't let us. We fought it, but it didn't matter. I didn't want to go to that damn party at Harsha's."

"It's not your fault, Vern." I held on to his elbow.

"I should've stayed. I should've stayed home from that damn party." I could see his heart thumping through his shirt. He caught his breath and backed away. He placed the fresh cigarette back in his mouth and let it dangle there a moment. "I suppose I should take him." He glanced at the box. Then, with his tobacco-stained fingertips shaking, he lit his cigarette.

"Do you want me to go with you?"

"No, darling. You take care of George. I'll take Chippie." Vern took a deep breath—the long, shoulder-heaving kind. It seemed like he was blowing out the last bit of heartbreak. "Jesus Katy Christ!"

"What?"

"I'll need to stop at the hardware store for a shovel." He bent over, placed his hands under the box on both sides, and heaved it up as if he were deadlifting a barbell.

"Are you sure you don't want me to go with you?"

"I'm sure."

With one arm cradling the box and the other arm under it for support, Vern carried Chippie across the family room floor and disappeared through the door. As soon as he backed the truck out of the driveway, I collapsed on the couch.

Later that afternoon, I opened the kitchen drawer over the

liquor cabinet and noticed Vern's gun was gone. I wasn't sure what it meant to Vern. Was he putting Ben's accident in the past? Was he showing his love and support to me? Whatever it was, it surprised me. It told me Vern wasn't as rigid and unyielding as I'd thought, that there *was* hope for change with him, and that recovering from Ben's death was a process, not something that could be healed with the birth of a new child. I placed Chippie with Ben in my mind's eye as a way of organizing events of Vern's past that I couldn't control and had no idea what to do with.

One day in early spring of 1986, we were sitting at the kitchen table. Vern was reading through a newsletter. I was feeding the kids—we had a daughter now, too—and I was thinking about how our lives had changed for the better since Stan had returned to his mother. We had adopted a new rhythm that was lighter and brighter, and significantly happier.

Vern turned to me as he dug in his chest pocket. "Darling, what do you think about our moving?"

"Moving where?" The question caught me off-guard.

He seemed to be rolling an idea around in his head. "What about 404?"

Vern's childhood home at 404 North High Street might be best described as a trophy house from the 1870s. It was a lovely hybrid of Italianate and Spanish Colonial detailing with a three-bay front, round-arch windows, a bracketed cornice, and an open front porch on a large lot at the intersection of North High and Willow Streets. Vern's parents and grandparents had shared the house; they'd split it down the middle, with his parents on one side and his grandparents on the other. Just before Vern was born, they'd built a two-story addition on the back, added an L-shaped porch with Spanish-style arches, and covered the whole house in stucco. For several years, Vern had haggled with the IRS over its value in his father's estate. Now, with all the changes in our lives, the house had sat neglected for more than three years, begging for a decision.

"It will take some effort, but you could fix it the way you want," Vern said. "New wallpaper, paint, maybe some different light fixtures. You have a good eye." He pulled out a cigarette and tapped it on the table.

His suggestion seemed to come from out of nowhere. I didn't know how to take what he was saying. The house was huge for our little family. What would we do with all that space?

Vern seemed to read my mind. "You could have a studio. Or an office. Or even an apartment that would bring in income." He set the cigarette in a small ashtray and smoothed my hair with his hand. "There are any number of possibilities, darling."

I gazed at Vern and saw the face I remembered from that first moment I met him. An expression of age and life experience, of joy and sorrow, in the lines of his eyes, coupled with a databank of humorous stories, quotes, and anecdotes. The idea welled up in me as absolutely right.

"Definitely. Yes. I would love it." I stood and went over to kiss him on the cheek.

He seemed surprised by my enthusiasm. He had the same pleased expression on his face as the first day I'd met him. "I need to apologize, darling."

"For what?"

"I've never felt right about the way I responded to all the work you did on Ben's room." He hesitated. "I'm sorry . . . I should say George's room."

"It's okay." I reached out my hand to squeeze his forearm.

"Let me just say I think you need a creative outlet. Here, I think you've been constrained by the aesthetic decisions made by Brand X." He tapped the ash from his cigarette into the ashtray, then rolled the tip in the ashes. "Do you know what I'm trying to say?"

I nodded. "I think so."

"We can take our time," he said, "and continue to live here and move in when the house is ready."

"Wow." I didn't have words for the feeling I had right then. It was the kind of dream I'd had all my life. I'd learned to accept our house as it was, but even with two children, it didn't feel like mine. Each time I stepped into the kitchen with its wallpaper of blue fruit, or sat down in one of Caroline's gold-upholstered wingback chairs in the living room, or passed by Cassie or Laura's bedroom doors, I was reminded of Vern's loss, regardless of my mood. I loved the idea of starting fresh, of not having to tiptoe around Vern's life with Caroline or loss of Ben. Since I had no history at 404, I would be free from limitations. I pursed my lips. "But what about all that furniture?" Vern had said the old gable roof had been leaking and much of the Victorian furniture was home to dead flies, yellow jackets, and cobwebs.

"Let's go there and take a look." Vern's eyes sparkled. "If you don't like what's there, we'll get rid of it."

It was late Saturday morning by the time Vern and I, with George in his red OshKosh overalls and Hannah in her pink snowsuit, finished breakfast at the Koffee Kup and drove slowly up North High Street to 404. The lawn was strewn with blown maple branches; the laurel hedge bordering it was holding back dry leaves and stray papers. For years, I'd admired this house from a distance but never imagined myself living there. This time it gleamed with promise.

We ambled slowly along the concrete path and up the steps to the side door, where Vern fumbled with the keys. I held Hannah in my arms as I peeked through the door's sheer curtain.

My God, even the back of the front hall looked magnificent. Its 1940s rose-colored wallpaper, which I remembered from Vern's sister's wedding pictures, danced in the light.

Vern held open the door and motioned for us to enter, and it seemed we were stepping into a movie. Once inside, Vern let go of George's hand, and he toddled forward in his white lace-up shoes. Even with no heat and that stiff, damp cold that chills to the bone, I felt a certain warmth. Sun poured in through two large double-hung windows and reflected in a giant hall tree—the largest coatrack I'd ever seen—with three beveled mirrors, a water-stained deacon's bench, and carved armrests.

"What do you think of that monstrosity?" Vern asked. It must've been seven feet tall.

"I love it . . . I absolutely love it." The hall tree fit perfectly in the house.

We faced a pair of French doors that opened to a bright office with thick crown molding and high baseboards. We entered slowly, taking in the tall windows with their white-painted wooden lou-vered shutters and heavy damask drapery panels. Some of the rooms had built-in glass-covered bookcases. The kitchen had 1920s white metal cabinets.

All the rooms—even upstairs—had their original mantels, including cast-iron fireplace enclosures. I loved the casement win-dows in back, and the built-in drawers. The large bathrooms, with their white hexagonal floor tiles and white brick wall tiles in run-ning bond, were a walk into a 1920s life of spare-no-cost. The tiled shower in the main bathroom had a series of exposed stainless pipes, including one in a horseshoe shape, that were filled with holes so you could shower from the neck down. I was imagining the Waldorf Astoria.

Vern steered me around to the various treasures—the horsehair slipper chair, the pier mirror, the 1880 Vose & Sons square grand piano with its massive cabriole legs and horsehair stool, and the wal-nut pedestal card table. There was a five-foot-tall bottle of wine from Cuba and, in front of one of the deep mossy marble mantels, dried brown hydrangea blossoms tastefully falling from an antique black wicker basket. I flitted from corner to corner in every room.

"What do you think?" Vern asked. "Does this look like a fun project?"

"Absolutely," I said. I could hardly wait.

Vern kissed me on the forehead, and we hugged with George standing and Hannah in my arms, sandwiched between us. "What do you think, George?" I cooed. "Do you like this house? Would you like to live here?"

Vern, hunched over, reached for George's hand and smiled sweetly. I didn't know what he was thinking, of course, but I imagined he saw himself as a young boy in that moment, toddling across the very same floorboards—his mother, father, and sister gathered around him—each day an open book with empty pages to fill and all the time in the world.

We descended the porch steps, and as I scanned the side yard, my eyes settled on the catalpa tree, bent sideways—an extraordinary piece of sculpture that seemed to define the house. I'd forgotten how even before I'd known Vern, my head had whirled around whenever I drove past that huge tree with its heart-shaped leaves, slender, dangling pods, and ivory blossoms.

Vern eyed the tree too. "Sometime in the early 1900s, that main branch started to bend away from the house. As I remember, a storm eventually took it down." He said he had climbed all over the tree as a kid. He'd gotten sick smoking the thick brown cigar-like pods. Though lightning had struck several times and branches had been removed, the tree continued to bend, filling the side yard like the St. Louis arch. Vern said someone—perhaps his parents—had tried to restrain it with a thick iron chain.

We approached the trunk, and I noticed that the tree, still rooted to the ground, had grown around the heavy chain, the bark bulging like cake over the edge of a baking pan. Someone had tried concrete to hold the tree upright, and later added tar.

I loved the tree's eccentricity. Its branches curved down and then upward and outward, hugging the yard as though it were bracing the house. I was reminded that this was no ordinary catalpa. The tree had fought every effort to make it look "normal." To make it like every other tree on the block.

In the end, it had healed in its own way.

EPILOGUE

A bout five years ago, I called Ruthann to tell her I was writing a book about Stan. So many vivid memories had stayed with me over the years. Stan's gobbling food, hoarding video tokens, maniacally riding Ben's bike, stabbing Chippie . . .

I was still carrying around questions from my brief five years with Vern, which ended with his death, and many of those questions related to Stanislaus. I'd never felt right about his coming to us, or our sending him home.

To my great surprise, Ruthann, at eighty-four, answered the telephone. When I asked if she remembered me, she immediately began to sing—*la-la-la-la-la*—to show me she still had her voice. "You have a daughter, don't you?" she asked. "Maybe she'd like to meet my Stanislaus. He lives in my basement."

My gut reaction was to cut the call short—so I did. I thought Ruthann was just strange enough, and I uncertain enough, that I needed to finish the Stan story before getting her version. Truth be told, I still didn't trust Ruthann. I didn't want to be influenced by anything she might say.

Sadly, by the time I reached out a second time, Ruthann and Stan were both gone.

When I learned that Stan's older brother, Sam, now in his fifties, was still living alone in the house on Sill Lane, the house his mother had fought so hard to save, I decided to go there to meet him and see what he could tell me. I still wondered about Stan. Had he turned out all right? Had he ever gone to school? Lived a normal life? His mother—had she had a mental disorder? Or was the stress of losing her husband, and nearly losing her home, what had made her so difficult? And what about Stan's father? What was his story? I wanted to know why Ruthann had called Vern in the first place. What was their connection?

I arranged to meet Sam at nine o'clock on a Monday morning. I flew to Hartford, rented a car, and drove south, over the Connecticut River.

When I reached Old Lyme's stately Main Street, I slowed. Like Hillsboro, the town was filled with manicured Federal, Greek Revival, and Italianate homes. Old Lyme had more confidence, though. Was it its proximity to New York City that had made a difference, or was it something to do with the thriving Lyme Academy College of Fine Arts? Whatever it was, the town gave off happy vibes.

I veered off to Sill Lane, smiling as I passed low rubble and cut-stone walls. When I reached the low girder bridge over Mill Brook, I recognized the Captain Thomas Sill House from the old newspaper clippings Ruthann had sent us. My eye went straight to its central open porch with its turned posts and pediment, which was now propped up with a four-by-four. What had happened? The house's front-facing windows, devoid of paint, were covered in plastic. Its stone and picket fence, visible in early photos, was gone; its yard was filled with tall weeds and towering black walnut, plum, and hazel trees.

Looking closer, I got goose bumps. The house still had its original clapboard siding; its double-hung windows—12/12 lights—and simple corner boards and window trim had retained their eighteenth-century simplicity and elegance.

"Hello? Hello?" I banged on the side door.

Sam drove up in a green Ford Focus, and I noticed immediately his enigmatic, buck-toothed smile. He had stark white hair, bald on top, and a short-cropped white beard. He looked nothing like the way I imagined a grown-up Stanislaus—he lacked the nervous energy, the deadpan expression I remembered.

He led me into a large living room, where a wood stove protruded from a fireplace. A 1980s sofa, patched with duct tape, faced the wood stove. A hint of kerosene mixed with the scent of burning wood. The place looked dirty, but there was an appealing openness to the room's austere simplicity. Nobody had carved into it with misguided renovation. It was as spare and open as a hollowed-out pumpkin.

Sam wore heavily soiled brown work pants and a dark, long-sleeved shirt, and I noticed his broad shoulders, his musculature. Something about him felt safe, unusually so. The total opposite of his anxious, fast-talking mother and brother. I trusted him instantly.

I mentioned the tragedy of Stan's dying at age forty-seven. He said Stan had gone to bed on the sofa, and the next morning he'd found him unconscious, in a diabetic coma.

Had he been on insulin? Other drugs? What about alcohol? I asked, but Sam didn't seem to know.

I asked if he could tell me about Stan's life. He said a lot of his own childhood memories had been clouded by the intensity of his mother's rage. What I gathered was that Stan was finished with homeschooling when he returned from Ohio. Ruthann had gotten him into the Sedberg School, a private boarding school in Canada, but Stan had been caught stealing beer and hadn't lasted there long. He'd returned to Old Lyme, where he'd decided he wanted to live with a family up the road. At some point, he'd been taken into temporary custody by the Department of Children and Youth Services and placed with the family he had chosen. They'd insisted on public school. But Ruthann had fought back. For at least five years, there had been threats and lawsuits and police showing up at the house or the high school. Each time, Stan had run back to the other family, pleading for help.

The mother of the family had been a nurse, the father, in construction, and as foster parents, they had offered Stan the kind of nurturing he'd wanted and needed. The father had taught Stan how to operate heavy machinery and had given him enough experience to become a skilled mechanic. He had learned to be a great cook. In his later years, he'd made and sold a delicious salsa, and he'd loved *The Simpsons*, race cars, and fishing. He had worked for Midas. At one point he had even owned his own Snap-On Tool franchise.

My mind fastened on the news that Stan had sold tools. Had his experience at the hardware store shaped his eventual livelihood? Again, Sam didn't seem to know. When he mentioned Stan had been married twice and had twin girls who were now six, I set my pencil down in the spine of my notebook for a moment, just thinking. What were the kids like? How often had Sam seen them? Had Ruthann been a part of their life? I had so many questions.

I told Sam I had found Stan's obituary online and was puzzled by a quote in it—*See how easy it is to be a man.* "What did the quote mean?"

"It was something Stan said once. The sense that he knew better. That he had a way forward. He found ways to get around my mother's strictures."

When he said this, I couldn't resist asking, "Do you think your mother was bipolar or had some kind of mental illness?"

"Who would know?" he said. "We never went to doctors." He leaned closer, his bright expression playful. "You know, she took us to Papua New Guinea. When we returned, she tried to smuggle bananas strapped to her waist, pretending she was pregnant. Who *does* that? She took us to Nicaragua in the middle of a revolution!"

Sam reminded me in this way of Vern, the way he answered but didn't answer, leaving small, oblique pieces of information for others to construct into a coherent narrative.

"What was the deal with the breast milk?" I asked. "Do you know if Stan was still breastfeeding when he came to us?"

Sam fidgeted for a moment. Then his voice raised to a high pitch. "I don't, um . . . I don't think so. Well, I don't remember with Stan." He hesitated. "But I was old enough to remember it myself."

He disappeared into the upstairs, and his feet thumped the floorboards above me. I looked longingly at the six-paneled front door—its original 1790s dark hardware, the decades of dirt and grime surrounding it. *My God*, I thought. *How I would love to restore this house to its former glory.* Why had it been so disregarded? So neglected? One possibility was a lack of money. But it was more than that. It was as if some tragic event had frozen the house in time. As that thought came to me, I felt an unearthly connection to Vern. I wanted to fix up that old house in the same way I'd wanted to fix up Vern. I loved the plaster walls, the carved elliptical trim over a set of double doors. The sags and cracks, nicks and scratches. I loved all of it. The house was a reflection of an earlier time that seemed lonely, neglected, and had shamelessly surrendered but not adapted to new conditions.

A few minutes later, Sam returned with a gold oval frame containing a beautiful photograph of Ruthann as a young woman. She wore a dark sweater with a white Peter Pan collar. Her thick brown hair, parted on the side and held with a barrette, fell in loose waves over her shoulders. It surprised me to see her wearing lipstick. She looked young, bright-eyed, and pure.

Which brought me back to the breast-milk fixation. The way she'd shoved the La Leche League literature on us every few days as if our lives had depended on it. I asked Sam if he knew why his mother was so rabid on the subject. I braced myself for his answer.

"I don't really know," he said. "She grew up on a farm. She lost her mother when she was only two."

"Whoa." My mind raced. Ruthann had been the adult version of Stan: profoundly shaped by the trauma of losing her parent, in this case, her mother. This news about Ruthann spoke volumes. Sam said she had been forced to help with her younger siblings. When she was nine, and her father remarried, she had watched her young stepmother breastfeed.

I asked Sam about his father, who, like Vern, had been a good-looking guy who'd served in WWII and come from a prominent family. Had they met in San Francisco, where Vern had lived after his stint in the Navy and where he'd met Caroline? Did Sam know the circumstances?

Again, Sam wasn't sure. "My mother used to describe a group in San Francisco that would get together over a jug of Gallo wine. Maybe that's where they met." He said his parents were both preservationists, that his mother wasn't the only passionate one in his family. He recalled his father's rewriting of Tennyson's "The Charge of the Light Brigade"—a tongue-in-cheek version—to criticize urban expansion.

I felt a chill. How could I forget Vern's "Ours not to wonder why; ours but to do or die"? He was always quoting his own version of that poem.

I glanced at the front wall, where a portrait of Sam's great-grandfather—Samuel Hanson Coxe, a famous Presbyterian abolitionist and Sam's namesake—loomed over us. At first, I'd complimented Sam on the painting. But as I looked closely, the image appeared dark and oppressive.

Something inside me clicked. Sam was dealing with the ghosts of *his* family too. The ghost of his father as the constitutional lawyer; his mother, the organic farming and La Leche League advocate; perhaps the ghosts of his family's ancestors as well, like his great-grandfather the abolitionist; and maybe even, in some way, the ghost of Stan. Sam had been eight years older than Stan. As the oldest, he, like me, had been groomed to keep things together. I considered the way I'd briefly felt pressure to continue my mother's gift business after she died, and also the tremendous relief my being fired and forced to close up shop had been.

One of the things that had drawn me to Vern was his love of

history. He had been such a packrat, holding on to things. And yet—what a paradox!—the very trait that had drawn me to him was also the trait that, at times, had unnerved me. It had created a dilemma: when to hold on and when to let go. Vern and I had shared a love for old houses that extended beyond the walls and wide floorboards to the thoughts, the loves, the passions of those who'd come before us.

I'd been living with Vern's family furniture for years, had even dragged some to Michigan to put it in storage for my children as a way of surrounding myself with his memory. With most of it, the intrinsic value was questionable. But the feel of Vern's grandfather's old rocking chair—its clean lines, its smell, its rhythmic squeak—connected me to a real person with flaws and struggles and heartache like ours.

Without much effort, I understood this house. It had been Stan's stomping ground. He'd run in and out, sat in that very chair in front of the wood stove. His life was in that room, his spirit lingering like Ben's spirit in *his* bedroom. I'm not a religious person, but I felt a weight pressing down in that house. The weight of unfinished business. Through Sam, I felt a connection to Stan, to his parents, and even, in a weird way, to Vern.

Something kept haunting me. I noticed a number of candlesticks with dripping wax scattered about. "What was the fascination with fire?" I told Sam that Stan had set his dresser on fire, and later, his bed. I was sure it was on purpose, and I wanted confirmation. I expected to hear a story like the one I tell of my father's racing us around in the backseat of his old Chevy to watch houses burning down that had created my own fascination. But Sam grew quiet.

He stood up from his chair to adjust the heat. His expression made me think he had dropped back into the past, that he was figuring something out.

I was giving myself a tongue-lashing, thinking I was being intrusive like my father, unable to restrain myself. "He stabbed our dog," I said calmly.

Sam's straight lips turned up at the corners. "You must've thought you had an ax murderer."

"Well . . . yes . . . Yes, I did." His words tightened the pit of my stomach.

Sam drew a sharp breath. "We had some fires here too. Unexplained fires."

"Where?"

"One was in the attic."

I raised my eyebrows. It seemed I'd handed Sam a missing puzzle piece.

We were quiet for a moment, and then Sam said, "Life is messy. It's the human predicament, isn't it? To be stuck in something you don't want to do?" He may've been speaking of himself, but in his way, he was validating Stan while at the same time validating me. "Once you come out of your shell," he said, "you realize how messy everything is. You have to work hard to keep up the illusion of non-messiness."

He returned to an upstairs room, where he gathered some promotional signs the family had made for their Essene Bread Company, as well as a couple of placards his mother had used to protest Stan's placement in foster care. They were sooty and tattered, some with yellowed tape clumsily sticking to their edges. He placed them on the table, under the light.

In one file was a threatening letter to the Old Lyme High School principal, copied to the superintendent, as well as to Joseph Lieberman, who had been the Connecticut State Attorney General, and to President Ronald Reagan. Ruthann's obituary had mentioned that her friend, Casper Weinberger, the Secretary of Defense at the time, had intervened to help her in their land dispute. I had been amazed when I first read that. Caspar Weinberger! Ruthann had a remarkable ability to use everything in her power to get what she wanted.

Sam wasn't able to give me Vern and Sam Sr.'s connection, or why Vern would have felt he owed so much to Ruthann. Vern had answered a call for help and had done what he thought was right for Stan. He also may've rationalized that Stan's visit would help me.

There are situations—like when you're having your own baby and someone asks you to take their son—where you can and should say no, no matter what the circumstances. To honor your own child and, for Godsake, yourself.

Some injuries take forever to heal. I'd carried the hurt from that summer more than thirty years. I hadn't wanted to examine it. It had been easier to blame the dull ache on an unreasonable woman who wouldn't take no for an answer—but in my heart, I knew the injury was more complicated. Putting it in the past would be putting Vern in the past. Stan had forced Vern and me to hold up a mirror to our marriage. Stan's time with us had also been an experience that helped prepare me for the terrible grief of losing Vern when our kids were only two and four. As much as I had bristled and resisted when Vern suggested Stan's visit would give me practice, Vern had been right: Stan *was* practice.

I lingered a moment as I scanned the room one last time.

"You've answered a number of questions," Sam said. "Thanks for explaining a few things."

I half nodded, half shrugged, and told him how much I appreciated his openness. He then escorted me to my car, ushering me slowly along the bluestone path.

I was having trouble leaving. I wanted to embrace the house, the city of Old Lyme, the memory of Stan and his mother. As I climbed into the driver's seat, I felt my heart contract. Sam had brought me back to the smells, the tastes, the sounds of that summer with Stan. He also had brought me back to the challenges Vern and I'd faced—our age difference, Vern's health issues, our individual struggles to come to terms with Vern's earlier marriage and losses—and to sealed memories, to these old homes that refused to give up their ghosts.

I started the engine, and as Sam stood there, ready to wave

good-bye, I leapt from the driver's seat and hustled around the car toward him.

"I want to hug you," I said as if I were apologizing. I threw out my arms, wrapped them around his warm waistline, and squeezed. Vern had seen the world differently than everyone else, and my visit today had helped me understand him a tiny bit more.

Sam had provided few answers. If anything, he had raised more questions.

But I realized I no longer had a need to know.

ACKNOWLEDGMENTS

This book would never have been possible without the help of my husband, Vernon Fairley. He provided a deep well of material and the encouragement to take time every day for the activities and people I love.

It's a wonderful feeling to get up in the morning eager to dive in and write. For that, I thank the Ann Arbor Area Writers, especially Anan Ameri, Michael Andreoni, Eleanor Andrews, Lisa Leona Bedbak, Charlotte Bowens, Kate Chenli, Jeremy Crosmer, Bill Feight, Lois Godel, Donnelly Haddon, Ellen Halter, Skipper Hammond, Karen Hildebrandt, Cheryl Israel, Yma Johnson, Raymond Juracek, Gayle Keiser, Fartumo Kusow, Wei Liu, Rachel Lash Maitra, Leslie McGraw, Don McKay, Bethany Neal, Barbara Richstone, Shelley Schanfield, Christina Shannon, Pat Tompkins, Dave Wanty, Anita Wilson, Marjorie Winful-Sakyi, and Karen Wolff, who continue to give me invaluable feedback and a reason to keep going.

From the very beginning, Karen Simpson never failed to take time to discuss this story with me, always providing a positive spin, for which I feel indebted. Her guidance, support, and friendship are true gifts in my life. Words cannot express my gratitude to Christi Mersereau, who has helped in myriad ways—reading, walking, discussing—and has given me invaluable feedback and support. I am deeply grateful to Dorothy Wall, who was generous with her time, patient, and always encouraging. Her insight and expertise made this a better book, and me a better writer.

I would like to thank my Hillsboro friends, especially Jim Gibbs, Ann Pence, and John Glaze, who have been in my corner and helped along the way. I owe special thanks to Jane Ratcliffe, who patiently read my earliest draft, and Zilka Joseph, who also was part of the journey. I owe a huge thanks to Katherine Sharpe for her knowledge and intuition, and special thanks and gratitude to Brooke Warner, Samantha Strom, Krissa Lagos, and Kirstin Andrews as well as all the design and production staff at She Writes Press.

Finally, I want to thank Stan's brother, Sam Coxe, one of the book's biggest champions, who provided me documentation to fill in Stan's history, and my son and daughter, George and Hannah, who convinced me to write the story and have provided unfailing support throughout the process.

ABOUT THE AUTHOR

Kim Fairley was born in Plainfield, New Jersey, and raised in Cincinnati, Ohio. She attended the University of Southern California and holds an MFA in mixed media from the University of Michigan. Her first book, *Boreal Ties: Photographs and Two Diaries of the 1901 Peary Relief Expedition* chronicles the Arctic expedition of her great-grandfather, Clarence Wyckoff and his friend, Louis Bement. She lives in Ann Arbor, Michigan.

kimfairley.com
Facebook.com/kimfairley11
Twitter.com/kimfairley1
Instagram.com/kimfairleywrites

BOOK CLUB QUESTIONS

1. Kim chose the James Baldwin epitaph: "History is not the past. It is the present. We carry our history with us. We are our history." Why do you think she used that reference in the beginning of the book?

2. The town of Hillsboro serves as both setting and character in the book. What was the impact of Hillsboro in the way the characters viewed each other?

3. Which character(s) did you relate to or not relate to, and why?

4. The age difference between Kim and Vern was thirty-two years. How much do you think the large age gap influenced the relationship?

5. How much do you think his grief and physical health played a part in informing the way Vern dealt with everyday challenges?

6. Why do you think Kim reluctantly parented Stan, even when Vern didn't?

7. Throughout the story, Vern is unyielding in his desire to mentor Stan. What in Vern's past experience, personality and beliefs fuel his deep desire to keep the boy?

8. How would you describe Stan? What would your first reaction to him have been?

9. Secrets play an important part in the story. Can you recall a moment when one of your own secrets had an impact on your life?

10. Sometimes in life we make decisions to support others even when we don't particularly agree. Which characters show that love and admiration can exist within conflict, and how do they show it?

11. What part do you think trauma played in the story and how do you think trauma influences the decisions we make?

12. What would you do if, like Kim, you were to gradually discover you had a disturbed child as a house guest?

13. In their relationship, Kim and Ruth appear an unlikely pair at first, but their relationship develops to be very supportive. What did you think about their relationship and how did it change over time?

14. Many people believe the way we are raised plays a major role in cementing the person we become later in life. In what ways does this story support that conclusion? How do you think Kim's experience as a child influenced her reaction to being recruited as Stan's stepmother?

15. Intergenerational and sibling relationships play a part in the story. In what ways do you think Kim's relationship with her parents, grandparents, and siblings influenced her relationship with Vern?

16. Is abandonment ever justified? Why or why not? How do you think the theme of abandonment is handled in the book?

17. Early in the story, it is clear there is an imbalance of power in the relationship between Kim and Vern. How do you think this imbalance complicated the relationship?

18. What is your opinion of the title, *Shooting Out the Lights?* Does it reflect the book's themes?

19. How do you think time and history, for example the antique furniture, the house, and family business played a part in influencing decisions that were made by characters in the story?

20. In one of his interesting statements, Vern says to Kim "You were a preservationist and I needed preserving." What do you think was the significance of historic preservation in the story?

21. How did the characters change throughout the story? How did your opinion of them change?

22. What scene in the book affected you the most and why?

23. Were there any surprises in the book?

24. This memoir is also about Kim's struggle to claim her agency. What do you think she has achieved by the end of the story?

25. If there is one question you wish the book had answered, what would it be and why?

SELECTED TITLES FROM SHE WRITES PRESS

She Writes Press is an independent publishing company founded to serve women writers everywhere. Visit us at www.shewritespress.com.

Filling Her Shoes: Memoir of an Inherited Family by Betsy Graziani Fasbinder. $16.95, 978-1-63152-198-0. A "sweet-bitter" story of how, with tenderness as their guide, a family formed in the wake of loss and learned that joy and grief can be entwined cohabitants in our lives.

Americashire: A Field Guide to a Marriage by Jennifer Richardson. $15.95, 978-1-93831-430-8. A couple's decision about whether or not to have a child plays out against the backdrop of their new home in the English countryside.

Fire Season: A Memoir by Hollye Dexter. $16.95, 978-1-63152-974-0. After she loses everything in a fire, Hollye Dexter's life spirals downward and she begins to unravel—but when she finds herself at the brink of losing her husband, she is forced to dig within herself for the strength to keep her family together.

Splitting the Difference: A Heart-Shaped Memoir by Tré Miller-Rodríguez. $19.95, 978-1-938314-20-9. When 34-year-old Tré Miller-Rodríguez's husband dies suddenly from a heart attack, her grief sends her on an unexpected journey that culminates in a reunion with the biological daughter she gave up at 18.

Breathe: A Memoir of Motherhood, Grief, and Family Conflict by Kelly Kittel. $16.95, 978-1-93831-478-0. A mother's heartbreaking account of losing two sons in the span of nine months—and learning, despite all the obstacles in her way, to find joy in life again.

A Different Kind of Same: A Memoir by Kelley Clink. $16.95, 978-1-63152-999-3. Several years before Kelley Clink's brother hanged himself, she attempted suicide by overdose. In the aftermath of his death, she traces the evolution of both their illnesses, and wonders: If he couldn't make it, what hope is there for her?